ON THE PATH OF THE PROPHET

Shaykh Ahmad Tijani (1737-1815)

and the Tariqa Muhammadiyya

Zachary Valentine Wright

ISBN 978-0-9913813-88

Revised & Republished
Fayda Books, Publishing & Distribution,
Atlanta, GA, USA.

Cover Design
ETHEREA DESIGN

On the Path of the Prophet

Shaykh Ahmad Tijani (173 7-1815) and the
Tarīqa Muhammadiyya

by

ZACHARY VALENTINE WRIGHT

Revised Edition

Fayda Books, Publishing & Distribution
www.faydabooks.com
Atlanta,2015

Contents

Publishers Preface   8

Acknowledgments   9

Introduction by Shaykh Hassan Cisse   11

Note on Transliteration   13

Preface   15

Introduction: Sufism within Traditional Islam   19

 The Tariqa Muhammadiyya and the 18th Century
 Revival of Sufism   21
 Economic and Social Factors in 18th Century Sufi Revival 25
 Ahmad ibn Idris and Shaykh Ahmad Tijani   29

Elements of the Tariqa Muhammadiyya   **33**

Note on Sources   **37**

Plan of Development   **47**

Chapter I   **49**

Biographical Portrait I: In Search of Knowledge   **49**

Early years and teachers   **51**

Pilgrimage East   **59**

Desert Illumination and the Vision of Prophet   **73**

Chapter II   **89**

Biographical Portrait II: The Shaykh and the Events of his Time   **89**

The Ottoman authorities of Algeria   **91**

Fes, Mawlay Sulayman and the solidification of a Tariqa   **97**

Chapter III   **109**

Shaykh Ahmad Tijani and Islamic Sacred Law (Shari'a)   **111**

Involvement in the World   **123**

Ijtihad and the Islamic Legal Tradition
(Fiqh and the Madhahib)   **127**

The Qur'an and Salat al-Fatih   **139**

Chapter IV   **145**

Shaykh Ahmad Tijani and the Sufism of his time   **147**

Prior Tariqa affiliation   **151**

The Tijaniyya within the ideology of earlier Sufism   **155**

Purification of the Self   **157**

Knowledge of God and Human Purpose   163

The Tariqa Muhammadiyya and the Muhammadan Reality   171

Chapter V   177

Towards a distinctive Tijani Sufi doctrine   179

Sainthood   181

The Shaykh al-Tarbiyya or Spiritual Initiator   187

The Principal of Shiikr and God's grace in an age of corruption   195

Conclusion   207

Epilogue: 213

Reflections on the later spread of the Tijaniyya   213

Appendix: 221

Some Prayers of Shaykh Ahmad Tijani   223

Prayer from "Forgiveness for all Sins."   225

"Ya Man Azhahara al-Jameel"   227

Other prayers expressing humility and asking for forgiveness.   229

Prayers expressing love for the Prophet Muhammad   231

Invoking the Glory of God   233

Bibliography   237

Index   253

Publishers Preface

The revising, reprinting, and redistribution of this book has been of paramount importance to me personally. I recall reading the university thesis of Professor Zachary Wright many years ago, and immediately knew that it would one day evolve into this current book. When it was initially published in 2005, I read the entire book in one weekend. It was as if it quenched a perpetual thirst after many years. This book removes the shroud covering one of Islam's most influential leaders and provides insight into the movement he initiated at the behest of the Prophet Muhammad (peace and blessings be upon him).

This work is a must read for anyone interested in understanding the importance of Allah's "Divine Balance." It is that balance which placed Islam's greatest proponents of theological rigidity (Wahhabism) and Islam's greatest proponents of spiritual unity (Tariqa Muhammadiyya), on opposite scales, in the world, at the same time in history.

Ibrahim Dimson
Publisher, Fayda Books

Acknowledgments

First and foremost, I would like to thank Shaykh Hassan Cisse for his assistance and inspiration in this work. Other Tijani scholars who have been of great help include Shaykh Muhsin Shalaby of the Tijani center (zawiya) in Heliopolis, Cairo, and Professor Abdelaziz Benabdellah in Rabat, Morocco. The actual publication of this work would not have been possible without the support of Dr. Dawud Jeffries and the African-American Islamic Institute based in Atlanta. *On the Path of the Prophet* was originally written as an M.A. thesis for the American University in Cairo. As such I am indebted to several professors there: my primary advisor, Dr. Mark Abd al-Azim Sedgwick, as well as Dr. Mohamed Serag and Dr. Nelly Hanna in the Arabic Studies Department. Thanks as well to Sawson Mardini in the Graduate Student Office. Others in Egypt include Azhar students Adam al-Islam and Zakir Khan for their help in translation. In Morocco I must also thank the Fulbright scholarship program, and particularly the program officers in Rabat, Dawud Casewit and Saadia Maskia. Professor Benabdellah's assistant in Rabat, Selma Bennani, was also of great help. In Fes, my gratitude is due to the descendents of Shaykh Ahmad Tijani in the Tijani zawiya there. Qarawin

University students Idris Watts and Mukhtar Sy also provided valuable help in translation and the procuring of texts. Besides Shaykh Hassan Cisse in Senegal, my thanks to Ibrahim Kafani Cisse for his advice and for helping to facilitate my stays there. Lastly, I must thank my mother, Um Salama Keller, for her support.

Introduction by Shaykh Hassan Cisse

This work is an important step both in elucidating the life and thought of one of Islam's seminal religious personalities, and in exposing the essential link between Sufism and the Islamic tradition. This work concerning Shaykh Ahmad Tijani (may Allah be pleased with him) is one of the only in the English language to which I have been able to lend my support. I hope it will help to dispel some of the myths surrounding the person of Shaykh Ahmad Tijani and to establish definitively the orthodoxy of the type of Sufism, which he practiced.

The concept of the *Tariqa Muhammadiyya* or "Muhammadan Way," is important because it expresses the absorption of Shaykh Ahmad Tijani and the path that bears his name, the Tijaniyya, in the example of the Prophet Muhammad (may Allah bless him and grant him peace). Indeed, Shaykh Tijani himself said, "If you hear something attributed to me, weigh it on the scale of the Shari'a (sacred law), if it balances, take it, if not, leave it." Outside the circle of Qur'an and Hadith (sayings of the Prophet), there is no such thing as the Tariqa Tijaniyya. In this way, Tijanis do not distinguish themselves from the larger Islamic community, for all Muslims are only trying

11

to follow the teachings of the Qur'an and the example of the Prophet Muhammad.

I, Shakyh Hassan Cisse, endorse this work as an accurate portrayal of Shaykh Ahmad Tijani and some of the important concepts of the Tijaniyya. The author, Zakariya Wright, visited us many times over the past years preparing this work. I worked with him helping him to interpret primary texts of the Tijaniyya, such as the *Jawahir al-Ma'ani*. I believe he has understood the importance of reading such texts from the perspective of one knowledgeable of the tradition of scholarship from which they emerge.

Shaykh Hassan Cisse

Imam of the Grand Mosque in Kaolack, Senegal.

Note on transliteration

All Arabic words have been italicized, except those common in English usage, such as shaykh (Islamic scholar or spiritual guide), Shari'a (Islamic sacred law) or Jihad (struggle, holy war). Words ending in ° are left to end in sound of the preceding vowel, unless followed by another word, thus *khalifa* vs *khalifat al-akbar.* Short vowels are transliterated as follows: *fatha,* **a;** *kasra,* **i;** *damma,* **u.**

a	ا	*d*	ض
b	ب	*t*	ط
t	ت	*zh*	ظ
th	ث	'	ع
j	ج	*gh*	غ
h	ح	*f*	ف
kh	خ	*q*	ق
d	د	*k*	ك
dh	ذ	*l*	ل
r	ر	*m*	م
z	ز	*n*	ن
s	س	*w*	و
sh	ش	*y*	ي
s	ص		

PREFACE

L ittle has been written about Islamic scholarship, and even less about Islamic mysticism, in the late eighteenth century of the Common Era. It was a period whose central actors were seemingly about to be obscured by the advent of modernity in Islamic societies. European colonialists and Muslim reformers generally had no taste for the delicately nuanced Islamic legal tradition, and certainly not for the intangible science of Sufism.

But in their own time, scholars such as Shaykh Ahmad Tijani and their followings were respected, cosmopolitan and popular movements; more-so than, say, the Wahhabi movement emerging at the same time in the east of Saudi Arabia. In scholarly and popular circles in the late eighteenth century, there is evidence that the sober mysticism associated with the *Tariqa Muhammadiyya* phenomenon was the talk of the town. *Tariqa Muhammadiyya* ideology, as it evolved in the late eighteenth century, was an attempt to orient Sufism more directly to the person of the Prophet Muhammad as the ultimate Sufi shaykh. With simultaneous emphasis on such concepts as the Prophetic Sunnah (code of behavior), the Muhammad Reality *(Haqiqa Muhammadiyya)* and visionary experience, the phenomenon was an interesting combination of external Islamic orthopraxy and some of the more complicated elements of Islamic esotericism.

Well traveled and well educated propagators made the *Tariqa Muhammadiyya* movements some of the primary agents of Islamic revival in the eighteenth and early nineteenth centuries. From the Khalwatiyya in Egypt, the Salihiyya in East Africa, the Sammaniyya in Sudan, the Sanusiyya in Central and North Africa, the Tijaniyya in the Maghreb and West Africa and similarly-minded movements in India and other parts of the Islamic world, scholars identifying with the ideology of the *Tariqa Muhammadiyya* helped to reinvigorate Islamic societies and institutions, to spread Islam among Christian and animist populations and even to lead resistance struggles against colonial occupation.

It is indeed surprising that the massively popular *Tariqa Muhammadiyya* movements of the late eighteenth and early nineteenth centuries were so marginalized by modernist rhetoric that many present-day Muslims can hardly recall the names of such scholars as Abd al-Ghani al-Nabulsi, Mustafa al-Bakri, Muhammad al-Hifhi, Ahmad Tijani, Ahmad ibn Idris or Muhammad al-Sanusi. In Egypt, the modernist reformer Muhammad Ali undermined the Azhari establishment and the *ulama* (class of Islamic scholars), which, in the late eighteenth and early nineteenth centuries, was often lead by Khalwati shaykhs. In Libya, Muammar Qadafi attempted to downplay and even erase the memory of the Sanusiyya order's resistance to Italian occupation. In Algeria, leftist revolutionaries and a new class of Salafi-influenced Islamists joined forces to malign the Sufi orders, particularly the Tijaniyya whose founder hailed from the Southern Algerian town of Ain Madi. Such attacks were not simply the result of a newly emerging power structure in competition for spheres of influence. They involved a struggle for the very identity of Islam itself. Simply put, modernist reformers were in need of a version of Islam that could be easily manipulated for political aims.

For the historian, the *Tariqa Muhammadiyya* movements represent some of the last examples of attempted Islamic re-vivification that might be said to be wholly indigenous to the Islamic tradition. With Europe's colonization of the Muslim world beginning in the nineteenth century, European-style modernity would become an inescapable reference point coloring all subsequent attempts at Islamic reform. Scholars such as Shaykh Ahmad Tijani thus provide us with an important window into the nature of the Islamic tradition before the coming of modernity, that would irrevocably imprint all forms of discourse in Islamic societies.

It is no accident that the personalities of figures such as Shaykh Ahmad Tijani have remained enigmatic. The polemics of the modernist discourse aside, Shaykh Ahmad Tijani was probably a somewhat mysterious person to his own contemporaries. He himself was not political, although his influence may be discerned on a wide range of political leaders. His life's work primarily centered on the standard Sufi shaykh ideal (that of helping people come to the knowledge of God), but neither did he require of himself or his followers to remain withdrawn from the world. He taught about the necessity of the heart's freedom from worldly preoccupation, but was himself rumored to possess great wealth. He claimed to have been graced with exalted spiritual stations, but was humble and frequently asked God for forgiveness. His presence inspired extraordinary love among his companions, but it never ceased to strike them with awe as well.

This book thus hopes to illuminate the double veils of a misunderstood time period and a saint who himself possessed a somewhat mysterious aura. This work does not pretend to be the definitive word on either subject, only a step in the process of reconstructing modern knowledge of the late eighteenth century in the Muslim world, and the Sufi shaykhs who dominated the stage.

17

Introduction: Sufism within Traditional Islam

T here remains a continued reluctance in some circles to admit the integral relationship between Sufism (Islamic mysticism) and the Islamic tradition. This reluctance exists despite the consensus of most contemporary academic research, not to mention the perspective of Sufis, or Muslim mystics themselves. While critics can always point to the executions of a few mystics such as al-Hallaj and Suhrawardi or the aberrant tendencies of some strands of popular Sufism such as those detailed in Jabarti's *History of Egypt*, elite or scholarly Sufism has more often than not found itself in the position of defining Islamic "orthodoxy" in the premodem period.

There is a long list of Sufi-scholars who have had a historically integral role in interpreting the Islamic message, including the likes of Abu Hamid al-Ghazali (d. 1111), Abu Zakariyya Yahya al-Nawawi (d. 1278) and Abd al-Rahman al-Suyuti (d. 1505), to name a few. Certainly there is much truth to the common assertion that it was the Sufi sages, whether in Malaysia, India, Anatolia, Upper Egypt or West Africa, who were responsible for spreading the religion of Islam. As long as the largely imagined barrier between Sufism and Islamic orthodoxy persists, Islamic history, from its supposed decline (Bernard Lewis), to its renaissance, to its spread, to the very personality of the Prophet Muhammad himself, are all in danger of being misunderstood if Islam is to be divorced from what might be defined as the essentially spiritual, mystical or "Sufi" nature of its message.

Even before modern ideas of Islam and Sufism's irreconciliability could be articulated, there emerged in the Muslim world a movement, the *Tariqa Muhammadiyya*, whose appearance indicates a decisive rejection of the idea of Sufisms alleged departure from Islamic orthodoxy. No wonder then, given the reluctance in the modem period to admit the close relationship between Sufism and Islam, that it has only been recently that this movement, despite its temporal proximity and popularity in the eighteenth and nineteenth centuries, has been granted any serious attention in the academic study of Sufism or premodern Islam.

The Revival of Sufism in the 18th Century: The Tariqa Muhammadiyya

At the end of the eighteenth century, a loose grouping of Sufis began to call their paths (*turuq*, sing., *tariqa*) the *Tariqa Muhammadiyya* or Muhammadan Path, as an expression of what they believed to be the essential link between the traditional Sufi *tariqa* and the Islamic message as taught and practiced by the Prophet Muhammad himself. Sufis have long conceptualized their practices as a path (*tariq* or *tariqa*) from the laws (Shariʿa) of the external or manifest (*zhahir*) to the reality (*haqiqa*) of the internal or hidden (*batin*). These paths often assumed the name of a seminal personality in their chains of spiritual knowledge transmission. Thus the followers of Shaykh Abd al-Qadir al-Jilani became known as the Qadiriyya or the disciples of the Abu Hassan al-Shadhili later took the name Shadhiliyya. It is easy for the critic to seize on the plethora of such paths by different names and accuse Sufism of dividing the Muslim community into a number of different sects. But each *tariqa* nonetheless believes itself to possess a chain of initiatory knowledge transmission (*silsilah*) legitimizing its ideas and practices from the Prophet himself. The emergence of a number of orders calling themselves the *Tariqa Muhammadiyya* is simply a further expression of the Muhammadan inheritance (*wiratha*) of which the Sufi orders have always believed themselves in possession. The development of the *Tariqa Muhammadiyya* phenomenon out of the tradition of earlier Sufism is indicative of this tradition's inseparability from the Islamic heritage and the inapplicability of the term "sect" to the different Sufi orders: being a member of a Sufi order was rarely grounds for a person to separate himself from the Islamic "orthodoxy" as it was defined at the time.

Aside from the popularization of the *Tariqa Muhammadiyya* nomenclature and the particular ways in which past Sufi ideas were combined in one spiritual path, the *Tariqa Muhammadiyya* phenomenon cannot be said to represent any particular innovation in the history of Sufism. Until recently, academic scholarship tended to lump the eighteenth-century renovators of Sufism under the colonial-inspired term of "Neo-Sufism." The "New Sufis" were the upstart reformers who departed from the tradition of benign Sufism and combined Sufi *tariqa* organization with Wahhabi style reactionism to resist European colonial incursion into Muslim societies.[1] Of course the Jihads led by the Tijaniyya in West Africa, by the Sanusiyya in Libya or by the Salihiyya in Somalia contributed to the tendency to see these orders, which had their roots in the new *tariqa* formation occurring at the end of the eighteenth century, as extremist cults created to resist the European "civilizing" mission. The "Neo-Sufi consensus" has been sufficiently deconstructed by O'Fahey (1990), Radtke (1993) and Sedgwick (1998) to obviate the need for the discussion of its shortcomings here. Clearly the most erroneous assumption of this consensus was the idea that the heightened Sufi activity at the end of the eighteenth century was actually a mirror of Wahhabi style puritanism and thus had little to do with the tradition of Sufism.[2]

---

1   H.A.R. Gibb, *Mohammedanism* (London: Oxford UP, 1949), p. 170.
2   Mark Sedgwick, *Heirs of Ahmad ibn Idris, The Spread and Normalization of a Sufi Order, 1799-1996* (Doctoral thesis at the University of

The historian is confronted then, with a period of increased Sufi organization on the brink of European occupation and the arrival of the modern age, but which cannot be said to represent anything particulary new when compaired to the earlier tradition of Sufism. The key to this development's categorization is perhaps found in how these movements perceived themselves, in other words, their use of the concept of the *Tariqa Muhammadiyya.* Moreover, if we cannot call this event a departure or innovation, then perhaps we can call it a culmination of certain elements of the Sufi and Islamic tradition in the affirmation of Islamic mysticism's essential connection to the Prophet of Islam.

Bergen, Norway, 1998), p. 49.

Economic and Social Factors in 18th Century Sufi Revival

Some writers have associated the eighteenth-century expansion of the Sufi orders in places like Egypt, to economic factors. Peter Gran, in his controversial book, *Islamic Roots of Capitalism,* describes the emergence of a new class of merchant-scholars, frequently involved with the Sufi orders, who were at the center of, if not an Islamic "Enlightenment," at least the beginnings of capitalism, class consciousness and the emergence of a "secular" culture. According to Gran, an increase in Hadith studies in the eighteenth century led to the affirmation of positivism and rationalism considered central to the capitalist project.[3] The Azhari *'Ulama,* many of whom were intimately involved with the Sufi orders, were behind an eighteenth-century commercial revival in Egypt, and they used the emphasis on Hadith study, where many traditions affirmed the value of trade and just profit, to justify their commercial activities.[4]

---

3   Peter Gran, *Islamic Roots of Capitalism: Egypt, 1760-1840* (Cairo: American University in Cairo Press, 1999), pp. 49-50.
4   ***Gran,*** Islamic Roots of Capitalism, ***p. liv.***

The Egyptian 'Ulama often used the medium of the Sufi order for trade, Gran contends, since it "provided the chief network of horizontal communication among the various trading communities in Cairo."[5] In general, the Sufi orders were "the institutions which mirrored the processes of social change during this period."[6] The reformist orders that were adopted by the Azhari 'Ulama, such as the Khalwatiyya (into which Shaykh Ahmad Tijani was initiated during his stay in Cairo), were particularly important in the rise of a new class of Sufi-scholar-merchants, who were able to influence both the Mamluk ruling elite and the Egyptian working class. This was because the orders possessed international trade links and were useful to the 'Ulama in sponsoring the religious revivalism needed to pacify the artisan (working) class in a state of turmoil caused by the dissolution of the medieval trade guilds.[7]

According to Gran, the "reformist orders" (mainly the Khalwatiyya) in Egypt owed much of their marked expansion in the eighteenth century to the wealth their leading members were able to accumulate, a wealth acquired, as Marsot has it, through the administration of *waqf* (trust) properties, tax farming, international trade and wages for scholarly services.[8] In a period of instability, the reformist Sufi orders that held within them several rich 'Ulama (many of whom had not been born into wealth), came to be seen as symbols of prosperity and upward mobility by the populace at large.

While social and economic factors cannot be excluded in explaining the growth of Sufism in the eighteenth century, the activities of some 'Ulama do not necessarily reflect the image of a Sufi order as a whole. More importantly, Egypt is a specif-

---

5 *Gran,* Islamic Roots of Capitalism, *p. 22.*

6 *Gran,* Islamic Roots of Capitalism, *p. liii.*

7 *Gran,* Islamic Roots of Capitalism, *pp. 178-179.*

8 Afaf Lutfi al-Sayyid Marsot, "The Wealth of the Ulama in late Eighteenth Century Cairo," in *Studies in Eighteenth Century Islamic History,* p. 205.

ic case, and there does not yet exist the data to make similar claims about the growth of Sufism outside of Egypt. Certainly this is true in the context of North Africa, where the Tijaniyya first spread. In many areas of the Islamic world during this time, there is even disagreement about whether the state was expanding or declining, so it becomes difficult to generalize as to the role of the 'Ulama or the Sufi orders in relation to the state and the people. This work thus does not attempt to relate the emergence of the Tijaniyya to social or economic factors, but rather limits itself to producing an intellectual portrait of its founder and his relationship to the *Tariqa Muhammadiyya* phenomenon.

Ahmad ibn Idris and Shaykh Ahmad Tijani

The period of increased Sufi activity towards the end of the eighteenth and beginning of the nineteenth centuries mostly revolves around two men, Sidi Ahmad ibn Idris (1750-1837) and Shaykh Ahmad Tijani (1737-1815). Ibn Idris, in the portrait painted for us by a number of excellent works including those by O'Fahey (1990), Vikor (1995) and Sedgwick (1998), was better known through the influence he left upon his students than through being the leader of any notable movement, and cannot himself be credited with the inception of one particular Sufi order. Ibn Idris was from Morocco but left Fes in 1798 to settle in the Hijaz. While there, his teachings influenced the likes of Muhammad al-Sanusi (1787-1859), founder of the *Sanusiyya* order in North Africa, Muhammad 'Uthman al- Mirghani (1793-1852), founder of the *Khatmiyya* or *Mirghaniyya* order in Sudan and Ibrahim Rashid (1813-1874), who provided the inspiration for three groups: the *Salihiyya* in Somalia, the *Dandarawiyya* in Sudan, Egypt and Syria and the *Rashidiyya* or the *Ahmadiyya*[9] in parts of Asia and Northeast Africa.

---

9   Not to be confused with the Qadiani Ahmadiyya movement started

It is tempting to suppose some sort of contact between Shaykh Ahmad Tijani and Ibn Idris since the former, although not installing himself permanently in Fes until after the departure of the latter, would have visited Fes when Ibn Idris was studying in the city. The two shared a student, Muhammad al-Sanusi, and there exist some similarities in certain prayers both men used.[10] But there is nevertheless no record of the two men ever meeting,[11] and we are left to conclude their shared contact with the Khalwati tradition in Egypt (discussed below and in chapter one) accounts for the similarities in thought and practice and, most importantly, their common use of the term *Tariqa Muhammadiyya*.

As for the Algerian-Moroccan Shaykh Ahmad Tijani (d. 1230/1815), his persona and teachings have remained somewhat shrouded in mystery notwithstanding previous academic research and despite the fact that the order to which he gives his name, the Tijaniyya, is today one of the most popular Sufi orders in the world. Shaykh Ahmad Tijani's conception of Islamic renovation through the *Tariqa Muhammadiyya* was to

---

in India by Mirza Ghulam Qadiani in 1871.

10   Both had links to the Moroccan Shadhili tradition and thus made use of Abu Hassan al-Shadhili's **Ahzab,** such as the **Hizb al-bahr** and **Hizb al-sayf.** Also some of the prayers in Ibn Idris's **Ahzab al-Awrad** are similar to those used by Shaykh Tijani, such as **Jawharat al-Kamal** (given to the Shaykh by the Prophet in a vision) and another reportedly used by him in Shaykh Ibrahim Niasse's **Jawahir al-Risala,** (Senegal, 1970), p. 165.

11   This, despite a tradition in the Sudan that Shaykh Ahmad Tijani had been a student of Ibn Idris. See Karrar, **Sufi Brotherhoods in the Sudan** (London: C. Hurst, 1992), p. 121. O'Fahey, however, declares this to be of doubtful authenticity. See Rex O'Fahey, **Enigmatic Saint, Ahmad Ibn Idris and the Idrisi Tradition** (London: C. Hurst, 1990), p. 46. Indeed, Shaykh Tijani was some thirteen years Ibn Idris's senior, and in any case, the **Jawahir al-Ma'ani** goes to great lengths to list all the teachers of Shaykh Tijani. Needless to say, Ibn Idris is not mentioned. If there was any contact, it would more likely have made Ibn Idris the student of Shaykh Tijani, itself a possibility maintained by al-Hasan al-Kuhin's **Tabaqat al-Shadhiliyya al- kubra** (O'Fahey, **Enigmatic Saint,** fh 58, pp. 46-47).

have a lasting inspiration on his followers to this day, who have often been at the forefront of the spread and renewal of Islam. Today, Tijani followers are found all over the world, from Indonesia to Albania to Egypt and Sudan to South Africa to North and West Africa to America to Canada to Europe to South America to china to Pakistan and India. The highest concentration of Tijanis is in West Africa, where a country such as Nigeria might possess up to thirty million adherents.[12] Indeed, Tijanis have been largely responsible for the spread of Islam in much of Africa, leading some to remark, "It is this Tijani push that Islamicized Africa. And if there had not been this [European colonial] occupant, all of Africa would have been islamicized."[13] But large populations of Tijanis exist outside of Africa as well. Indonesia, for example, possibly is the home of some two million Tijanis.[14]

The emergence of the Tijaniyya in the later part of the eighteenth century was neither an anomaly nor can it be discarded as an uninspired combination of past ideas. However, academic research, contrary to the case of Ahmad ibn Idris, has yet to really contextualize the order's emergence nor has it adequately elaborated on Shaykh Ahmad Tijani's teachings. As was mentioned, the Shaykh considered his new path or order to be a *Tariqa Muhammadiyya*. In applying this term to the Tijaniyya, he indicated the new *tariqa*'s links with a number of reform movements present in the Islamic world at the same time.

---

12   Mervyn Hiskett, "The Community of Grace and its opponents, the rejectors," in *African Language Studies* (17, 1980), pp. 99-140.

13   Chakib Arsalane, *The Presence of the Islamic Civilization,* cited by Abdelaziz Benabdellah, interview with author, Rabat, October 2002; also Benabdellah, interview with the Senegalese daily, *Le Soleil* (see www. abdelaziz-benabdellah.org, date not included in reprinting).

14   Benabdellah, *La Tijania, une Voie Spirituelle et Sociale* (Marrakech: A1 Quobba Zarqua, 1999), p. 66. For more on the Tijaniyya in Indonesia, see Martin Van Bruinessen, "Controversies and Polemics involving the Sufi orders in Twentieth Century Indonesia," in de Jong and Radtke ed.s, *Islamic Mysticism Contested* (Leiden: Brill, 1999).

Since Shaykh Tijani's links, whether physical or ideological, to these other thinkers of the time have not yet been thoroughly examined, the ideas specific to the order have not been properly understood, as they have been divorced from the context in which they sprang.

Elements of the Tariqa Muhammadiyya

Researchers have tentatively defined the late eighteenth-century *Tariqa Muhammadiyya* phenomenon as possessing a few basic elements:

1) Emphasis on the Sunna of the Prophet, leading to an objection to certain popular manifestations of Sufism and a deemphasis of the *madhahib* (schools of jurisprudence, sing., *madhhab*).

2) Prominence of the idea of the *Haqiqa Muhammadiyya* (Muhammadan Reality) in esoteric conceptualizations, leading to a form of spiritual concentration on the spirit of the Prophet and a deemphasis of the role of the shaykh in spiritual instruction.

3) Stress on the transmission of knowledge through dreams and visions of past saints or prophets, particularly through the waking vision of the Prophet.

4) A tendency to restrict the disciple's adherence to one preeminent *tariqa'*.

The *Tariqa Muhammadiyya* phenomenon saw a gradual evolution until its final culmination in the above form by the end of the eighteenth century, with most elements witnessed among a variety of scholars well prior to this time. The line of development has been traced by historians such as Mark Sedgwick in his thesis concerning Ahmad ibn Idris, and will be discussed later in chapter one. For now, it is enough to know that by the end of the eighteenth century the idea had become popular around the Muslim world, from Morocco to India. Shaykh Ahmad Tijani would have had contact with the idea both through the general context of Maghrebi Sufism and through direct interaction with the Khalwatiyya order under Mustafa Bakri (d. 1749) in Egypt and the Hijaz. During his pilgrimage, he himself became a propogator (*muqaddam*) of this order that was apparently at the center of the dissemination of the *Tariqa Muhammadiyya* idea and generally the impetus for a period of heightened Sufi activity and renewal, especially in Egypt.

What is clear in relation to Shaykh Ahmad Tijani is that he did not invent the idea of the *Tariqa Muhammadiyya*, which he used to describe the nature of his own path. Certainly the notion witnessed a gradual historical development until its final fruition at the end of the eighteenth century, but its essential features, such as the transcendent spirituality of the Prophet and mysticism's close relationship to the Law, were to be found very early in the history of Sufism, and probably from the very beginnings of Islam itself. The Shaykh's own contributions to the phenomenon were more quantitative than qualitative, meaning that his emergence simply represents an increased frequency of reported visionary contact with the Prophet, or the mystic's complete submersion in (and mastery of) the Law, or a more pronounced emphasis on the preeminence of the *Tariqa Muhammadiyya* over other *tariqa* affiliations.

Shaykh Ahmad Tijani's qualitative contribution to the *Tariqa Muhammadiyya* ideal revolves mostly around another idea resuscitated from earlier Sufi and Muslim conceptions, that of God's preference, bounty or grace *(fadl)* to His Prophet and those close to him. The Shaykh successfully endowed this idea of grace flowing through the Prophet with a sense of historical destiny embodied by the Tijaniyya order in heretofore unprecedented proportions. Tijanis quote the Qur'an in this regard in verses often cited in the primary source book of Tijani doctrine, the *Jawahir al-Ma'ani* (1799),

> *It is He Who has sent amongst the unlettered a messenger from among themselves, to rehearse to them His Signs, to sanctify them and to instruct them in Scripture and Wisdom - although they had been before in manifest error - As well as (to confer all these benefits upon) others among them, who have not already joined them: and He is Exalted in Might, Wise. Such is the Bounty (fadl) of Allah, which He bestows on whom He will: and Allah is the Lord of the highest bounty.[15]*

In describing his own *Tariqa Muhammadiyya* as the receptacle of this bounty or grace God had conferred on the creation through the medium of His Prophet, Shaykh Ahmad Tijani was making no small claim. Despite the deterioration of true guidance since the time of the Prophet, there remained, according to him, a continued possibility of accessing Divine favor, and the Shaykh saw himself in the position of defining the elements of such a path of grace, mostly through the principle of *shukr,* or giving thanks to God, which took precedence over spiritual mortification and worldly renunciation.

In order to perceive the distinctive contributions of the order of Shaykh Ahmad Tijani, we must first examine the historical and intellectual context of its emergence. The phenomonon of the *Tariqa Muhammadiyya* provides a useful framework for study of the order because it is endowed with both an academic, historical definition (even if it is still in the process of being

---

15   Qur'an, 62:2-4, 'Abdullah Yusef'Ali translation.

worked out) and the term has itself been used by Tijanis themselves. Of course, it is not presumed that academics and Tijanis have perceived the *Tariqa Muhammadiyya* in the same manner, the academic historian being preoccupied with the idea of historical change while the Tijani being concerned with actual practice and the historically contiguous nature of his ideology. But unless a historical work is to be divorced from making any sense to his subject, the historian cannot afford to neglect this latter essential question of how Tijanis have themselves conceived the nature of their *Tariqa Muhammadiyya*. This work thus presents the emergence of Shaykh Ahmad Tijani's *Tariqa Muhammadiyya* as an important historical "elaboration" of the Islamic and Sufi traditions, meaning its originality or newness is a question of a degree of emphasis rather than any significant innovation. In so doing, I hope to satisfy both types of readers, one interested in the processes of historical change, another curious as to what Tijanis actually believe and practice.

Note on Sources

There are few secondary sources in European languages that are of much use for the study of the Tijaniyya, but those that exist include Jamil Abun-Nasr's *The Tijaniyya, A Sufi Order in the Modern World* (1965); the section on Shaykh Ahmad Tijani entitled "Le Confrerisme et les Lumieres" in Jacques Berque's *L'interieur du Maghreb XVe-XIXe siecle* (1978); the brief remarks about the Shaykh's thought on key doctrinal issues in Bemd Radtke's "Sufism in the 18th Century: an attempt at a provisional reprisal" (1996); Abdelaziz Benabdellah's *La Tijania: Une Voie Spirituelle et Sociale* (1998); and two articles by Jillali El Adnani summarizing his doctoral work in Karthala's *La Tijaniyya* (2000), entitled "Reflexions sur la naissance de la Tijaniyya" and "Les origines de la Tijaniyya."[16]

Of the five authors, Berque and Radtke contain excellent, if altogether too brief for any kind of in-depth understanding, discussions of the Shaykh Ahmad Tijani's thought. They do not, however, contain much information about the person and life of the Shaykh. Benabdellah's work has proved valuable for this work, containing both information of Shaykh Ahmad

---

16   Adnani's articles are contained in Jean-Louis Triaud and David Robinson ed.s, *La Tijaniyya, Une Confrerie musulmane a la conquete de l'Afrique* (Paris: Karthala, 2000).

Tijani's life and thought based on primary sources. Himself a Tijani savant, Benabdellah's book is a useful reconstruction of how Tijanis have come to interpret their own doctrine. But it does not contain much concerning the intellectual context out of which the Shaykh emerged, nor does it provide the order with much in the way of historical distinction, mentioning only in passing the Shaykh's ideas of the Divine grace embodied in his own *Tariqa Muhammadiyya*.

Abun-Nasr's book is a systematic study of both the Shaykh's life and thought and the later history of the Tijaniyya in the lands of its spread. But unfortunately, it divorces Shaykh Ahmad Tijani from the context of Sufism in general and from the eighteenth-century *Tariqa Muhammadiyya* phenomenon in particular. It likewise contains many distortions of the Shaykh's life and thought, as well as the later history of the order, that seem rooted in an a *priori* agenda concerning Sufism's superstitious irrationality and betrayal of the Arab nation. Abun-Nasr, himself of Lebenese orgin, believes the Sufi orders have been responsible for the spread of superstition and sorcery in the Muslim world in general, and in the Maghrib in particular."[17] Elsewhere he attempts to demonstrate the complicity of the orders in European colonialism and concludes: "Their story is, therefore, that of adjustment and reconciliation, which would have enabled them to survive politically had it not been that the doctrines which they preached and the functions they performed were no longer suited to modem times."[18] It is easy to see how a work with such presuppositions might serve to marginalize what appears to have been the cosmopolitan and scholarly nature of Shaykh Ahmad Tijani.

El Adnani's two articles provide some valuable insight in attempting to lift the veil of mystery surrounding the Shaykh and

---

17   Jamil Abun-Nasr, *The Tijaniyya, a Sufi Order in the Modem World* (London: Oxford UP, 1965), p. 8.
18   Abun-Nasr, *The Tijaniyya*, p. 14.

his companions. But his starting point seems to be the "routin-ization of charisma" theory of Max Weber, where Shaykh Ah-mad Tijani becomes an example of a religious leader's attempts to construct a personality cult around his own person. As such, Adnani's articles are more concerned with combing the order's primary sources for clues about conflicts between the Shaykh and his followers than with the actual doctrines or history of the order. The resulting construction of saintly authority was so strong in the case of Shaykh Ahmad Tijani, according to Adnani, that Tijani disciples "forget that the emanation comes from God" and "have surrendered the weapons of reason in order to embrace the faith in their master."[19] Such an attempt to discredit the religious authenticity of the order[20] only serves to further confuse its history and doctrine, imposing as it does dubious notions of the formation of religious movements that suppose some sort of clandestine will to power in the shaping of doctrine. What suffers most in this sort of analysis is the movement's actual history, its own self-identity and what the founder is actually saying.

* * *

The most important primary source for this work, and in-deed for any study of the Tijaniyya, is 'Ali Harazem al-Barada's *Jawahir al-Ma'ani wa bulugh al-amani fi fayd Sidi Abi al-'Abbas al-Tijani,* "The Jewels of the Meanings and the attainment of hopes in the flood of Sidi Abu al-'Abbas al-Tijani." This book, completed in 1799, possesses a certain mystique as the work approved by Shaykh Ahmad Tijani and kept in his possession for a number of years. The Prophet himself, in a visionary

---

19   Adnani, "Les origines de la Tijaniyya: quand les premiers disciples se mettent a parler," p. 63.
20   Adnani compares the founding of the Tijaniyya to the founding of Islam in its supposed lack of authenticity. See Adnani, "Les origines de la Tijaniyya," p. 63.

appearance to the Shaykh, is said to have ordered the book's compilation, recompilation and approved its final redaction.[21] It contains two volumes consisting of about nine chapters in total which cover rather traditional subjects for such a genre of literature: the Shaykh's biography, a description of his character, knowledge and miracles, his litanies, his interpretations of specific passages from the Qur'an and Hadith, his letters and his rulings on specific legal issues.

The *Jawahir* has served as the major source of doctrine for Tijanis since the time of the Shaykh, even if some admit that Muhammad ibn al-Mushri's *Kitab al-Jami' li al-'ulum al-fa'ida min bihar al-Qutb al-Muktum* ("The Comprehensive Book for the bountiful sciences from the seas of the Hidden Pole") is more authentic since its later compilation (1808) demonstrates its author's longer period of companionship with Shaykh Ahmad Tijani.[22] Jillali El Adnani has presented a convincing case for the study of this latter book,[23] but given the fact it has remained unpublished[24] and lacks the official status of the *Jawahir*, and because a good portion of the book simply comprises a summary of al-Barada's text (in some cases the exact same passages), this work gives more attention to the *Jawahir*.

The *Jawahir* itself is a text shrouded in controversy, since its uncredited relationship to a previous work was brought to light by the reform-minded Salafiyya movement in Morocco in 1932 as a means to discredit the Tijaniyya.[25] It seems 'Ali Harazem al-Barada lifted the introduction and some of the poetry from an earlier book of the Wazzaniyya Sufi order (to

---

21   Ali Harazem al-Barada, *Jawahir al-Ma 'ani* (Cairo: Dar al-Fikr, 2001), p. 27.
22   Shaykh Hassan Cisse, interview, Medina Kaolack, Senegal, November, 2002; Abdelaziz Benabdellah, interview, Rabat, Morocco, October, 2002.
23   Adnani, "Les origines de la Tijaniyya," pp. 42-48.
24   Tijani tradition, according to Shaykh Hassan Cisse, has it that whoever should publish the book will die.
25   Abun-Nasr, *The Tijaniyya,* pp. 23-24; Adnani, "Les origines de la Tijaniyya," p. 50.

which Harazem had previously been affiliated) concerning the Moroccan saint Ahmad ibn Abdullah Ma'n al-Andalusi (d. 1708), called the *Kitab al-Maqsid al-Ahmad fi al-ta 'rifbi Sayyidina ibn 'Abdullah Ahmad,* written by Muhammad Abd al-Salam al-Qadiri. The accusation of plagiarism has been contested by later Tijanis, such as the Moroccan savant Ahmad Sukayrij, by referring to the well-established tradition of writers borrowing from previous manuscripts in classical Arabic literature, thereby minimizing the notion of exclusive authorship, which was not so important then, according to Sukayrij and many others, as it has become in modern times.[26] In any case, the *Jawahir*'s relationship to the *Kitab al-Maqsad* in no way affects the authenticity of the *Jawahir* as a source for the study of the Tijaniyya. What is important for our purposes is that it dates from the time of Shaykh Ahmad Tijani and that he himself approved the work in the presence of his companions.

Nonetheless, the present-day Senegalese Tijani Shaykh Hassan Cisse has charged the published version of the *Jawahir* with deviation from its original form. Shaykh Hassan seems to have inherited the original manuscript of the book that was itself in the possession of Shaykh Ahmad Tijani from the time of its writing until his death. The story of how the book came to be in Shaykh Hassan's possession is itself of interest. The manuscript was given to Shaykh Hassan's great-grandfather, al-Hajj Abdullah Niasse, when he visited Fes in 1903. Al-Hajj Abdullah obtained the book from the head of the Fes Zawiya at that time through the visionary intervention of Shaykh Ahmad Tijani himself. In 1915, the manuscript was borrowed from the Senegalese Shaykh by a Moroccan scholar and returned in 1922, but with a few pages missing, which Shaykh Ibrahim ibn Abdullah Niasse had replaced with copies from the published

---

26   Ahmad Sukayrij, *Kashf al-Hijab*, cited in Adnani, "Les origines de la Tijaniyya," p. 51. See also an article concerning authorship in Sufi poetry by Midrad Frishkopf, in *ALIF Journal of Comparative Poetics* (Cairo, AUC Press, Spring, 2003).

version by Sidi 'Ali Cisse. In Fes in 1986, Shaykh Hassan Cisse (the son of 'Ali Cisse and grandson of Shaykh Ibrahim) identified the missing pages of the original *Jawahir al-Ma 'ani* from a seller of ancient manuscripts and had them placed along with the original in his possession.[27] Shaykh Hassan's copy matches the other oldest known copy of the *Jawahir*, which exists in the *Biblioteque Nationale* in Paris, and matches other older unpublished copies.[28] The original manuscript, which is currently in the process of being published in Egypt by Shaykh Hassan's brother, Shaykh Tijani Cisse, differs slightly from the published version.[29] Shaykh Ibrahim Niasse once cited such a discrepancy as evidence that the words of Shaykh Ahmad Tijani were victims of tampering with malignant intention in the same way some of Ibn 'Arabi's works were distorted.[30]

Despite having obtained a photocopied version of the original manuscript from Shaykh Hassan, this paper cites the most recently published version (Egypt, 2001) for the reader's benefit in verifying my citations, should the desire exist. While the publishing of the original version of the *Jawahir* is certainly a matter of great importance, it does not seem the two texts differ so much as to render the currently published version unreliable. But to be safe, I have checked the published version of the *Jawahir* both against the manuscript version and relevant passages in the *Kitab al-Jami'* on esoteric or disputed issues,

---

27   Interview with Shaykh Hassan Cisse, Medina Kaolack, Senegal, November, 2002.
28   Shaykh Ibrahim Niasse, "Lumieres sur la Tijaniyya et les Tijan," (trans. Gane Samb Lo, Dakar: GARSIS, unknown date of publication), p. 7.
29   Shaykh Hassan once compared the two texts line by line, underlining all the additions in the published version.
30   Shaykh Ibrahim Niasse, "Lumieres sur la Tijaniyya et les Tijan," p. 7. Such an occurrence in the case of Shaykh Ahmad Tijani was also recognized by Shaykh al- Azhar 'Abd al-Halim Mahmud in a 1982 *fatwa* (Jean-Louis Triaud, "La Tijaniyya, voie infaillible ou voie soufie inventee: autour du pamphlet anti-tijani d'Ibrahim al- Qattan," in Triaud and Robinson ed.s, *La Tijaniyya,* p. 172).

such as those concerning the *Haqiqa Muhammadiyya* (Muhammadan Reality), the nature of the *Qutb al-Aqtab* (Pole of the poles) or the benefits of the prayer, *Salat al-Fatih*, and have not found any discrepencies of note.

Beside the *Jawahir al-Ma'ani* and the *Kitab al-Jami '*, another primary source includes the *Kitab Ifadat al-Ahmadiyya li murid also'ada al'abadiyya* by a companion of Shaykh Ahmad Tijani, Muhammad al-Tayyib al-Sufyani (d. 1843).[31] This short book was written after the founder's death for the purpose of recording some of his words not contained in either the *Jawahir* or the *Jami '*. Other early Tijani sources include al-Hajj 'Umar al-Futi's (d. 1864) *Kitab Rimah hizb al-Rahim 'ala nuhur hizb al-rajim,*[32] completed in 1845 and long considered such a worthy commentary on the *Jawahir* and a compendium of Sufism in general that it has always been printed with the *Jawahir,* either in the margins or immediately following. There is also the *Mizab al-Rahma al-Rabbaniyya fi al-tarbiyya hi al-tariqa al-tijaniyya,* a book written in 1851 by 'Ubayda ibn Muhammad al-Saghir that emphasizes the order as a path of gratitude (*shukr*) for Divine grace.[33] Also of importance is Muhammad al-'Arabi ibn Sa'ih's late nineteenth-century *Bughyat al-Mustafid li sharh muniat al-murid,*[34] considered a more easily accessible summary of Tijani doctrine than the contents of the *Jawahir.* The work of Ahmad al-Amin al-Shinqiti (d. 1913), the *Fath al-Rabbani* is likewise considered an important summary of Tijani doctrine.[35] Two other sources of importance for this

---

31   Al-Tayyib al-Sufyani, *Ifadat al-Ahmadiyya li murid al-saiada wal-abdiyya* (ed. Muhammad al-Hafiz, Cairo: Khairiya, unknown date).

32   Al-Hajj 'Umar al-Futi, *Kitab al-Rimah* (printed with *Jawahir al-Ma 'ani,* Cairo: Dar al-Fikr, 2001.

33   Ubayda ibn Muhammad al-Saghir al-Shinqiti al-Tishiti, *Mizab al-Rahmat al- Rabbaniyya* (Beirut: Dar al-'Ilm, 1973).

34   Muhammad al-'Arabi Ibn Sa'ih, *Bughyat al-Mustafld* (Cairo: al-Babi, 1959).

35   Ahmad al-Amin Shinqiti, *Al-Futuhat al-Rabbanniyya fi al-Tariqa al-Ahmadiyya al-Tijaniyya*, in Muhammad al-Tasafawi al-Tijani, *Al-Fath al*

work are Ahmad Sukayrij's *Kashf al-Hijab*, [36] containing the biographies of all of Shaykh Ahmad Tijani's important disciples, and Shaykh Ibrahim Niasse's *Kashf al-'Ilbas*,[37] a twentieth century justification and application of classical Tijani doctrine. Lastly, I have also obtained a copy of a letter that is believed to have been written by Shaykh Ahmad Tijani himself, from the private collection of Shaykh Hassan Cisse.[38]

The secondary sources in European languages all make use of the *Jawahir al-Ma'ani* to varying degrees, with the work of Berque representing the most in-depth study of the doctrines contained in it thus far. Adnani is mostly concerned with the *Kitab al-Jami '*, although he seems uninterested in most of the essential doctrinal issues it contains. Abun-Nasr cites from nearly all of the important Tijani sources, but his use of the *Jawahir* is selective and usually out of context with the larger picture of Sufism presented in the work. Benabdellah gives voice to most of the essential Tijani works, with preference given to the *Jawahir*, the *Kitab al-Rimah* and the *Bughyat al-Mustafid*, the latter which he considers the key to understanding the *Jawahir* and Tijani doctrine itself.[39] This book is primarily concerned with a more systematic study of the *Jawahir al-Ma'ani*, but other sources that have proved important include the *Kitab al- Jami '*, the *Kitab al-Rimah*, the *Kashf al-Hijab* and the *Kashf al-'Ilbas*. This book obviously does not pretend to present a comprehensive study of Tijani sources, but rather to offer a significant step in

---

Rabbani fima mahtajliyhi al-murid al-Tijani (Casablanca: Dar al-kitab, unknown date)

36   Ahmad Sukayrij, *Kashf al-Hijab* (Casablanca: Dar al-Kitab, unknown date).

37   **Shaykh Ibrahim Niasse,** Kashf al- 'Ilbas 'an al-Khatm Abi al-Abbas **(Cairo, 2001).**

38   The content of this letter, mostly concerning sainthood and the nature of the shaykh-disciple relationship, matches closely similar discussions in the *Jawahir al- Ma 'ani*, a further credit (besides the testimony of Shaykh Hassan Cisse himself) to its authenticity.

39   Benabdellah, interview, Rabat, Morocco, October, 2002.

reconstructing a clearer picture of the Tijaniyya based on these sources, starting from the first and most important source, the *Jawahir al-Ma'ani.*

Frequent recourse has been made to interviews with some contemporary scholars from within the Tijani tradition in order to help interpret Tijani doctrine. The academic field of history is largely concerned with the analysis of primary texts, but many researchers, especially in the field of Sufism, have concluded that the historian is also in need of the oral tradition. As Seyyed Hossein Nasr has explained, Sufi doctrines and practices, as with other fields of traditional Islamic knowledge, are handed down generation after generation in unbroken transmission through qualified scholars. Sufism is one of the traditional Islamic sciences, according to Nasr, where the oral tradition must be relied on to interpret the written tradition. Not only do the texts available not represent the entirety of the knowledge contained in a particular Sufi tradition, they can also be misleading as they were sometimes purposefully written as a sort of a code to be deciphered by scholars who had inherited the relevant oral tradition directly from their predecessors. [40] Nasr's approach runs the obvious risk of obscuring the historical development of the oral tradition surrounding the interpretation of written texts, a danger of which the historian must necessarily be mindful, although it should not prevent him from engaging or even relying on the oral tradition, especially in the case of an unclear or esoteric text. I have thus attempted to judiciously involve the contemporary, largely oral, understanding of how scholarly Tijanis have interpreted their own tradition. My primary source in this regard has been

---

40   Seyyed Hossein Nasr, "Oral Transmission and the Book in Islamic Education: The Spoken and Written Word," in George Atiyeh ed., *The Book in the Islamic World, The Written Word and Communication in the Middle East* (Albany, SUNY Press, 1995), pp. 57-70. Also Nasr, "An Intellectual Autobiography," in Hahn, Auxier and Stone ed.s, The Philosophy of Seyyed Hossein Nasr (Peru, Illinois: Open Court, 2001), pp. 40-41.

Shaykh Hassan Cisse, the Senegalese Imam who is one of the foremost scholars and propogators of the Tijaniyya in the world today.[41] Other scholars that have been helpful include Professor Abdelaziz Benabdellah, a Moroccan Tijani savant and one of the most prolific contemporary writers on the order; al-Hajj Muhsin Shalaby, a shaykh of the Tijaniyya in Heliopolis (Cairo), Egypt; as well as some of the descendents of the Shaykh Ahmad Tijani in Fes.

The field-work that forms the basis of these interviews includes a year in Medina Kaolack and Dakar, Senegal (comprising about seven trips of one or more visit per year, 1997-2003), nearly a year in Fes, Morocco (2002-2003), as well as some interviews conducted while in Cairo (2000-2002). Aside from interviews of important Tijani scholars in their own homes, 1 also had opportunity to meet with Shaykh Hassan Cisse in France (August, 2001) and Morocco (March, 2003) and al-Hajj Muhsin Shalaby in Morocco (December, 2002 and March, 2003) and New York (January, 2003).

---

41   Although he has never publically pronounced such a claim, Shaykh Hassan possesses the necessary prerogative to be *khalifa* of the entire order. Before dying, Shaykh Ibrahim Niasse named him his *khalifa* (successor). Shaykh Ibrahim was himself named *khalifa* by Ahmad Sukayrij, who in turn received the title from Ahmad Abdalawi, receiving from Ali Tamasin, named *khalifa* by Shaykh Ahmad Tijani. In any case, it does not seem that any attempt has ever been made to organize the order exclusively around one leader.

Plan of Development

As no history, according to the more recent principles of historiography, can claim to be more than a narrative, this work does not claim any definitive reconstruction of Shaykh Ahmad Tijani's life and thought. I am attempting to emphasize a narrative that has been left out in most previous academic works concerning the Tijaniyya; namely that the order was more than a contrived anomaly, but sprang out of the vibrant context of eighteenth-century Sufism with a remarkable enthusiasm and conviction to define one of the more important movements of Islamic renewal. Far from being an outmoded phenomenon, Sufism, and particularly the Tijaniyya (due to its structural entrenchment and continuity in places like West Africa), remains an important element of vibrancy and Islamic traditionalism in a Muslim world that often seems on the verge of being torn apart by radicalized ideological movements.

This work will attempt to reconstruct such a narrative through three main parts. First, I attempt to clarify, based on primary sources, some basics of Shaykh Ahmad Tijani's biography in order to establish his scholarly influences and his contacts with some of the important people and historical events of his time. Secondly, I discuss the Shaykh's relationship to the external elements of the *Tariqa Muhammadiyya* phenomenon, namely his conception of the Shari'a, the Sunna of the Prophet, involvement in the world and *ijtihad,* or scholarly interpretation. Some attention is given here as well to the accusations of the Shaykh's departure from Islamic orthodoxy. Finally, I situate Shaykh Ahmad Tijani's esoteric doctrines within the context of the earlier Sufi tradition (extending, in the *Jawahir,* from Junayd well into the fifteenth century), attempting to provide the ideological context for the emergence of the distinctive esoteric doctrines of the *Tariqa Muhammadiyya,* such as *Haqiqa Muhammadiyya* or the vision of the Prophet. This section develops into a discussion of the Shaykh's specific ideas of Divine grace, which he associates with the *Tariqa Muhammadiyya.* My conclusion defines the emergence of Shaykh Ahmad Tijani and the Tijaniyya more as a culmination of the tradition of classical, scholarly Sufism than as a departure from it. Rather than another indication of Islam's supposed eighteenth-century decline into superstition and self-gratification (Abun-Nasr), the order may be described as a movement of Islamic renewal in a time of uncertainty. As a final note, I briefly touch on the later spread of the Tijaniyya, particularly in West Africa, both as a means to demonstrate the forceful impact the order has often had in the lands of its spread and to demonstrate how the history of the order has sometimes been obscured by modem polemic.

Chapter I

Biographical Portrait I: In Search

of Knowledge

Early years and teachers

Sidi Abu Abbas Ahmad al-Tijani (hereafter referred to as Shaykh Ahmad Tijani) was bom in the Southwest Algerian oasis town of Ain Madi on the twelfth of Safar in the year 1150 (1737 C.E.).[42] He was a descendent of the Prophet Muhammad through Fatima Zahra's first son Hasan and later through Mawlay Idris, the celebrated founder of Morocco.[43] His father was Sidi Muhammad b. al-Mukhtar b. Ahmad b. Muhammad b. Salam, a prominent scholar whose family hailed from the Moroccan Abda tribe and whose grandfather had immigrated to Ain Madi fleeing a Portugese invasion less than a century before Shaykh Tijani's birth.[44] This same ancestor was perhaps one of the more renowned of the Tijani line prior to Shaykh Ahmad Tijani, and it is reported that he used

---

42   The year, as some later Tijanis have pointed out, happens to be the numerical equivalent of the Arabic words **mawlid al-khatm** ("birth of the Seal"), and thus was significant for them in fulfilling the coming of the "Seal of the Saints."

43   As with many claimants of Sharif status in peripheral areas to the Islamic world proper, Shaykh Tijani's claim to be Sharif was not without contestation. See Abun- Nasr, *The Tijaniyya,* p. 16.

44   Benabdellah, *La Tijania,* p. 9.

to engage so much in spiritual retreat *(khalwa)* that he would have to walk to the five prayers in the mosque with his face covered, otherwise onlookers would fall so heedlessly in love with him that they would thereafter never be able to separate from him.[45] Shaykh Tijani's mother, Aisha, was the daughter of Muhammad b. Sanusi (no known relation to Muhammad al-Sanusi, the founder of the Sanusiyya Tariqa), and was noted for her piety and generosity.[46]

The Tijani family was apparently not the dominant family in Ain Madi prior to the nineteenth century; that position was held by the descendents of Sidi Ahmad al-Dahsa. A seventeenth-century pilgrim's witness to the city describes it as being primarily composed of scholars and students, who were known for excellence in jurisprudence and who mostly studied the *Mukhtasar* (a summary of the Maliki school of jurisprudence) of Sidi Khalil.[47]

The young Shaykh Tijani continued in the scholarly tradition of his family and city, memorizing the Qur'an by the age of seven before turning to the study of jurisprudence *(fiqh and usul al-fiqh),* Prophetic traditions (Hadith), explanation of the Qur'an *(tafsir),* Qur'anic recitation *(tajwid),* grammar *(nahw)* and literature *(adab),* among other branches of the traditional Islamic sciences. According to the *Jawahir,* the Shaykh mastered all of these fields at a very young age, in part due to the force of his resolve but also because of the quality of his teachers. Among his first instructors were masters of their fields, such as Sidi Mabruk Ibn Ba'afiyya Midawi al-Tijani (not mentioned in the *Jawahir* as being a relation to Ahmad Tijani), with whom he studied the *Mukhtasar* of Sidi Khalil, the *Risala*[48] and

---

45   Muhammad ibn Mishry, **Kitab al-Jami '** (manuscript copy attained in Morocco), b. I, pp. 6-7.

46   Jawahir, p. 11.

47   The testimony of A.b. Nasir, cited in Adnani, "Reflexions sur la naissance de la Tijaniyya," p. 22.

48   The *Risala* was an integration of Sufism and 'Ashari theology. See Abu-Nasr, *The Tijaniyya,* p. 17.

the *Muqaddama* of Ibn Rushd (Averoes) and the *Kitab al-'Iba-da* of al-Akhdari.[49] What is striking to the modem reader, who might tend to distinguish between scholars of the "external" sciences (such as law, grammar or Qur'anic exegesis) and esoteric gnostics, is that many of those who taught Tijani the so-called exoteric or external Islamic sciences in this early period were simultaneously known for their spiritual energy and Sufi inclinations. His teacher of the Qur'an, for example, Sidi Muhammad ibn Hamw al-Tijani, was acknowledged for having his knowledge of the Qur'an deepened by visionary experience.[50]

In trying to contextualize Shaykh Tijani's early period of learning, we should not underestimate his own commitment to the path of knowledge. In this regard, the *Jawahir* reports the saying of his, "When I begin something, I never turn from it."[51] In another passage describing his love for the people of religion, the *Jawahir* describes him as a youth of powerful intelligence, such that nothing escaped his realization.[52] Thus, after he had mastered the sciences available in Ain Madi and had become by the age of twenty, according to the *Jawahir*, a great scholar, jurist and man of letters such that people were coming to partake of the knowledge of this newest Mufti (a scholar licensed to issue legal decisions), his thirst for more knowledge pushed him to leave the city of his birth in 1171/1758. It should be recognized that such accounts of an important shaykh's biography, as contained in the *Jawahir*, nearly always stress the youthful achievements of their subject, but this is not to say these events did not actually happen.

There are of course other ways to explain his departure from Ain Madi at the age of twenty-one. Five years before, his parents had died on the same day from a devastating plague, and although he was already married at this time (a marriage

---

49   *Jawahir*, p. 17.
50   Jawahir, *p. 17.*
51   *Jawahir*, p. 19.
52   *Jawahir*, p. 19.

contracted by his father, which Tijani dissolved prior to his leaving Ain Madi), it seems he was left as the sole surviving member of his family.[53] However, more importantly, he had early on become interested in another branch of the traditional Islamic sciences, that of the soul's purification (*tassawuf*) or Sufism. Even prior to his formal association with any of the Sufi orders, he would, according to the *Jawahir,* spend much of the night in prayer, and certainly the spiritual interest and vigor of his early teachers could only have served to reinforce his inclinations towards Sufism. That Sufism should be the natural means of seeking a path to the further realization of the knowledge of God was a sentiment Shaykh Tijani shared with the majority of Islamic scholars in the pre-modem context,[54][13] so it is fruitless to explain his early interest in Sufism other than it being a natural extension of his mastery of the traditional Islamic sciences.[55]

The obvious destination for any seeker of Islamic knowledge in the Maghrebi context was Fes, the long-established political, intellectual, cultural and religious capital of the area. According to the Moroccan professor Abdelaziz Benabdellah, Ain Madi was at the time of Tijani's birth still considered part of the Moroccan sultanate despite Ottoman attempts to claim Morocco's eastern provinces, areas now part of Algeria. Whatever the political and military maneuvering in the area of Ain Madi between the Moroccan and Ottoman governments during Tijani's younger years,[56] it is probable that people in the

---

53   Adnani, "Reflexions," p. 25. He would later free two slaves, Mabruka and Mubaraka, and marry them.

54   See, for example, the biographies of prominent eighteenth century scholars in Jabarti's **History of Egypt,** most of whom became affiliated with some Sufi shaykh as a matter of course in their general course of study.

55   Adnani feels it appropriate to suggest a sense of loss at his parents' death occasioned al-Tijani's proclivity towards esotericism. See Adnani, "Reflexions," p. 25.

56   In 1150/1737, Mawlay Abdullah sent an expedition under Caid Jilali Ben Muhammad Saffar against the Turks, who were trying to instigate the secession of Morocco's eastern provinces, such as Mhaya, Benou Hachem,

area would have perceived travelling to Fes as nothing but the move from one Moroccan city to another.[57] But clearly Tijani was interested in more than escaping the political intrigues of his times in setting out for what would be the first of many journeys. According to the *Jawahir*, the young Shaykh Tijani spent his time in Fes studying Hadith and generally seeking out the people of piety and religion.[58]

Among his teachers in Fes were many famous for their knowledge and saintliness. Their names are provided here to demonstrate Shaykh Ahmad Tijani's contact with some of the more significant luminaries of eighteenth-century Moroccan Sufism. Al-Tayyib b. Muhammad al-Sharif of Wazan (d. 1180/1767), who was head of the Wazzaniyya Sufi order at the time and the student of the famous Shaykh Tuhami, descending from the Jazuli shaykh Ahmad al-Sarsari,[59] gave Tijani permission to give spiritual instruction, only to have the young scholar refuse so that he might work harder on himself before becoming a spiritual guide.[60] Sidi Abdullah b. 'Arabi al-Mada'u (d. 1188) was likewise impressed with his student, telling him that God was guiding him by the hand, and before Tijani left him, the old scholar washed his student with his own hands. Another scholar to predict to Tijani an exalted spiritual attainment was Sidi Ahmad al-Tawash (d. 1204).[61] From Sidi Ahmad al-Yemeni, Shaykh Tijani took the Qadariyya Sufi order, and from Abu Abdullah Sidi Muhammad al-Tizani he took the Nasiriyya order. He also took the order of Abu Abbas Ahmad al-Habib al-Sijilmasy (d. 1165), who came to him in a dream, put his mouth on his, and taught him a secret name.[62] Although

South Oran, Chellala, Aflou, Ain Madi and Laghwat (territories part of Morocco for 150 years). Later, Turkish troops under the Bey of Mescara began openly attacking these eastern provinces. See Benabdellah, *La Tijania,* p. 19.
57   Abdelaziz Benabdellah, interview, Rabat, October, 2002.
58   *Jawahir,* p. 20.
59   Benabellah, *La Tijania,* p. 11.
60   *Jawahir,* p. 23.
61   *Jawahir,* p. 23.
62   *Jawahir,* p. 24.

Tijani did receive spiritual permission *(idhni)* in these orders, his association with them should not be considered the essential element in his spiritual development. But the imprint of his early affiliation with these orders was not completely lost with the later development of the Tijaniyya, and their emphasis on an elite "orthodox" Sufism, firmly rooted within the bounds of the Qur'an and Sunna, was an essential component of Shaykh Tijani's new order, as will be seen later in chapter three.

Shaykh Ahmad Tijani's encounters with shaykhs prior to his 1784 illumination, which resulted in the foundation of his own *Tariqa Muhammadiyya,* brings up an important question of the nature of the relationship between a saint who would later claim the height of the saintly hierarchy and his teachers who obviously imparted to him knowledge and whose understanding of Sufism was closely related to that of Shaykh Tijani himself. It does not seem that the latter's later claims to an exalted spiritual status were meant to belittle the roles of his past teachers, and the *Jawahir* contains the most glowing descriptions of the saintliness of these shaykhs and the meetings with them often appear to have been intense spiritual encounters. Nevertheless, it is clear Shaykh Tijani was not overly interested in any one *tariqa* affiliation or becoming the lifelong disciple of any of his teachers. The implication of the *Jawahir* is that Tijani was seeking a position beyond that which his teachers could grant him, infact each of them assured him of a position beyond which they had attained.[63]

It is also likely that some sort of reluctance towards a life-long affiliation to one shaykh was manifested on the part of Shaykh Tijani himself. For someone to whom the visionary experience of the Prophet Muhammad was later to become such an important reality, presumably his early dream visions of the Prophet

---

63   According to Shaykh Hassan Cisse (interview, Rabat, March 2003), al-Tijani did not have any life-long obedience to one shaykh, since all his teachers pushed him onwards, assuring him of "good tidings."

during this time were enough to alert him, "*Divine Providence wanted him to have as master the only universal master and most sublime of creatures, the Prophet Muhammad.*"[64] Professor Benabdellah writes that, due to his foreseen initiation at the hands of the Prophet, Shaykh Tijani in fact insisted upon "the temporary nature of all engagements" with other shaykhs.[65] All of this does not, however, downplay the necessity in Tijani thought, of having a shaykh of spiritual education *(shaykh al-tarbiyya)*, and the central role of such a guide is emphasized by al-Tijani himself, as will be discussed later in chapter five.

Evidence from the *Jawahir* suggests that it was not through a lack of desire for spiritual instruction or an abscence of respect for his teachers that Shaykh Tijani never found himself the exclusive student of any one teacher. [66] Rather, his lack of complete commitment to any of his shaykhs is testament to the Prophet's presence as a very tangible reality in his life. According to the *Jawahir,*

> *As for the source of his Tariqa Muhammadiyya, he, Shaykh Ahmad Tijani informed us, "We studied under numerious shaykhs (may God be pleased with them), but God did not decree that they should be the means of attaining the goal. Where this Path is concerned, our authority and our confirmation are derived from the master of existence (God bless him and grant him peace). Our success and our attainment were destined*

---

64   Al-'Arabi b. Sayah, *Bughyat al-Mustafid;* quoted in Benabdellah, *La Tijania,* p.11.
65   Benabdellah, *La Tijania,* p. 15. This is also the finding of Ibrahim Sail, *La Prophetie, la Saintete et leurfruits* (Dakar: Multi-Services-Excellence G.I.E., 1997), p. 36.
66   For evidence of this, see a letter of the Shaykh's included in the *Jawahir* asking the Prophet to guarantee Paradise for any of his teachers. The letter is translated in Abun-Nasr, *The Tijaniyya,* pp. 43-44.

to be at his hands. None of the other shaykhs had any controlling influence over us."[67]

Whatever the case, his shaykhs did not seem to expect any more or less of him; according to the *Jawahir,* they only served to strengthen his commitment and encourage him on the path that seemed destined for him. For the historian, such accounts in the *Jawahir* can only be considered a partial source, especially since predictions of future greatness of this kind seem standard to the literary genre of accounts of renowned scholars and Sufi shaykhs. But, particularly in the lack of a contradicting account, it cannot be denied that such stories quite possibly reflect actual events.

Even from the time of Shaykh Tijani's first visit to Fes, the young scholar's ascendent motivation seemed to be the attainment of a spiritual opening *(fath)*. So when another of his teachers, Sidi Muhammad al-Wanjili (d. 1185), a man known for his saintliness, predicted for him a *maqam* (spiritual station) of *Qutbaniyya* (Polehood) similar to that of Abu Hasan al-Shadhili, but that his *fath* would come in the desert, Tijani hastened his departure from Fes.[68] The *Jawahir* reports that he spent some time in the desert Zawiya of the famous Qutb Sidi Abd al-Qadir b. Muhammad al-Abyad (known as Sidi al-Shaykh) before returning to Ain Madi, only to leave his home soon again to return to al-Abyad before moving on to Tlemcen. His activities during this time consisted of teaching Qur'anic exegesis *(tafsir)* and Hadith in whatever town he happened to be staying, while continuing an apparently rigorous practice of asceticism, including frequent fasting and superogatory worship.[69] During his stay in Tlemcen, he received through Divine inspiration, greater assurance of his coming grand illumination.[70]

---

67   Jawahir, p. 54.
68   *Jawahir,* p. 20.
69   *Jawahir,* p. 20.
70   This according to the *Bughyat al-Mustafid;* quoted in Benabdellah,

Pilgrimage East

It was from southwest Algeria, then, that Shaykh Ahmad Tijani
set out in 1186/1773 to accomplish the requisite Islamic pilgrimage *(Hajj)*. As with other noteworthy Islamic scholars who have
made the pilgrimage, especially in pre-modem times, Shaykh
Tijani partook of an arduous and lengthy journey that would
not only bolster his personal faith and societal renown, but
which linked him with the foremost Muslim scholars of the age.
It is indeed ironic that in the time before modem travel meth-
ods, renowned scholars from diverse areas of the Islamic world
would often become personal acquaintances of each other,[71]
whereas the boundaries imposed by colonial occupation and
the modem nation-state seem to have gone a long way towards
stifling Islamic scholarly exchange in the present day. Shaykh Tijani's pilgrimage was a testament to the "travelling scholar" par-
adigm of the pre-modem Muslim world and the ability for eminent scholars to communicate, befriend and share ideas with

---

La Tijania, p. 13.

71   Stefan Reichmuth, "Islamic Scholarship between Imperial Center and Provinces in the 18th Century: The case of Murtada al-Zabidi (d.
1205/1791) and his Ottoman Contacts," in *The Great Ottoman-Turkish Civilization, v. ///*(Ankara: Yeni Turkiye, 2000).

each other, despite the great geographical and cultural diversity of their homelands. The most important contacts the Shaykh was to make during his pilgrimage were with the Khalwatiyya tradition associated with Mustafa al-Bakri (d. 1749).

Shaykh Tijani's first stop of note en-route to Mecca was at Algiers, where he met Sidi Muhammad b. Abd al-Rahman al-Azhary (d. 1793),[72] a prominent *muqaddam* (spiritual guide) of the Khalwatiyya Sufi order who had received initiation at the hands of Shaykh al-Azhar Muhammad al-Hifnii (or al-Hifnawi, d. 1181/1767).[73] The Khalwatiyya, originating in four-teenth century Anatolia, had become by the eighteenth century, under the tutelage of Mustafa al-Bakri, one of the most prominent orders in Egypt and a locus for Islamic and Sufi renewal, with ideology similar to that expressed by the term *Tariqa Muhammadiyya,* as will be discussed below. Shaykh Tijani's affiliation with this order was perhaps the most significant influence upon his thought prior to his waking meetings with the Prophet, and he did not leave Algiers before receiving initiation at the hands of al-Azhary. No doubt such an encounter would have provided additional impetus to meet, as he later would, some of the day's most renowned Khalwati scholars, such as Mahmud al-Kurdi and Muhammad al-Samman, while passing through Egypt and the Hijaz.

Shaykh Ahmad Tijani's journey East brought him also to Tunis, home of the famous Zaytuna mosque and university, which predates both the Azhar in Cairo and the Qarawin in Fes. Indicative of the ease with which foreign scholars could integrate into diverse Islamic communities, upon his entry into Tunis, Shaykh Tijani immediately met with the people of saint-ly renown, such as Sidi Abd al-Samad al-Ruhwij, and took up teaching at Zaytuna, this time his syllabus including Ibn 'Atta Allah's *Kitab al-hikam.* It seems he made enough of an impres-

---

72   *Jawahir,* p. 24. This shaykh would later become the eponym for the Rahmaniyya order that spread widely in Algeria.
73   Benabdellah, *La Tijania,* p. 13.

sion on the scholars there for the Emir, Bey Ali (r. 1757- 1782), to offer him a lucrative permanent teaching position at Zaytuna. But the Emir's request had the opposite effect on Shaykh Tijani to that which was hoped for and, reportedly not wanting to accept dependence on state authority, he continued his journey East. It is probable that Shaykh Tijani's reputation in the city from this visit partly facilitated a later rector of Zaytuna, Ibrahim Riyahi, to pay him homage in Fes and become a propagator of his *Tariqa* in Tunis. Shaykh Tijani's stay in Tunis is of note for other reasons as well. He was encouraged on his path by a dream vision of the Prophet, who told him, *"Pray for wise knowledge and for your desired goal, and I will guarantee your prayer."* Another dream of of the illustrious Mahmud al-Kurdi strengthened his desire to meet the Egyptian shaykh.[74]

Shaykh Ahmad Tijani at last met this Egyptian Khalwati shaykh when he arrived in Cairo. Mahmud al-Kurdi (d. 1195/1780) was by origin an Iraqi Kurd but had moved to Cairo at the age of eighteen following a dream in which Muhammad al-Hifni was shown to him as his shaykh. Although he had previously belonged to another order (that of al-Qushayri), al-Kurdi received initiation into the Khalwati order at al-Hifhi's hands, and was reportedly so beloved of al-Hifni that he used to send many of his disciples to receive initiation from al-Kurdi.[75] He also had the opportunity to learn directly from al-Hifni's shaykh, Mustafa al-Bakri, who encouraged him to offer exclusive obedience to the Khalwatiyya,[76] and next to whom he is buried in Cairo. Al-Kurdi was known for his saintliness from an early age and apparently had frequent visionary encounters with the Prophet Muhammad and Khidr, the mystical guide of Moses, as well as past saints such as Ibn 'Arabi, from whom he received the impulse to write the *Risala fi'l-hikam*.

---

74   *Jawahir,* p. 24.
75   Moshe Perlman ed.s, *'Abd al-Rahman al-Jabarti's History of Egypt* (Stuttgart: Franz Steiner Verlag, 1994), pp. 98-111.
76   Jabarti 's History of Egypt, *p. 100.*

Al-Kurdi's visionary experience was also marked by assurances of sainthood and the acquisition of litanies. He was said to see the Prophet in visions nearly every night, and once, upon telling the Prophet of his love for him, was assured that anybody who so loved the Prophet would enter Paradise.[77] In a vision of Khidr, al-Kurdi received a prayer called the *Musab'at al-'ashr,* which he gave to Shaykh Tijani and which the latter was to continue doing morning and evening even after the development of his own order.[78] Other famous students of al-Kurdi, besides Shaykh Tijani, included the afore-mentioned Ahmad ibn Idris, as well as Abdullah Sharqawi (d. 1812), the latter of whom would, after al-Kurdi's death, become Shaykh al-Azhar.[79]

Shaykh Tijani's first meeting with al-Kurdi, as recorded in the *Jawahir,* is included below as an example both of the kind of welcome the Shaykh received from eminent scholars and of the intensity with which he pursued his aim of spiritual enlightenment. Another aspect of this meeting, of course, was the before-mentioned ease and directness with which scholars from as far away as Iraq and Morocco could interact and exchange knowledge. Upon first seeing Tijani, al-Kurdi reportedly said, "You are the beloved of God in this world and the next."

Shaykh Tijani asked, "From whence has this come to you?" Al-Kurdi replied, "From God."

Tijani then related to him, "I saw you when I was in Tunis and I said to you, 'My whole essence is copper [meaning flawed].' You answered, 'That is true, but I will change your copper to gold.'"

---

77   Jabarti's History of Egypt, *p. 101.*

78   *Jawahir,* p. 63.

79   Frederick De Jong, "Mustafa Kamal al-Din al-Bakri (1688-1749): Revival and Reform of the Khalwatiyya Tradition?" in Levtzion and Voll ed.s, *Eighteenth Century Renewal and Reform in Islam* (Syracuse: Syracuse University Press, 1987), p. 127.

Al-Kurdi assured him that what he saw was the reality and then asked the traveler, "What is your desire?"

"My desire," said Tijani, "is for the great polehood (*al-Qut-baniyya al-'Azhami*)."[80]

"For you there is much more than that," al-Kurdi informed him. Then he told Shaykh Tijani about his own travels and his meetings with al-Hifni and al-Bakri.[81]

* * *

Arriving in Mecca just after Ramadan in the year 1187/1774, Shaykh Ahmad Tijani stayed long enough to accomplish the rites of the *Hajj*. During his stay there he also, as was his custom, sought out the people of "goodness, piety, righteousness and happiness."[82] His search led him to a mysterious saint from India, Ahmad b. Abdullah al-Hindi, who had made a vow to speak to no one except his servant. On knowledge of Tijani's presence at his house, al-Hindi sent him the message, "You are the inheritor of my knowledge, secrets, gifts and lights,"[83] and informed the pilgrim that he himself was to die in a matter of days (it came to pass on the exact day al-Hindi had predicted for himself), but that he should go visit the *Qutb* (Pole of the Age) Muhammad al-Samman when in Medina.[84]

---

80   A position refering to the height of the hidden hierarchy of saints at any given time.

81   *Jawahir*, p. 24.

82   *Jawahir*, p. 24.

83   *Jawahir*, pp. 24-25.

84   *Jawahir*, p. 25. It is tempting to assume some sort of connection between this mysterious Indian saint and the school of Muhammad Andalib, who was known to have proselytized the idea of the **Tariqa Muhammadi-yya**. This would provide a link between the Arab and Indian versions of the phenomenon, although this still would not explain how the idea came to be found in India in the first place. In any case, pending further research, Shaykh Ahmad al-Hindi remains a figure sufficently shrouded in mystery to

After accomplishing the *ziyara* (visitation) to the Prophet's tomb, where *"God completed his aspiration and longing"* to greet the Prophet,[85] Shaykh Tijani went to visit the renowned Shaykh Muhammad Abd al-Karim al-Samman (d. 1189/1775). Like al- Kurdi, al-Samman was a member of the Khalwatiyya order, being one of two students given full *ijaza* (permission) by Mustafa al-Bakri; the other was al-Kurdi's shaykh, Muhammad al-Hifni. Al-Samman was a prolific scholar and one of the foremost advocates of the *Tariqa Muhammadiyya* ideal. One of his more famous works, called *Futuhat al-ilahiyya fi'l-tayvajjuhat al-ruhiyya* ("Divine openings in the spiritual pursuits"), treats the concept of the *Nur al-Muhammadi* (the Prophetic light) and the method of attaining union with this light (i.e., *Tariqa Muhammadiyya*). The book also describes the author's own visionary encounters with the Prophet and emphasizes that the mystic must continue to follow the external elements of the Prophet's Sunna [86] Al-Samman elsewhere elaborate on the process by which the aspirant attained the waking vision of the Prophet and the results achieved by such an event.[87]

Aside from his own intellectual and spiritual prowess, al-Samman has become famous on account of another disciple, Ahmad al-Tayyib (d. 1824), who spread his ideas in the Sudan as the Sammaniyya order. Despite the assertions of some modem writers that Tijani took the Sammaniyya order from al-Samman,[88] there is no evidence in the *Jawahir* that he took any new order while in the Hijaz, or even that there existed at that time any such order known as the Sammaniyya.

---

preclude any attempt to connect him with the Andalib school, although one might assume his familiarity with the *Tariqa Muhammadiyya* idea current both in his home country and the Middle East proper.

85   *Jawahir,* p. 25.

86   Radtke, "Sufism in the 18th Century," in *Der Welt des Islams* (36, 3, 1996), p. 332.

87   Radtke, "Sufism in the 18th Century," p. 355.

88   See Karrar, Sufi Brotherhoods, p. 120 and Sedgwick, Heirs of Ahmad ibn Idris, p. 15

The *Jawahir* does however report a close connection between Tijani and al-Samman. Upon his arrival, al-Samman met Tijani and informed him of the "names"[89] and told him that he was to be the *al-qutb al-jami* ' (the comprehensive Pole).

On his return from the Hijaz, Shaykh Tijani stopped again in Cairo and once more visited Mahmud al-Kurdi. The *Jawahir* reports that many of the *'ulama* of the city came to visit the travelling scholar during this second visit.[90] Demonstrating his profound respect for his teachers of the Khalwati tradition, Tijani accepted from al-Kurdi to be a *muqaddam* (propagator) of the Khalwati order in North Africa. Although Tijanis later initiation at the hands of the Prophet would obviate its need, the *Jawahir* reproduces the chain of transmission (*silsilah*) of the Khalwatiyya, stretching from the Prophet through Ali ibn Abi Talib, Hasan al-Basri, Junayd, Muhammad al-Khalwati (from whom the order derives its name), Bakri, and Kurdi (not to mention all the names) to Shaykh Tijani.[91]

Prior academic research on the Khalwatiyya has demonstrated its central position in the eighteenth-century period of reform in Egypt. According to Frederick De Jong and Rachida Chih, Egypt witnessed the flowering of the order under the efforts of Mustafa Bakri, Muhammad al-Hifni and their disciples.[92] Chih writes, "In a period of decline of Ottoman power, al-Hifni and his disciples were indeed the bearers of

---

89   The Jawahir is elusive here, but could these be the same seven names of God taught by the Khalwati order to correspond to seven levels of the soul? See Rachida Chih, "Le debuts d'une tariqa, la Halwatiyya," in Chih and Gril ed.s, Le Saint and son milieu, ou Comment lire les sources hagiographiques (Cairo: 1FAO, 2000), p. 143. For a fuller discussion of this issue, see chapter four.

90   Jawahir, p.25

91   Jawahir, p.25

92   De Jong, "Mustafa Kamal al-Din al-Bakri," p. 118, and Rachida Chih, "Les debuts d'une tariqa, la Halwatiyya." De Jong concludes, however, that al-Bakri cannot actually be credited with any distinctive reform of the Khalwatiyya tradition.

a new religious spirit, the propogators of reform in a muslim society in agony."[93] Many of the prominent scholars of the time became associated with the order, including most of the highest shaykhs of Azhar. The order saw a rapid spread even in Upper Egypt. Its name quickly became associated with a form of elite, scholarly Sufism synomous with Islamic "orthodoxy," or the Muslim scholarly establishment at the time. Some of the order's fundamental teachings which were later incorporated by the likes of Shaykh Ahmad Tijani included the situation of Sufism firmly within the Shari'a and the Prophetic Sunna, the detailing of the inner states of the soul, the enthusiasm for Ibn 'Arabi and the propensity towards visionary experience of the Prophet Muhammad or other important personalities in the Islamic and Sufi traditions.

Of primary significance for Shaykh Ahmad Tijani was the Khalwati use of the term, *Tariqa Muhammadiyya*. His contact with the Khalwati masters of the time would have been his first initiatory experience with the phenomenon that would later comprise such an important aspect of the Tijaniyya. In order to understand its significance, it is useful to trace the development of the *Tariqa Muhammadiyya* until its flowering in the end of the eighteenth century. To summarize the essential elements of the phenomenon as were detailed earlier, the *Tariqa Muhammadiyya* came to mean, emphasis on the external Sunna of the Prophet, use of the concept of *Haqiqa Muhammadiyya*, experience of the waking vision of the Prophet and restriction of the disciple to one transcendent *tariqa*. According to Mark Sedgwick, these ideas, though not always found together, seem to have been evidenced much prior to the eighteenth century in such thinkers as Ibn 'Arabi (d. 1240) and Abd al-Karim al-Jili (d. 1402), Ahmad Imad al-din al-Wasiti (d. 1311) and Muhammad ibn 'Ali al-Birgawi (d. 1573), and in the context of Moroccan Sufism with some of the branches of the Shadhili order such as the Jazuliyya.[94]

---

93   Chih, "Les debuts d'une tariqa," p. 149.
94   Mark Sedgwick, Heirs of Ahmad Ibn Idris, revised version, chapter

It is thus possible to trace the development of the *Tariqa Muhammadiyya* phenomenon until its more or less, final version that culminated at the end of the eighteenth century. Ibn 'Arabi and his student al-Jili did not themselves use the term *Tariqa Muhammadiyya* but they were famous for elaborating the idea of the Muhammadan Light *(Nur Muhammadi)*, the Muhammadan Spirit *(Ruh Muhammadi)* and the Muhammadan Reality *(Haqiqa Muhammadiyya)*. Ibn 'Arabi and al-Jili advocated a form of spiritual concentration on the Prophet's *dhat* or essential reality, which was endowed with a singular power to reflect fully the Divine Countenance.[95] Al-Wasiti was a Shadhili Sufi and student of Ibn Taymiyya who paid lip service to Ibn Taymiyya's rejection of the idea of the *Haqiqa Muhammadiyya*, but who nonetheless emphasized the Muhammadan Spirit *(ruh)*, which continued to remain present to provide guidance to the community. He himself left his own Shadhili *tariqa* affiliation in preference for the all-assuming "*Tariqa Muhammadiyya*", following the spiritual path of the Prophet.[96] The Ottoman Turk Muhammad al-Birgawi wrote a book called *al-Tariqa al-Muhammadiyya wa al-sira al-Ahmadiyya* in which he condemned the perceived excesses of popular Sufism and argued that the only legitimate Sufi or-

---

II, "Tariqa Muhammadiyya."

95   Ibn 'Arabi writes in his Futuhat al-Makiyya, "Know that you do not have [this perfection] and you do not have this constitution which belongs to Muhammad, peace and blessings be upon Him, and that no matter how much the Real discloses Himself to you in the mirror of your heart, your heart will only show you what is according to its own constitution and the form of its shape... So cling to faith and follow him! Place him before you like the mirror in which you see your form and the form of others. If you do this, you will know that God must disclose Himself to Muhammad in his mirror." See Valerie Hoffman, "Annihilation in the Messenger of God: the Development of a Sufi Practice," in International Journal of Middle East Studies (31, 1999), p. 353.

96   Eric Geoffrey, "Le traite de soufisme d'un disciple d'Ibn Taymiyya: Ahmad 'Imad al-din al-Wasiti (m. 711/1311)," in Studia Islamica (82, 1995), pp. 92-93, 95. Also Mark Sedgwick, A Sufi Reform of Islam, the Defeat of the Rashidiyya (Leiden: Brill, forthcoming).

der was the Muhammadan Path, the *Tariqa Muhammadiyya,* to which the entire Muslim community should belong.[97] The Shadhili-Jazuli Shaykh 'Abdullah al-Ghazwani (d. 1529) also wrote on the idea of the *Tariqa Muhammadiyya* as an alternative term to refer to the *madhhab al-sunna al-Muhammadiyya* (the school of the Muhammadan Sunna). Al-Ghazwani combined Ibn 'Arabi's and al-Jili's ideas of the saint's absorption (or annihilation) in the Muhammadan essence (*dhat*) with an emphasis on the necessity of the saint's involvement in society, although his use of the term *Tariqa Muhammadiyya* has more to do with the latter emphasis than the former.[98]

Scholars closer to Shaykh Tijani's time who expressed the ideas of the *Tariqa Muhammadiyya* in an increasingly comprehensive manner included Abd al-Aziz al-Dabbagh (d. 1719), Abd al-Ghani al-Nabulsi (d. 1731), and the Khalwati Shaykhs: al-Bakri, al-Hifni, al-Samman and al-Kurdi. Al-Dabbagh emphasized the ability of the saint to attain direct contact with the essence (*dhat*) of the Prophet in a waking vision, and added that a scholar who had attained this vision was permitted to transcend the *madhhab* (school of jurisprudence) in the interpretation of the Shari'a.[99] Al-Nabulsi is credited with rescuing the term *Tariqa Muhammadiyya* from the anti-Sufi implications of al-Birgawi's work. The famous Damascene Qadiri and Naqshbandi scholar was a proponent of Ibn 'Arabi who emphasized the spiritual component of the *Tariqa Muhammadiyya* (including visionary contact with the Prophet) as well as the importance of the external *Sunna* of the Prophet. He also spoke against the excesses of popular Sufism, but warned

97   Sedgwick, The Heirs of Ahmad Ibn Idris, pp. 36-37.
98   Vincent Cornell, Realm of the Saint, Power and Authority in Moroccan Sufism (Austin: University of Texas Press, 1998), pp. 219, 227.
99   Bernd Radtke, "Ibriziana: Themes and Sources of a Seminal Sufi Work," in Sudanic Africa (7, 1996), pp. 113-158.

against the practice of *takfir* (excommunication) that had become the vogue of Birgawi's followers, the Kadizadelites.[100]

The Khalwati Shaykh al-Bakri was the student of al-Nabulsi, and although his use of the term *Tariqa Muhammadiyya* was not known, he experienced visionary spiritual initiation,[101] spoke against some aspects of popular Sufism[102] and required the disciple's exclusive affiliation with one Sufi order.[103] Al-Bakri in turn initiated al-Hifni as well as al-Samman. Al-Samman wrote a book explaining the notion of the *Tariqa Muhammadiyya*, as previously discussed, involving all the elements mentioned above, except that he, like Shaykh Tijani, did not specifically reject the *madhahib* nor did he de-emphasize the role of the living spiritual guide.[104] Mahmud al-Kurdi (d. 1780) received the Khalwatiyya from al-Hifni and from al-Bakri himself, and although he was not such a prolific writer as al-Samman, he was known to have experienced the waking vision of the Prophet and to have emphasized Sufism's relationship to the *Shari'a*.[105]

The end of the eighteenth century also witnessed the popularization of the *Tariqa Muhammadiyya* in India. The Naqshbandi Sufi Muhammad Nasir 'Andalib (d. 1758), a spiritual descendent of Ahmad Sirhindi (d. 1624), reportedly received the fundamentals of the idea from a vision of Hasan ibn 'Ali, an idea he later transmitted to his successor, Mir Dard (1785). There exist no known contacts between the Indian and Arab versions of the *Tariqa Muhammadiyya*, but Mark Sedgwick concludes that the Indian rendition, emerging slightly after its Arab counterpart, "could hardly have arisen independently."[106]

---

100 Sedgwick, Heirs of Ahmad Ibn Idris, pp. 38-39.
101 Sedgwick, Heirs of Ahmad Ibn Idris, p. 39.
102 Radtke, "Sufism in the 18ᵗʰ Century," p. 341.
103 Jabarti's History of Egypt, pp. 99-100. Also, Ifadat al-Ahmadiyya, p. 36.
104 Radtke, "Sufism in the 18ᵗʰ Century," pp. 327-328.
105 Jabarti's History of Egypt, pp. 98-112.
106 Mark Sedgwick, Heirs of Ahmad Ibn Idris, revised version, chapter II, "Tariqa Muhammadiyya." For more on the Tariqa Muhammadiyya in In-

Due to the fact that the Arab manifestation of the *Tariqa Muhammadiyya* is more easily traceable and was perhaps more influential, but what concerns us here is the phenomenon as it developed in the Middle East.

In the Middle East proper, the *Tariqa Muhammadiyya* thus sprang from such diverse sources as Ibn 'Arabi, al-Wasiti, al-Birgawi, al-Dabbagh and al-Nabulsi to culminate in the end of the eighteenth century with the Khalwati masters such as al-Kurdi and al-Samman. These Khalwati shaykhs were in turn primarily responsible for passing on the idea to be implemented in heretofore-unprecedented proportions by the likes of Shaykh Ahmad Tijani and Ahmad ibn Idris and their followers.

* * *

When returning from the Middle East, Shaykh Ahmad Tijani passed by way of Tunis and Tlemcen, spending some time in the latter city in worship, before travelling once again to Fes to visit the shrine of Mawlay Idris, where he arrived in 1191/1779. On the way, he met his first two permanent disciples, Muhammad ibn al-Mishry of Constantine, whom he met in Tlemcen (1188/1776), and Ali Harazem al-Barada, whom he met in Wijda (1191/1779). Both received the Khalwatiyya order from him,[107] all the while being forewarned of a forthcoming grand enlightenment of which Shaykh Tijani apparently sensed the close proximity.[108] Another disciple gained prior to his 1196/1784 illumination was Muhammad Ibn al-'Arabi al-Tazi al-Damrawi.[109]

dia, see Arthur F. Buehler, Sufi Heirs of the Prophet, the Indian Naqshbandiyya and the Rise of the Mediating Sufi Shaykh (Columbia, South Carolina: University of South Carolina Press, 1998), p. 72.

107   Ahmad Sukayrij, Kashf al-Hijab, pp. 54-55, 115-116.
108   Benabdellah, La Tijania, p. 16.
109   Salah al-din Tijani, Kashf al-Ghuyum 'an ba'd israr al-Qutb al-Muk-

The circumstances of the affiliation of these first disciples not only represent Shaykh Tijani's range of appeal to seekers of knowledge, but also provide an interesting insight into the dynamics between Tijani and his disciples. Muhammad ibn al-Mishry was a prominent *Faqih* (doctor of law) in Western Algeria who was also renowned for his stature as a poet and mystic, being previously a disciple of the Khalwati shaykh, Muhammad Ibn Azzuz (d. 1819).[110] He would serve for a time as the *Imam* (leader of the prayer) for Tijani's group of followers and authored the *Kitab al-Jami.* Al-Mishry was apparently attracted to Shaykh Tijani for his vast erudition and was in turn beloved by Tijani because of his thirst for knowledge.[111] Ali Harazem al-Barada, often referred to as the Shaykh's *khal ifat al-akbar* (greatest successor), was a scholar of clear spiritual determination who would eventually be charged with the compilation of the *Jawahir al-Ma'ani.* It seems he had been forewarned in a dream that his guide on the path was to be a man named Shaykh Ahmad Tijani. When the two first met in Wijda, al-Barada did not immediately recognize Tijani until the unknown Shaykh approached him and said, *"You have long been notified in dreams that your guide on the path is a man named Ahmad Tijani."* Much surprised at the stranger's ability to tell him the content of his dreams, al-Barada replied in the affirmative, whereupon the man said, *"I am Ahmad Tijani."*[112] Al-Tazi al-Damrawi's attachment to Shaykh Tijani was also explained by an esoteric connection, and especially their common ability to experience the waking vision of the Prophet.[113]

---

tum (Cairo: Dar al-Taysir, 1999), pp. 78-80.

110   Adnani, "Les origines de la Tijaniyya," pp. 37-39. Azzuz, from the Baij oasis in Algeria, had received initiation from Muhammad ibn Abd al-Rahman al-Azhary, and thus was one of the successors of the founder of the Rahmaniyya order, itself a branch of the Khalwatiyya.

111   Benabdellah, La Tijania, p. 15; Sukayrij, Kashf al-Hijab, pp. 115-119.

112   Jawahir, p. 26; Sukayrij, Kashf al-Hijab, p. 55.

113   Jawahir, p. 187.

Desert Illumination and the Vision of the Prophet

In 1196/1784 Shaykh Ahmad Tijani was graced by the much anticipated *fath al-kabir,* or grand illumination/enlightenment. While residing in the desert oasis town of Abi Samghun, he saw the Prophet Muhammad "waking, not dreaming." The Prophet informed him that he himself was his initiator on the Path and told him to leave the shaykhs he had previously followed. The Shaykh then received the basis of a new *wird* (basic litany of a Sufi order) and was given permission to give "spiritual training to the creation in [both] the general and unlimited (*itlaq*)." To understand the extraordinary nature of the new *tariqa* that had been unveiled, special emphasis must be given to the Prophet's words to Tijani as they are recorded in the *Jawahir:*

> *"And when he, God's blessing and peace be upon him, initiated him in this Tariqa Ahmadiyya and [this] mode of life (sira) Mustafuwiyya Nabuwiyya (of the chosen Prophet), and Allah illuminated [al-Tijani] at his hands, may God's blessing and peace be upon him, he [the Prophet] informed him that he was his educator (murabbi) and guarantor (kafil), and that nothing arrives from God except by his hands and at his media-*

tion, may God's blessing and peace be upon him. And
he said to him, "You are not indebted for any favor from
the shaykhs of the Path, for I am your means (wasita)
and your support in the [spiritual] realization, so leave
the entirety of what you have taken from all the tariqas."
And he said to him, "Hold to this tariqa without retreat
(khalwa) or withdrawal from the people until arrives
the station that is promised you, and you will attain
your state without constriction, difficulty or excessive ef-
fort. And leave [or stop seeking from, itrak] the assembly
of the saints."

Such a citation reveals immediately the distinctive elements of the *Tariqa Muhammadiyya*: *Tariqa Muhammadiyya* nomenclature (the term "*Tariqa Ahmadiyya*" is meant to refer to the path of the Prophet, whose inner name is said to be Ahmad, and thus should be considered the same as the term "*Tariqa Muhammadiyya*"), visionary contact with the Prophet, the role of the Prophet as the transcendent guide to God *(Haqiqa Muhammadiyya)* and the emphasis on worldly involvement.

It might be possible to interpret Shaykh Tijani's report of the Prophet's words as a rejection of saintly authority. But given the history of Tijani's own relationship to prominent saints, and his continued respect for other saints after the founding of the Tijaniyya, it is difficult to see the above words as a rejection. They seem more a reemphasis of sainthood's essential connection to the Prophet Muhammad, where the Prophet himself becomes the center and source of saintly authority.

From this time on the Shaykh reportedly began having regular visionary contact with the Prophet and his companions began hearing "from him what we had not heard before in regard to the sciences and the secrets."[114] The time from 1196/1784 until his 1213/1798 arrival in Fes was marked by an increase in his following and the solidification of this new

---

114   Jawahir, p. 26.

Tariqa Ahmadiyya or *Muhammadiyya* as a distinctive order, with the completion of the order's *wird* in 1200/1787, and the sense among his followers that their shaykh, due to his knowledge and miracles (which he ordered them to keep hidden), was of an unparalleled spiritual station.[115]

* * *

In order to understand how it was that Shaykh Ahmad Tijani could have established a whole new Sufi order more or less on the basis of visionary experience (even if many of its elements resonated with the Khalwati tradition into which he had been previously initiated), it is important to examine the context of dreaming and visionary experience in pre-Modern Islamic history, and specifically the role of the dream or vision of the Prophet Muhammad. Even if modernist Islam seems to have inherited the Orientalist disdain for subjects such as visions and dreams, which writers like Grunebaum would have us believe evidence the superstitious nature of the traditional Muslim mind,[116] they nonetheless played a significant part in the shaping of Islamic identity and history. In her discussion of Ibn Abi al-Dunya's *Kitab al-Manam* (Book of Dreams), Leah Kinberg attests to the "great prestige that dreams had in the classical period of Islam."[117]

---

115   Jawahir, p. 26.

116   Grunebaum declares that, "As a result of our [Western] scientific advancement we have become able to afford a renunciation long overdue..." in rejecting the significance of dream or visionary experience. "To us, the symptomatic, revelatory, 'prophetic' significance of the dream points inward to the dreamer (and to his society), not outward into areas of reality inaccessible by rational or 'natural' means. (In fact, to many of us the existence of such areas of reality has become quite doubtful)." G.E. Von Grunebaum, "Introduction, the Cultural Function of the Dream as illustrated by Classical Islam," in Grunebaum and Caillois ed.s, The Dream and Human Societies (Berkely and Los Angeles: UC Press, 1966), pp. 20-21.

117   Leah Kinberg, Ibn Abi al-Dunya: Morality in the Guise of Dreams, a

While all dreams were of course not of value,[118] the true dream was thought to be an expression of an unseen reality. The Prophet once said, *"Nothing is left of Prophethood but glad tidings."* On being asked, "What are glad tidings?" he replied, *"True dreams (ru'yas, visions)."*[119] In traditional formulations such as that of al-Nabulsi, the dreamer's soul (*ruh*) was thought to stretch out to "see through the light of God's illumination what the archangel of dreams reveals to it. It then withdraws to return to the *nafs,* like the sun when it gets covered by a cloud."[120] It logically followed that the more purified the dreamer's *nafs* or ego, the more clearly he could perceive and remember the unseen world of his dream. Moreover, since the true dream provided access to an unseen world that actually existed, a truly purified individual might have the veils lifted from his sight such that he would witness the hidden while in a waking state. Al-Ghazali maintained that after the seeker's purification of his heart and complete absorption in God, "there begin the revelations and visions. The mystics in their waking state now behold angels and the spirits of the Prophets; they hear these speaking to them and are instructed by them."[121] The same is emphasized by Ibn 'Arabi, "The person who undergoes unveiling sees while he is awake what the dreamer sees while he is asleep,"[122] and, according to Chittick, it is rarely clear in

Critical Edition of Kitab al-Manam (Leiden: Brill, 1994), p. 15.

118   The Prophet explained three different types of dreams, that inspired by God, that inspired by Satan, and that coming from the talk of the self still active after sleep. See Yehia Gouda, Dreams and their Meanings in the Old Arab Tradition (New York: Vantage Press, 1991), pp. 3-4.

119   Hadith reported by Abu Hurairah, recorded in Bukhari, quoted in Gouda, Dreams, p. 5.

120   Nabulsi, Taatirul Anam fi Taabir al-Manam (Introduction to the Scented Sleep and What our Dreaming Mind Expresses), quoted in Gouda, Dreams, p. 4.

121   Abu Hamid al-Ghazali, Deliverance from Error and the Attachment to the Lord of Might and Majesty. Montgommery Watt, Faith and Practice of al-Ghazali (London: Unwin Brothers, 1953), p. 61.

122   Muhiyy al-Din Ibn al-'Arabi, Futuhat al-Makkiyya, quoted in William Chittick, Imaginal Worlds: Ibn al-'Arabi and the problem of religious

Ibn 'Arabi's accounts whether his visions happen during sleep or wakefulness.[123] The same might be said of Shaykh Ahmad Tijani, who also believed that visionary experience was a mark of distinction. For the truthful person, he said, the vision might go so far as to indicate his own end or destiny, in other words, what sort of fate had been written for him. The *Jawahir al-Ma 'ani* reports in this regard that the Shaykh never had a vision but it happened.[124] Thus, he reported a dream from his youth where the throne for a great kingdom was erected for him to sit on, and when he sat, he noticed himself in possession of a great many soldiers at his command.[125] The *Jawahir* likewise reports Shaykh Tijani's visions of the famous twelfth-century mystic Abu Madyan, who predicted for him the attainment of *Qutbaniyya* (the highest level of sainthood), as well as of the Prophet Moses, who spoke to him of God's greatest name.[126]

However, the best sort of vision that might be hoped for by the pious Muslim, and what primarily concerns us in the case of Shaykh Tijani, is the vision of the Prophet Muhammad himself. There are a variety of Hadith attesting to the validity of seeing the Prophet in a dream. One says, *"Seeing me in a dream is like seeing me in reality, because Satan neither incarnates nor impersonates me. Whoever has dreamt of me has actually seen me. And he who has dreamt of me will not go to Hell."*[127] Another Hadith states, *"Who has seen me in a dream will see me in a waking state and Satan cannot take my form."*[128]

---

diversity (Albany: SUNY Press, 1994), p. 84.

123   Chittick, Imaginal Worlds, p. 90.

124   Jawahir, p. 27.

125   Jawahir, p. 27. This metaphor is obviously meant to indicate a predication spritual authority.

126   Jawahir, pp. 27-28.

127   Hadith of Bukhari, quoted in Gouda, Dreams, p. 281.

128   Hadith of Bukhari, quoted in "Ithbat jawaz ru'ya sayyidina rasulullah salla Allahu aleihi wa salam fi al-yaqzha ba'da intiqalihi ila al-rafiq al-'ala" ("The proof of the permissibility of seeing our master the Messenger of God, the blessings and peace of God upon him, in a waking state after his passage to the Most High Companion.") (article prepared for author by the Tijani

We are not so much concerned here with the theological arguments surrounding the validity of seeing the Prophet in a waking state (and indeed it seems that visionary experience was well enough accepted in pre-modem Islamic societies that visionaries rarely bothered to explain the legitimacy of their visions) or to make much of a distinction between their occurrence in a dreaming or waking state. But it is important to note that Tijanis have been able to make a convincing defense of the legitimacy of visionary experience even if many in the muslim world today might prefer more material or "rational" contact with their tradition. A paper prepared the Tijani zawiya of Heliopolis, Cairo, states that the passage of the prophets from this world doesnt mean that they have died; they are alive in the *barzakh,* or between worlds.[129] According to the paper, one Hadith reports that the Prophet said God prohibited the earth from eating the bodies of the prophets.[130] Just as the Prophet Muhammad saw Moses standing in prayer in his grave and Jesus circumambulating the Kaba, so too can the righteous servants of God see the Prophet after his passing from this world.[131] As for a person taking knowledge from the waking vision of the Prophet, this is but a manifestation of God's ability to instill knowledge directly to His servant, as in the Qur'an, *"Fear Allah and He will teach you."*[132]

The vision of the Prophet occupied a central position in Islamic history from an early date. One of the Prophet's companions, Ibn Sirin, devoted an entire chapter of his book on dreams, *Tafsir al-Ahlam al-Kabir,* to seeing the Prophet in a dream.[133] The *Kitab al-Manam* of Baghdad's Ibn Abi al-Dunya (d. 281/892) contains some forty-seven accounts of dreams of

Zawiya of Heliopolis, Cairo, Ramadan, 1422/2002), p. 1.

129   "Ithbat," p. 3.

130   Hadith reported by Ahmad, Abu Dawud, Ibn Majjah and Ibn Hayyan. "Ithbat," P* 4.

131   "Ithbat," p. 4.

132   "Ithbat," p. 2.

133   Gouda, Dreams, p. 21.

the Prophet.[134] The famous Sufi poet Abd al-Rahman al-Jami (d. 1492) even wrote a poem that would induce the dream of the Prophet.[135] Jalal al-Din al-Suyuti's (d. 1505) book, *Tanweer al-Halak fi imkan ru 'yat al-nabiyy wal-malak* ("The Enlightment of the Darkness in the Possibility of Seeing the Prophet and the Angels"), not only discusses the dream of the Prophet but elucidates the possibility of sitting with the Prophet in a waking state.[136] The book entitled, *History of the Uwaysis* (c. 1600) of Khirghizia's (Central Asia) Ahmad Uzgen, contains many references to the dream and vision of the Prophet.[137]

Visionary experience dealing with the Prophet has served a variety of functions, from deciding theological or legal issues, to endorsing a particular scholar or his work, to investiture of political authority, to knowledge of future events or just commentary on a contemporary situation. The tendency of the Prophet to appear to pious Muslims in times of difficulty is affirmed by Goldziher in his study of the dream of the Prophet in Islamic history:

> *It is no uncommon thing in Islamic literature to find both theological doubts and questions of practical controversy solved by the decision of the Prophet, who appears in a dream ... decisions that extend as well to isolated cases affecting individuals, as to matters affecting the interests of the community at large.*[138]

---

134   See Kinberg, Ibn Abi al-Dunya.

135   Annemarie Schimmel, And Muhammad is His Messenger: The Veneration of the Prophet in Islamic Piety (Chapel Hill, UNC Press, 1985), p. 79.

136   Sa'di Abu Habib, Hayat Jalal al-Din al-Suyuti (Damascus: Dar al-Manahil, 1993), pp. 154-156

137   Julian Baldick, Imaginary Muslims: the Uwaysi Sufis of Central Asia (London: I.B. Tauris, 1993), p. 1.

138   Ignaz Goldziher, "The Appearance of the Prophet in Dreams," in Journal of the Royal Asiatic Society (1912), p. 503.

There is not the space to cite all the relevant examples here, but a few of the more prominent include Umar ibn al-Khattab, who learned from the Prophet in a dream not to kiss his wife while fasting,[139] Uthman ibn 'Affan, whose dream of the Prophet predicted for him his own assassination the night before he was killed,[140] and Umar ibn Abd al-Aziz (Umayyad Khalif, d. 102/720), who dreamed of God's judgement in the presence of the Prophet between Ali and Mu'awiya ibn Abi Suffyan and later of the Prophet (together with Jesus, Abu Bakr and Umar) supporting his policy of tolerance towards Christians.[141] Indeed, it would seem that crucial junctures of Islamic history often had their outcomes influenced by a guiding dream of the Prophet. The Andalusian conqueror Tariq ibn Zayd dreamed of the Prophet and his companions entering Andalusia before his own fateful incursion into that country in 93/711.[142] Abu al-Hasan Ali al-Ash'ari (d. 324/936) founded the Ash'ari school of theology in opposition to the dominant Mu'tazilite doctrine on the repeated urging of the Prophet in a number of dreams.[143] The Prophet also appeared on other occasions to solve minor points of legal dispute, such as the number of prayer cycles in the superogatory early morning prayer (salat al-duha)[144] or the efficacy of raising the hands before and after bowing in the prayer.[145] Ibn al-Subqy's important fourteenth century work

---

139   Al-Ghazali, Remembrance of Death and the Afterlife (trans. T.J. Winter, Cambridge: Islamic Texts Society, 1989), p. 156.

140   Toufic Triad, La Divination Arab (Leiden: Brill, 1966), p. 81.

141   Fahd, Divination, pp. 297-298. Of the former dream, God decided in favor of Ali, but forgave Mu'awiya.

142   Fahd, Divination, pp. 288-289.

143   Abu al-Qasim Ibn 'Asakir, "The Exposure of the Calumniator's Lying concerning what has been imputed to the Imam Abu'l-Hasan al-Ash'ari," in Richard McCarthy, The Theology of al-Ash'ari (Beirut: Imprimerie Catholique, 1953), pp. 152-155.

144   This in a dream to Abu Bakr Muhammad al-Jaziri (10th cent C.E.), the doubt was solved in favor of Imam Malik's opinion. See Goldziher, "Appearance of the Prophet," pp. 503-504.

145   This in a dream to Ibn al-'Arabi. See Chodkiewicz, Seal of the Saints:

containing the biographies of prominent Shafi'i legal scholars frequently details how the Prophet appeared to clarify an unclear *ijtihad* (legal interpretation) or to solve a particular problem.[146] Likewise did certain trends of Sufism gain ascendancy in part through the dream of the Prophet, such as sobriety in mysticism[147] or the emphasis on loving the Prophet.[148]

Even if the dream of the Prophet was always a significant event in Islamic history, at a certain point, perhaps from the sixteenth century, it seems the emphasis on its occurrence increased, and in particular, the accentuation of the waking vision of the Prophet became more prevalent. There is of course the case of Uways (d. 657 C.E), who lived during the time of the Prophet and became Muslim through visions of the Prophet without ever having met him.[149] It is from Uways that the term "Uwaysi transmission," meaning learning from the Prophet or a saint through visionary contact, has gained currency. Other early figures, such as Imam Shafi'i (d. 9th century C.E.), reportedly used to see the Prophet in a waking state.[150]

Likewise the vision of the Prophet was a frequent enough occurrence within the specific realm of Sufism for centuries prior to Shaykh Tijani. Abu Maydan, Ahmad Rifa'i, Abd

---

Prophethood and Sainthood in the Doctrine of Ibn 'Arabi (trans. Liadain Sherrard, Cambridge: Islamic Texts Society, 1993), p. 99.

146   Abu Nasr 'Abd al-Wahhab Ibn al-Subqy, Tabaqat al-Shafiyya al-Kubra (10 volumes, Cairo: Hijr, 1992). Interview with Muhammad Serag, April, 2003. Serag wrote a paper on the subject.

147   This in a dream to Abu Sa'id al-Kharraz, to whom the Prophet counseled against beating oneself while making dhikr. See al-Ghazali, Remembrance of Death and the Afterlife, p. 163.

148   This in a dream to Ahmad al-Kharraz (d. 899), whose repetition of Rabia al- Adawiyya's profession that her love for Allah left no room for loving the Prophet, was told by the Prophet in a dream, "He that loves God must have loved me." See Annemarie Schimmel, And Muhammad is His Messenger, p. 130.

149   Baldick, Imaginary Muslims, pp. 16-21.

150   Sa'di Abu Habib, HayatJalal al-Din al-Suyuti, p. 155.

al-Qadir Jilani, Ibn al-'Arabi and al-Shadhili's first khalifa, Abu al-Abbas al-Mursi, all reported waking visions of the Prophet. Al-Jilani's emphasis on the true teacher's guidance from the Prophet almost seems comparable to later formulations of the *Tariqa Muhammadiyya*: "A living teacher must have connection with our master the Prophet of Allah (SAW), that is, if he is truly the inheritor of the state of the Prophet. In his teaching he receives guidance from the Prophet and is taught to be a true servant of Allah." Al-Jilani later clarifies that such guidance is obtained through direct contact with "the spirit" of the Prophet.[151] Al-Mursi's statement that, "By God, were the Messenger of God concealed from me for a twinkling of the eye, I would not count myself among the Muslims," is often quoted by Tijanis as an earlier manifestation similar to what their Shaykh would himself later claim. The famous *Tadhkira al-Awliya* (Memorial of the Friends) of 'Attar (d. 1221) speaks of a whole class of "Uwaysi" Sufis, who learned from the Prophet directly and therefore had no need of another instructor.[152] The renowned Hadith scholar Jalal al-Din al-Suyuti (d. 1505) reportedly met with the Prophet on numerous occasions to question him about the validity of various Hadith, but urged his close companions to conceal the fact until after his death.[153] Some might contend that the above statements of renowned Sufis do not necessarily mean a waking vision of the Prophet, but neither is the intimacy with the Prophet and the direct nature of their contact with him that is revealed in their statements explained by the simple dream. In any case, in Sufism the distinction between the waking and dreaming state, between the Prophet's spirit (*ruh*) or his actual self (*dhat*), rarely seems to have been made, so there is no basis to reject the Tijani claim that the waking vision of the Prophet was an event witnessed before Shaykh Ahmad Tijani by some of the greatest Sufis.

---

151   Abd al-Qadir al-Jilani, The Secret of Secrets (trans. Tosun al-Helveti, Cambridge: Islamic Texts Society, 1992), p. 113.

152   Baldick, Imaginary Muslims, p. 25.

153   Abu Habib, Hayat Jalal al-Din al-Suyuti, pp. 154-156.

But even if reports of the vision of the Prophet are available from earlier periods of Islamic history, it is hard to dispute Julian Baldick's point that such reports increased from the sixteenth century onwards.

> *The position of the Uwaysi is really, as we have seen, the position of every Muslim with regard to Muhammad: like Uways himself, the believer has not met the Prophet in the flesh, but wishes to know him and learn from him. Given the political and economic decline of Islam from the sixteenth century onwards, it is understandable that the Uwaysi phenomenon should have gained in importance from then on.[154]*

While personal visionary experience cannot necessarily be explained by an alleged external decline of society, it is apparent that reports of the Prophet's appearance attained a level of increased circulation in all parts of the Muslim world. This seemed to be the case from Ahmad Sirhindi (d. 1624)[155] and Shah Waliullah (who wrote a treatise devoted to hadith taught by the Prophet to a scholar in a vision)[156] in India to the Maghreb, where waking visions of the Prophet were reported by such diverse sources as the Moroccan Grand Qadi Abu Zayd Abd al-Rahman al-Tamanarti (alive 1633)[157] to the Sufis of the Jazuliyya and Nasiriyya orders, among others.[158] Indeed we find in the *Ibriz*, the book concerning Abd al-Aziz al- Dabbagh (which contained most of the essential elements of the *Tariqa Muhammadiyya* phenomenon and which had a large influence on eighteenth-century Sufism), that the waking

---

154   Baldick, Imaginary Muslims, pp. 226-227.
155   Baldick, Imaginary Muslims, p. 26.
156   Schimmel, And Muhammad is His Messenger, n. 58, p. 281.
157   Jonathan Katz, "Visionary experience, Autobiography and Sainthood in North African Islam," in Princeton Papers in Near Eastern Studies (v. 1, 1992), p. 99.
158   Katz, Dreams, Sufism and Sainthood: the Visionary Career of Muhammad al- Zawawi (Leiden: Brill, 1996), pp. xv, 100, 102, 226-227.

vision of the Prophet seems such a part of the scholarly understanding that the *Ibriz*'s author does not feel obliged to explain
Abd al-Aziz al-Dabbagh's tendency to postpone answering a
question posed to him until he had occasion to consult the
Prophet.[159] Moreover, even if modernist distaste for intangible
phenomena has perhaps occasioned a decline of the dream's
integral importance in Islamic societies, pious and well respected Muslim leaders, as well as ordinary people, still report
visionary contact with the Prophet. A special 2002 Ramadan
program on Egyptian national television reported that the
popular Egyptian Shaykh Muhammad Mutwali al-Sharawi (d.
1998), whose weekly television program enthralled millions
around the Muslim world, saw the Prophet on his deathbed,
greeted him out loud and repeated the Islamic testimony of
faith.

It is difficult to speculate as to the reasons for the apparent rise in frequency of the vision of the Prophet. Certainly, it
could be said that Muslims generally have seen themselves in
a state of increased decline the further history progresses from
the time of Prophet, since a widely accepted Hadith predicts
just this. So perhaps, as Baldick states, pious Muslims' longing
for the Prophet's countenance augmented according to the increased need for guidance in an uncertain time. In any event,
this was evidently the case with Shaykh Ahmad Tijani, who
spoke specifically of the difficulty of attaining knowledge of
God in his time except through the grace channeled through
the saints on account of their close proximity to the Prophet, a
proximity which manifested through frequent visionary contact with him.[160]

Before discussing the exact nature of Shaykh Ahmad Tijani's visionary experiences with the Prophet Muhammad, we

---

159   Ahmad ibn Mubarak Lamati al-Sijilmasi, Al-Ibriz min Kalam Sidi
'Abd al-'Aziz al-Dabagh (Beirut: Dar al-Kutub, 1998), p. 57.
160   **Kitab al-Jami'**, b. I, p. 17

must conclude that visionary contact with the Prophet prior to the Shaykh was far from unprecedented. Even closer examination of the nature of these prior visions reveals that the specific characteristics of his own experiences, such as asking the Prophet for advice or the receiving of particular prayers, or even the saint and his followers being promised intercession or salvation by the Prophet (such was reported in the Maghrebi context by Muhammad al-Jazuli, the fifteenth century founder of the Jazuliyya order, and Muhammad ibn Nasir, seventeenth century founder of the Nasiriyya order),[161] all were elements of Tijani's visions which had been reported by visionaries before his own time. Neither did Shaykh Tijani's visions transcend the bounds of orthodox or acceptable visionary experience, established in formulations such as that of Imam Nawawi (thirteenth century C.E.), who objected to visions being used as the source for practices contradicting the Sunna.[162] The only new development with Shaykh Tijani's visionary relationship to the Prophet Muhammad was perhaps simply one of degree. The intensely personal and vivid descriptions of his meetings with the Prophet represent a degree of intimacy difficult to be matched, and certainly with no other saintly tradition did visions of this kind have such a compelling and lasting effect on the visionary concerned and the inheritance he left behind.

There seems to have been roughly two phases of Shaykh Ahmad Tijani's visionary encounters with the Prophet. What might be called the early period can be characterized by mostly dreams (although the distinction between sleeping and awake is not always made) where the Prophet's appearance plays a more "background" or personal role. In the later period, be-

---

161   Katz, Dreams, Sufism and Sainthood, pp. xv, 226-227.
162   Goldziher, "Appearance of the Prophet," p. 506. Tijani scholars themselves agree upon the same limits of visionary experience. Shaykh Hassan Cisse maintains that a vision is not of general applicability if it contradicts the established Shari'a (Interview in Medina Kaolack, Senegal, November 2002).

ginning with his 1784 spiritual opening *(fath)* in Abi Samghun, Tijani is told to take the Prophet as his only spiritual guide, the accent is on the Shaykh's visions of the Prophet while in a waking state, where the Prophet takes on an appropriately more intimate and public capacity in his life. An early dream of the Prophet presented in the *Jawahir* indicates these two distinct phases of his life prior to and after his illumination. The conclusion of the dream finds the Shaykh in the presence of the Prophet at the time of prayer. As he goes to pray with the Prophet, he is unable to respond to the prayer summons until half way through the prayer, *"so that was the case that half of my life was lost, and I did not realize anything, but in the last half I realized my aim."*[163]

Still the Shaykh was not bereft of the Prophet's visionary guidance in the first half of his life. The *Jawahir* reports a variety of dreams that demonstrate the fulfillment of a range of functions of the dream of the Prophet - from advice to solving of controversies to simple encouragement - previously witnessed in Islamic history. While in Tunis, Shaykh Tijani dreamt that the Prophet read to him *Surat al-Duha* ("The Early Morning Light") from the Qur'an, and when the Prophet reached the fifth verse, *"and soon will thy Guardian-Lord give thee (that wherewith) thou shalt be well pleased,"* "he gazed at me with his noble sight, and finished the Sura, may God's blessing and peace be upon him."[164] In another vision, the Shaykh asked the Prophet to tell him which of two hadith dealing with the length of Jesus's stay on earth following his return was correct, whether forty years or seven. The Prophet replied Jesus would stay seven years.[165] The Prophet also appeared to Tijani to clarify minor points of *fiqh,* such as dealing with alms giving or ablution for example. The Shaykh explained that one dream

---

163   Jawahir, p. 27. Presumably the aim referred to here is the Shaykh's attainment of Qutbaniyya.
164   Jawahir, p. 27.
165   Jawahir, p. 27.

helped him to be less severe *(shadid)* about the prerequisites for making ablution as the Maliki School of jurisprudence laid them out. Where before he had considered the water for ablution impure if drops had fallen from oneself back into the bucket, he saw the Prophet making ablution out of a container into which had fallen some water from his washing.[166]

By the time the *Jawahir al-Ma'ani* was written, Shaykh Tijani was clearly in frequent visionary contact with the Prophet. Often, it is stressed that a certain vision, especially those with relevance to his followers, occurred in a waking state. Consonant with the role of the Prophet's visionary appearance in Islamic history, the Prophet is seen appearing to Shaykh Tijani to give advice, inform him of spiritual states, and instruct him of hidden knowledge or to provide consolation. A widely quoted description of Shaykh Tijani's visionary relationship to the Prophet is the following provided in *al-Fath al-Rabbani*:

> *Among the graces with which God honored him, (Shaykh Ahmad Tijani) was the waking vision of the Prophet, continuously and ever, so that it was never absent from him for the twinkling of an eye. Moreover, his questioning of the Prophet on everything and asking for counsel in small things and great, and undergoing training at his hands. This is the highest of all graces granted to the people of knowledge.[167]*

Even if Muslims prior to Shaykh Tijani had experienced visions of the Prophet, the intensity or degree of his visions seems quite exceptional. According to the *Jawahir*, the Prophet assured him *"of everything he asked for, even in the dunya (material world)."*[168] Even though the Shaykh continued with

---

166   Jawahir, p. 28.
167   Ahmad al-Shinqiti, Al-Fath al-Rabbani, translated in Constance Padwick, Muslim Devotions: a study of prayer manuals in common use (London: SPCK, 1961), p. 150.
168   *Jawahir,* p. 28.

some of the prayers he had learned from his previous teachers, following his spiritual opening he insisted that he did not use any prayer unless the Prophet gave him final permission and arranged it for him.[169] A major section of the *Jawahir* contains information from the Prophet about the benefits of various prayers, from portions of the Qur'an to prayers reported in Hadith to well known Sufi invocations to those specific to the Tijaniyya.[170] However, mostly what is apparent, from the visionary reports in the *Jawahir* is the profound intimacy and love between Shaykh Tijani and the Prophet. Even the contact of the Shaykh's companions with the Prophet serves to reinforce and even further explain this love. One of his most beloved companions, Ibn al-Arabi al-Tazi al-Damrawi, reportedly used to see the Prophet twenty-four times a day, but in one vision he is told by the Prophet that if it were not for al-Damrawi's love for his Shaykh, the Prophet would never have appeared to him at all.[171] It seems many of his companions, taken with the idea of seeing the Prophet in a waking state, saw Shaykh Ahmad Tijani's ascendent proximity to the Prophet as the means by which they could achieve their aim.[172]

---

169   *Jawahir,* p. 36.
170   Jawahir, pp. 51-65.
171   Jawahir, p. 187.
172   ***Kashf al-Hijab,*** p. 372.

Chapter II

Biographical Portrait II:

Shaykh Ahmad Tijani and the

Events of his Time

The Shaykh and the Ottoman authorities in Algeria

Although the *Jawahir* does not mention the political atmosphere of the times, being primarily intended as a book of spiritual guidance, such a learned traveler as Shaykh Ahmad Tijani would not have been able to escape some sort of entanglement with the political turmoil of the times. The attempted distance from politics but inevitable involvement was apparently a legacy the Shaykh left his later followers, especially his descendents in Algeria, such as Muhammad al-Saghir (d. 1853), who is discussed in the epilogue. The Turkish authorities in Algeria were apparently apprehensive of independently minded scholars such as Shaykh Tijani,'[173] especially when they started to attract around them, large followings that might challenge the central government in Algiers. Most of the major Sufi orders established in rural Algeria, such

---

173 [1] Benabdellah, *La Tijania,* p. 19. Tal Shuval has related how many of the country's prominent 'ulama in the eighteenth century were either executed, exiled or destituted by the Ottoman government in Algiers if they were thought to have become too influential *vis a vis* the central government. See Tal Shuval, *La ville d'Alger vers la fin du XVIIIe siecle: population et cadre urbain* (Paris: CNRS Editions, 1998), p. 121.

as the Rahmaniyya, the Darqawiyya and the Tijaniyya, thus came into armed conflict with the Turks.[174]

It was on account of a Turkish need to generate increased revenues, and, according to Benabdellah, of Shaykh Tijani's growing influence,[175] that Algiers imposed an annual tribute on Ain Madi in 1785. By this time, Ain Madi seems to have been home to a good number of Tijani's followers, even though the Shaykh himself did not reside there and had only made "very rare appearances in the city"[176] after his departure for study at the age of twenty-one. A 1788 Turkish expedition against Ain Madi represented both a general need to make an example of independently-minded oases and a more personal attack to curtail the influence of a leader whose growing following no doubt perturbed the Ottoman authorities. The accusation of the contemporary North African writer al-Zayani that Shaykh Tijani was collecting about him "the dregs of the Berbers and the Arabs,"[177] a common elitist charge of associating with the poor often made against religious leaders, indicates a possible source of Turkish apprehension of the Shaykh.

The story of Turkish hostility towards Shaykh Ahmad Tijani is corroborated by Abun-Nasr and Adnani. Adnani adds that Shaykh Tijani not only suffered the enmity of the Turks, but probably of the jurists of Ain Madi's Tijajna tribe as well, who formed an alliance with the Turkish government in Algiers against what they would have perceived as an usurper of their traditional position of ascendence.[178] Benabdellah and Abun-Nasr both suggest that Shaykh Ahmad Tijani did his best to avoid confrontation with the Turks, implying that

---

174   ² Julia Clancy-Smith, Rebel and Saint, Muslim Notables, Populist Protest, Colonial Encounters: Algeria and Tunisia, 1800-1904 (Berkeley and Los Angeles: UC Press, 1997), pp. 67-68.
175   Benabdellah, La Tijania, p. 21.
176   Adnani, "Reflexions," p. 26.
177   Al-Zayani quoted in Abun-Nasr, The Tijaniyya, p. 19.
178   Adnani, "Reflexions," pp. 22-23.

many of travels from city to city teaching following his return from the East could have served the double purpose of evading the Turkish authorities.[179] It is indeed possible that Shaykh Tijani's emigration to Fes was as much motivated by a desire to finally be free of Turkish hostility as it was to install himself in the center of learning in the Maghreb.

Turkish apprehension of Shaykh Ahmad Tijani is best understood in the context of what has often been described as the eighteenth-century decline of the Ottoman state. With the Turkish government in Algeria facing a drop in Mediterranean privateering revenues, Algiers tried to strengthen its hold on the inland oases with the hope of generating more tax revenues. It was a trend that "met with radical, rural-based opposition,"[180] and often the government found it necessary to send out tax-collecting expeditions designed to force the oases into submission. For their part, the tribes of the interior, usually led by the Sufi orders, largely viewed the Turkish government as an alien presence. This was exacerbated by the fact that, in Algeria, "unlike Morocco's 'Alawi dynasty, the Turks enjoyed little Islamic justification for their rule."[181] Clancy-Smith and others have recently called into question the idea of the Turko-Algerian decline in the late eighteenth century, indicating a move towards greater centralization of the Algerian state as the reason for increased intervention in the interior of Algeria.[182] Whatever the reason, the point remains that the eighteenth century witnessed heightened tensions between the Turkish government in Algiers and the interior of Algeria, and so the oases-based Sufi orders.

For his part, it is clear Shaykh Ahmad Tijani could not have had the most favorable opinion of the Turkish government in Algiers. Indeed, it is reported that, following notification in 1805 that the Turks had executed one of his followers in Tle-

179   Benabdellah, La Tijania, pp. 19-20. Abun-Nasr, The Tijaniyya, p. 19.
180   Julia Clancy-Smith, Rebel and Saint, p. 65.`
181   Clancy-Smith, Rebel and Saint, p. 65.
182   Clancy-Smith, Rebel and Saint, p. 67.

mcen (for reasons unknown), the Shaykh prayed for the Turks to lose Algeria in the same way God had permitted Muslim Spain to be lost to the Christians.[183] But this stance against the Turks in Algeria seems to have been somewhat exaggerated by writers such as Abun-Nasr who are intent on demonstrating the easy subservience of Sufi orders to the non-Muslim colonial powers, which is contrasted with their rebellion against indigenous Muslim state-building. The argument has obvious implications in the context of twentieth century nationalist agendas. In fact, Abun-Nasr himself relates several examples of a more complicated relationship between Shaykh Tijani and the Turks, although he apparently fails to see their significance for his narrative. In one letter, Shaykh Tijani responded to a request from Ain Madi for help against an advancing Turkish regiment by cautioning against rebellion and saying, "give the Bey whatever [money] may improve matters between you and him."[184] Nor can it be forgotten that the Shaykh, as was mentioned in chapter one, was well received by the Turkish Bey in Tunis on his way East. Even if the Turkish government in Tunis was often at odds with the central Ottoman authority, the fact remains the Shaykh can not be said to have completely rejected all Turkish Muslim authority.

If the divide between Shaykh Tijani and the Turkish authorities was indeed so wide, then it likewise becomes difficult to understand the close relationship of several later Tijani scholars and the Turkish governments in various places. The Bey of Tunis as the country's Chief Mufti and rector of the prestigious Zaytuna mosque and university appointed Ibrahim Riyahi (d. 1850). Muhammad ibn al-Mukhtar (known as Wad al-'Aliyya) met with the Ottoman Sultan Abd al-Hamid in 1897 and was reportedly so well received that the Sultan

---

183   This according to Ahmad Sukayrij, Raf al-Niqab, as cited in Abun-Nasr, The Tijaniyya, p. 61.
184   Al-Tijani's words quoted by Sukayrij, Kashf al-Hijab, included in Abun-Nasr, The Tijaniyya, p. 60.

took the Tijaniyya at al-Mukhtar's hands.[185] It is more likely that Shaykh Tijani's stance towards the Turks was defined by a characteristic unease towards any sort of political authority, in this case exacerbated by being a first-hand witness to Turkish corruption and heavy-handedness in Algeria. Clearly the Islamic dressing of the Turkish government was not enough to stave off the Shaykh's censure of certain unjust practices on a local level, such as expropriation and summary executions, but there seems no justification for the view that he was possessed of an irreconcilable enmity to the Ottoman Sultanate as a whole.

---

185   Abun-Nasr, The Tijaniyya, pp. 58-59, 61. Sultan Abd al-Hamid seems to have taken on a variety of tariqa affiliations, largely for political reasons (Mark Sedgwick, interview, Cairo, April, 2003).

Fes, Mawlay Sulayman and the Solidification of a Tariqa

Before examining the nature of the Shaykh Ahmad Tijani's *Tariqa Muhammadiyya* movement, it is important to trace its spread and establishment during his lifetime. The milieu of Moroccan religious reform and politics, particularly centering around the Moroccan Sultan, Mawlay Sulayman, into which the Shaykh's new order was introduced, provides valuable insight into the nature of the Shaykh's own doctrine.

Shaykh Ahmad Tijani and an entourage of his closest companions took up residence in Fes beginning in 1213/1798.[186] The "Baghdad of the Maghreb,"[187] Fes was at the time the greatest center of learning in Northern Africa outside of Cairo, and for a number of centuries had been the political, religious and cultural capital of the Moroccan Sultanate. Home of the Qarawin mosque and university, the city boasted a host of scholars famous for the study of Maliki jurisprudence and Hadith.

---

186   The correct date as given by the Jawahir al-Ma'ani has been recognized by a number of academics since Abun-Nasr's mistaken assertion of 1789 as the date of permanent residence. See Jawahir, p. 26.
187   Benabdellah, La Tijania, p. 21.

In part due to the pious reputation of its legendary founder, Idris II, whose mausoleum can still be found in the heart of the old city, it had acquired an almost unrivaled renown for being an abode of saints, and many of the famous *'Awliya* had at one time resided there, including Abu Madyan, Ibn 'Arabi and al-Shadhili.

By the time of his arrival in Fes, Shaykh Tijani's fame as a scholar possessing religious charisma or blessing (*baraka*) had spread throughout the Maghreb,[188] so that his entry into the city was a matter of some importance for the political and religious establishment. The Shaykh was met by a delegation of scholars selected by the Sultan. There is little record of this first meeting, except that some of the scholars came to discuss theological questions with him.[189] But an early nineteenth-century French source, reporting oral accounts of Shaykh Tijani's 1798 entry into Fes, recounts the exchange between the scholars and the Shaykh in some detail, and is included here for the lack of a better description. It seems the Sultan's aim in sending the delegation was to test the reputed knowledge and saintliness of the newcomer, a task to which the scholars readily agreed, since they were jealous of his reputation and wanted to reveal him to the Sultan as an ordinary man and an imposter. However, upon entering Tijani's presence, they became unable to speak except to exchange pleasantries.[190] Guessing the real purpose of the welcoming delegation, Shaykh Tijani said, "*I am nothing by myself, it is only with the aid of Him who knows all that I have been able to acquire any of the sciences. If someone among you wishes to discuss with me the subjects that the Eternal has permitted the human soul to know, let him raise his voice and*

---

188   Bughyat al-Mustafid, p. 180.

189   Abun-Nasr, The Tijaniyya, p. 20.

190   A similar inability to speak in the Shaykh's presence is reported about one of his sharpest critics in Fes, al-Tayyib ibn Kiran, the head of the royal council of 'Ulama to which Shaykh Tijani would later be appointed. See Sukayrij, Kashf al-Hijab, quoted in Adnani, "Les origines de la Tijaniyya," p. 47.

I will do my best to respond."[191] Whatever the case, the delegation's report to the Sultan must have been sufficiently favorable
for him to further inquire after this newest saint in his kingdom.

The relationship that developed between Shaykh Tijani and
Sultan Mawlay Sulayman is important in understanding the
religious personality of both men. After a series of tests to ascertain the veracity of Tijani's claims to sainthood, such as giving the saint money in a manner he would not have been able
to accept as a man of religion,[192] Mawlay Sulayman became
closely linked to the newcomer, appointing him to his council
of religious scholars and giving him a large house ("the House
of Mirrors"). The Sultan's initiation into the Tijaniyya has often
been denied by non-Tijanis, but Tijanis have maintained his
discipleship to their Shaykh. Tijani tradition has chronicled a
series of letters between Shaykh Tijani and the Sultan clearly
indicating a shaykh-disciple relationship. In one exchange, the
Shaykh writes the Sultan urging him to fear God and keep to
His command and then informs him of some of the benefits of
the Tijani *wird* as told to him by the Prophet, and tells him of
the proper manners for experiencing the vision of the Prophet.
The Sultan replied,

> *The ransom of our parents, our master and our shaykh
> and our Muhammadan example, Abu 'Abbas Sidi Ah-
> mad. I praise God to you and to Him and I send bless-
> ings and peace upon His noble Prophet. Your most bless-
> ed lines have reached us, and we praise God the Most
> High on account of what He has made special for us by
> them from the pleasure of the master, the Messenger of
> God ... and this matter I do not want that I should al-
> low myself to leave its performance, and I am not safe
> from losing or neglecting its fulfillment ... [and I pray*

191   Francois de Neveu, Ordres Religieux chez les Musulmans de l'Algerie (Paris, Imprimeriede A. Guyot, 1846), pp. 133-135.
192   Kashf al-Hijab, pp. 372-376. Apparently, the Shaykh followed the
Prophet is refusing charity.

that you] remove me from all that prevents me from looking at his [the Prophet's] noble face, that [you may] surround me with the degree of those close to the glory of the Messenger of God. And [this] is needed of you, since you know that my righteousness is a righteousness from my guardianship of God over them [the people], and that my corruption is their corruption, so the prayer for me is a prayer for the general [population].[193]

In the *Kashf al-Hijab*, Ahmad Sukayrij relates the story of the Sultan's coming to be affiliated with the new order. It seems the Sultan, as was hinted in his letter, was very much interested in the idea of seeing his ancestor, the Prophet Muhammad, in a waking state, and incessantly asked of Shaykh Tijani to facilitate his meeting with the Prophet. The Sultan was not only motivated by the pious desire to meet his forefather, but was also interested in this as a means of assurance of Shaykh Tijani's claims concerning sainthood.[194] The Shaykh at first refused the Sultan, saying the latter would not be able to bear the experience, but at his insistence, wrote for him a prayer and gave him instructions as to how to go about seeing the Prophet. But when it came time for the Sultan to recite the prayer, he was seized by a great fright, and returned to the Shaykh to ask him if he would be with him during the meeting. The saint agreed, but when the light of the Prophet entered the room, the Sultan fainted. He awoke an hour later to find the Shaykh by his side with his hand on his chest. Then the Sultan heard what the Prophet had assured him, and he offered profuse thanks to Shaykh Tijani, no doubt fortified in his love for both his ancestor and his new shaykh.[195]

---

193   Salah al-Din al-Tijani, Kashf al-Ghuyum, pp. 415-419. Also Sukayrij, Kashf al- Hijab, pp. 374-376.

194   Sukayrij, Kashf al-Hijab, p. 372.

195   The story is related in Sukayrij, Kashf al-Hijab, pp. 372-373, and Ibn Sa'ih, Bughyat al-Mustafid, pp. 180-185.

However, others, such as the contemporary historian Muhammad Mansour, have disputed the Sultan's affiliation with the Tijaniyya, indicating the Sultan's rank of *Muqaddam* (propagator) of the Nasiriyya order, as well as his family's traditional affinity with that order.[196] Nevertheless, the romance of the Tijani story aside, the Sultan's adherence to Shaykh Tijani's new order makes historical sense in the context of the Sultan's reign. From the beginning of the nineteenth century, Mawlay Sulayman was engaged in a reform campaign, which included, among other things, an attack on the excesses of popular Sufism. Such a campaign left hardly any of the traditional orders unscathed, including the Nasiriyya, against the Beni Touzine (Rif region) zawiya of which he launched a military campaign in 1808.[197] It does not seem likely he would have attacked the zawiya of an order to which he still exclusively adhered. Other secondary evidence for the Sultan's association with the Tijaniyya include his warm reception of Shaykh al-Tijani and the open Tijani affiliation of both his son, Mawlay Abd al-Salam, and one of his closest advisors, Muhammad Ikanasus, as well as many of the government and business elite.[198] It seems Mawlay Sulayman's warm reception of the Tijaniyya set an example for his posterity as well, and several of Morocco's later Sultans have been followers of the Tijaniyya, possibly including the late Sultan Hassan II (d. 2000), who some say held the rank of *Muqaddam* in the order.[199]

Aside from whatever esoteric connection existed between the Sultan and the founder of the Tijaniyya, another explanation of Mawlay Sulayman's warm reception of Shaykh Ahmad Tijani was the fact that the Sultan "found, in the person of

---

196   Mohamed el-Mansour, Morocco in the reign of Mawlay Sulayman (London: ME and N. African Studies Press, 1990), pp. 161-162.
197   Mansour, Mawlay Sulayman, fh 75, pp. 177-178.
198   Abun-Nasr, The Tijaniyya, p. 94.
199   Interview with Sidi Ibrahim al-Tijani (fifth descendent of Sidi Ahmad al-Tijani), Fes, Morocco, October, 2002.

Shaykh Tijani, the symbol that personified by his behavior and his teaching, the indelible precepts of the Shari'a."[200] Certainly, the Shaykh's situation of Sufism firmly within Islamic sacred law, while maintaining the ascendancy of a *Tariqa Muhammad-iyya* over both Sufi and *Fiqh* (jurisprudence) historical traditions, would have been attractive to the reform-minded Sultan.

Mawlay Sulayman was himself famous for his personal piety and as an Islamic scholar in his own right. It seems he at first shied away from political office, preferring instead to further pursue religious studies. But when his brother died after only two years as Sultan, the political establishment prevailed upon the then twenty-six year old Sulayman to take the throne in 1792. Even as Sultan, he "continued to govern more like an *'alirn* (religious scholar) than like a statesman; referring constantly to the *Shari'a* and the *'alims* before taking any important decision."[201]

It is not surprising then that such a Sultan should use his office to affect a series of religious reforms aimed at elevating the status of Islam in his country. Since Mawlay Sulayman is often credited with helping to centralize the Moroccan state, it has often been said that such reforms were a politically motivated measure to take power away from the local *marabouts* (shaykhs, religious leaders) or zawiyas in order to strengthen the power of the central government. That some of his reforms had this effect cannot be disputed, and clearly his role as Sultan required that he respond to the *Crise Maraboutique*, where rural zawiyas often set up independent governments and sometimes went so far as to levy their own taxes.[202] Other reforms, such as abolishing the tobacco trade,[203] reveal an almost idealist attempt to protect his country from what he perceived as

200   Benabdellah, La Tijania, p. 22.
201   Mansour, Mawlay Sulayman, p. 134.
202   Francisco Manas, "Supplanting the Ruler: the Levying of Taxes by Sufi Zawiya-s in the Maghrib," in Islamic Quarterly (v. 40, no. 2, 1996).
203   Mansour, Mawlay Sulayman, p. 134.

detrimental influences despite adverse political or economic results (the tobacco trade being quite profitable).

Through a sequence of enactments and his own writings, Mawlay Sulayman embarked on a series of religious reforms mostly aimed at popular Sufism. As such, his reforms are often compared to the contemporary Wahhabi movement in the Hijaz, and it is tempting to conclude some sort of contact between the two countries, which would have inspired the young Sultan. However, Morocco's first significant contact with the Wahhabiyya did not occur until the Sultan, after receiving a letter from the Wahhabis, sent his son Mawlay Ibrahim, together with some prominent religious scholars, to investigate the new movement in 1811, by which time Mawlay Sulayman's own reforms were already in full swing. These reforms included objection to ornate domes being built over tombs, sacrificing animals on the tombs of saints to attain their intercession, the use of dancing and music in formal Sufi group *dhikr* (liturgical remembrance of God), and the extravagance and mingling of the sexes occurring at religious festivals sponsored by Sufi zawiyas. These objections on the part of the Sultan seem to have been rather standard on the list of *bida'* (innovation) targeted by late eighteenth- century reformers. To reform such practices, one of the most significant decrees during Mawlay Sulayman's reign was the banning of some of the *mawlid* festivals (commemorating the birth of the Prophet or of a saint) held by rural zawiyas. On a theoretical level, the Sultan's condemnation of popular Sufism was motivated by his belief that the worship of God should not be equated with amusement and that Sufis should remain productive members of the society instead of beggars creating a burden on the rest of the community.[204]

---

204   Mansour, Mawlay Sulayman, p. 136. The Sultan was obviously identifying with the strand of Sufism, represented in the Maghrebi context by the Jazuliyya, emphasizing worldly involvement as opposed to another, represented at the time of the Sultan by the Darqawiyya, emphasizing renunciation of the world.

The similarity of these reforms with the Wahhabi agenda is striking, and indeed the twentieth-century Moroccan Salafi movement (whose ideology has come to closely resemble that of the Wahhabis) would later claim Mawlay Sulayman as the country's first Salafi. Indeed, the report of the Moroccan delegation to the Hijaz generally gave a favorable impression of the Wahhabiyya,[205] but it is possible this early form of the Wahhabiyya with which the Moroccan delegation came into contact was significantly less radical than its later interpretation.[206] The Moroccan delegation reportedly met with the Saudi leader, Sa'ud Ibn 'Abd al-'Aziz, and received assurance that the Wahhabis did not oppose the *ziyara* (visitation) of the Prophet's tomb or even the sanctity of the saints, only how the common people sometimes exaggerated in these respects.[207]

Nonetheless, the Moroccan Sultan's reply to the Wahhabiyya did not entail a blanket acceptance, and there remained three significant points of divergence. The first was the issue of *takfir* (excommunication). Wahhabi doctrine generally made it easy to label somebody an unbeliever, a practice to which the Sultan vehemently objected, writing, "Excommunication should be pronounced only against an infidel about whom there can be no ambiguity."[208] He therefore urged the new movement to practice greater tolerance towards diverging interpretations. A second issue Mawlay Sulayman held at variance was affiliation with a *madhhab* (school of jurisprudence), which the wahhabi movement sought to bypass entirely. The Sultan, along with Shaykh Ahmad Tijani and the rest of North and West Africa, held firmly to the Maliki *madhhab*. Lastly, the Sultan disagreed with the Wahhabis that seeking the interces-

---

205   Mansour, Mawlay Sulayman, p. 141.
206   This is one of the major subjects of a recently published book by Natana J. DeLong Bas, Wahhabi Islam, from Revival and Reform to Global Jihad (New York: Oxford UP, 2004).
207   Mansour, Mawlay Sulayman, p. 143.
208   Mawlay Sulayman and al-Tayyib Ibn Kiran, Jawab f i Mas 'alat al-Kasb, quoted in Mansour, Mawlay Sulayman, p. 134.

sion of the saints was an act of polytheism *(shirk)* or disbelief *(kufr)*. In a letter citing from the Qur'an and Hadith, he upheld the intercessionary powers of the Prophet and the saints, while admitting that the common people sometimes transgressed the limits and forgot that it was God who was fulfilling their request and not the saint.[209]

The reforms of Mawlay Sulayman can thus be characterized as a move towards an elite, scholarly accentuation of the Islamic tradition, where both law and mysticism were affirmed from within the traditions at hand, namely Maliki *fiqh* and *tariqa*-based Sufism, rather than given a radical redefinition, as was the case with the Wahhabiyya. As will be seen, Shaykh Ahmad Tijani's thinking, like that of the Sultan, seems more a revitalization or even a culmination of past traditions rather than a rejection of them in an attempt to create something new. Given the connection between Shaykh Tijani and the Sultan, the latter's reforms prove an interesting commentary on the Shaykh himself and the light of revivification with which he saw his own movement. And certainly the later spread of the Tijaniyya can be characterized by the diffusion of an elite class of scholarly mystics whose emphasis on Sufism might be described as erudite, sober and socially conscious. There are clear parallels between the Mawlay Sulayman's reforms and the later impact of the Tijaniyya in societies where it spread, but more research needs to be done as to the exact nature of Shaykh Ahmad Tijani's influence on the Sultan's reform agenda.

* * *

Aside from his relationship to the Sultan, the Shaykh's time in Fes was largely occupied with the solidification of the *tariqa* and its doctrines and the training and sending out of *muqaddams* (propagators). Before the end of his life, he had

---

209   Mansour, *Mawlay Sulayman*, p. 142.

attracted thousands of followers[210] and sent out *muqaddams* such as Ali Harazem al-Barada, Muhammad Ghali and Muhammad al-Hafiz as far away as the Hijaz and Mauritania. Before the completion of the Tijani zawiya, his followers met at the Shaykh's own house, the House of Mirrors. This house can still be visited today, and although it has fallen into a state of disrepair, its original majesty has not been lost. It has an expansive courtyard decorated entirely with blue and yellow *zellij* tile work with a large fountain in the middle, flanked by a number of rooms that include what was the Shaykh's library, a room for *khalwa* (spiritual retreat), a salon, the bedroom, the kitchen, etc., with rooms for the Shaykh's family and guests on the second floor. It is easy to imagine the house serving as the center of prayer and for the teaching and diffusion of the Shaykh's ideas.

Although his main bases of support came from outside of Fes, he did maintain some popularity in the city itself, even if some of the established 'Ulama (legal scholars), such as al-Tayyib ibn Kiran (d. 1802), rejected his claims to sainthood.[211] No doubt Shaykh Tijani opened himself up to such attacks by his announcement in 1214 (1799), in a city where nobody had yet claimed a spiritual authority higher than Fes's founder, Mawlay Idris II, of having attained the station of *Qutb al-Aqtab* (the Pole of poles). Clearly this, along with his reports of frequent visionary contact with the Prophet (and the superceding of traditional structures of scholarly authority that this entailed), would have incited the indignation of many of the Fassi 'Ulama. But the Shaykh's following nonetheless continued to increase, prompting him in 1215 (1800),

---

210   The primary sources do not give us any exact number, so it is difficult to ascertain exactly how many followers Sidi al-Tijani had during his life. But he apparently had large followings stretching from Tunisia through Algeria to Southern Morocco to Mauritania. Ibrahim Sail gives the number as 124,000 (Sail, La Prophetie, la Saintete et leurfruits, p. 45). This number cannot be verified, however

211   Abun-Nasr, The Tijaniyya, p. 21.

by order of the Prophet,[212] to begin construction of the Tijani zawiya that still serves as a place of congregation for the order to this day. The construction of this fabulous specimen of Moroccan artistry was financed by Tijani's followers as well as from his own funds.[213] Shaykh Tijani was himself of reputed great wealth because of property and trade interests in Southern Algeria.[214] Clearly, his example of saintliness while being successfully involved in the world was a source of attraction for many religiously minded business and government elite. It seems that such a reputation of worldly *baraka* (blessing) became attached to taking the order that later Egyptian *muqaddams* found it necessary to screen potential initiates to establish whether they were taking the order for genuine spiritual enlightenment or just to become rich.[43]

Shaykh Ahmad Tijani passed from this world in 1230 (1815) at the age of eighty. He left behind him a firmly established order, the *Tariqa Muhammadiyya* emphasis of which inspired many of his later followers to renew and spread Islam in diverse communities far from the mother zawiya in Fes, where the Shaykh's tomb can still be found. The exact nature of this *Tariqa Muhammadiyya* left by Shaykh Ahmad Tijani demands further explanation in both its external and esoteric components.

212   Kashf al-Hijab, p. 18.
213   Kashf al-Hijab, p. 18.
214   Abun-Nasr, The Tijaniyya, p. 22; Abun-Nasr cites the Moroccan writer, al-Nasiri, Kitab al-Istiqsa

Chapter III

Shaykh Ahmad Tijani and Islamic Sacred Law (Shari'a)

Shaykh Ahmad Tijani and Islamic Sacred Law (Shari'a)

One of the more pertinent questions for any Sufi order claiming to be a *Tariqa Muhammadiyya* is its relationship to the external attribute of the Muhammadan Path, namely the Shari'a or Islamic sacred law. The connection between Sufism in general and the Shari'a has been a sometimes contentious issue, especially since the nineteenth century. It is important to understand the *Tariqa Muhammadiyya* phenomenon in the context of the sporadic charges of unorthodoxy leveled against the Sufi orders. The *Tariqa Muhammadiyya*'s emphasis of the Shari'a has many precedents in the history of Sufism, and the notion of Sufism's inherent opposition to the Shari'a must be considered more as a modem polemic than as a truism emerging from the pages of history. Recent Wahhabi and Salafi reformers have branded Sufism with the disreputable indictment of *bida'* (innovation), a charge perhaps as much motivated by a modem nationalist political agenda than any perceived doctrinal impurity.[215]

---

215   Elizabeth Sirriyeh, Sufis and Anti-Sufis: The Defense, Rethinking and Rejection of Sufism in the Modern World (Great Britain: Curzon, 1999),

Western scholarship has likewise contributed to the stereotype, whose "wishful thinking" has until recently desired to "see Sufism as congenial but Islam as oppressive, or who finds Islam's spiritual teachings exciting but its attention to ritual details tiring."[216] But, notwithstanding the few Sufi sages, like al-Hallaj (executed in tenth century Baghdad for allegedly denying the necessity of the Pilgrimage), whose publicized mystic utterances have drawn the ire of the jurists, Sufis have traditionally comprised some of Islam's most eminent jurists.[217] The respect for the Shari'a thus evidenced by many Sufis seems to indicate a vital link between Islamic Law and mysticism. As Bernd Radtke has observed,

> *Sufism concerns itself with the activation and cultivation of those powers and spheres from within the totality of the soul that under the impress of enlightenment and science have been neglected ... Traditionally, a Muslim has understood these phenomena of the soul within the Islamic religious framework, that is the Koran and Sunna. Within this framework, the Sunna, orthopraxy and mysticism are not in opposition to each other. On the contrary, the Law is fulfilled by mystical experience.*[218]

---

p. 102; George Joffe, "Maghribi Islam and Islam in the Maghrib, the Eternal Dichotomy," in Westerlund and Rosander eds., African Islam and Islam in Africa, Encounters between Sufis and Islamists (Ohio: Ohio UP, 1997), pp. 66-67; Jamil Abun-Nasr, A History of the Maghrib (Cambridge: Cambridge UP, 1975), p. 368.

216   William Chittick, Faith and Practice of Islam (Albany: State University of New York, 1992), p. xii.

217   Nuh Ha Mim Keller lists about thirty of the most eminent Islamic scholars who were known to have undergone Sufi training. While not claiming to be comprehensive, it includes such seminal men as Abu Hanifa and Imam Malik. See Ahmad ibn Naqib al-Misri, Reliance o f the Traveler (trans. and commentary by Nuh Ha Mim Keller, Maryland: Amana, 1991), p. 863.

218   Bernd Radtke, "Ijtihad and Neo-Sufism," in Asiatische Studien (v. 19, issue iii, 1994), pp. 909-910.

The famous Sufi Hakim al-Tirmidhi (d. 910), for example, stressed the necessity of the Law's outward interpretation and application, and conceived the *'ilm al-batin* (esoteric knowledge, attained through an act of Divine grace and the aspirant's purification of his *nafs,* ego or carnal self) as an aid in this process insofar as it is the means by which one understands the essential foundations of the legal prescriptions.[219] Ibn 'Arabi, known as the **Shaykh al-Akbar** (the greatest Shaykh), also emphasized the unity of external and esoteric knowledge: "Know that God addressed man in his totality, without giving precedence to his exterior *(zhahir)* over his interior (**batin**)."[220]

The respect scholarly Sufism has always had for the Shari'a does not mean that popular Sufism has not often been the object of juridical censure. The scholars associated with the eighteenth-century *Tariqa Muhammadiyya* phenomenon were themselves foremost in criticizing this perceived corruption of religion. Mustafa al-Bakri spoke against Sufism's adulteration by immoral practices and ideas such as consorting with young men and strange women and the practice of magic.[221] Likewise 'Abd al-Aziz al-Dabbagh, the Moroccan Shadhili shaykh who was the subject of the widely popular *Kitab al-Ibriz,* believed that Sufi practices had over time become corrupted through the impure intentions of disciples and the use of magic.[222] Although Shaykh Ahmad Tijani was considerably less outspoken in the criticism of other Sufis than were some of his predecessors, the marked sobriety of Tijani practices and the Shaykh's own close relationship with Mawlay Sulayman may be considered evidence of his belonging to this tradition of scholarly Sufism.

---

219   Radtke, "Ijtihad," pp. 912-913.
220   Ibn al-'Arabi, Futuhat al-Makkiya, quoted in Michel Chodkiewicz, An Ocean Without Shore: Ibn 'Arabi, the Book, and the Law (trans. David Straight, Albany: SUNY, 1993), p. 24.
221   Radtke, "Sufism in the 18th Century," p. 341.
222   Radtke, "Sufism in the 18th Century," p. 341.

In any case, the eighteenth-century reformist Sufis were just a few examples of a longer tradition of elite Sufis criticizing the practices associated with popular Sufism, from al-Junayd, Abd al-Qadir al-Jilani to al-Suyuti, to name a few. Thus, it is an oversimplification to see the close connection to the Shari'a of such *Tariqa Muhammadiyya* Sufis like Shaykh Ahmad Tijani as a reactive attempt to justify Sufism to an incredulous "orthodoxy." Rather the emphasis on the Shari'a was an inevitable accent given the links of such Sufis with the tradition of Islamic scholarship and their own enthusiasm for the Sunna of the Prophet. Some elements of this emphasis do, however, represent a significant historical development, mainly in the notion of *ijtihad* (scholarly interpretation) and Sufism's ability to have an impact on the society at large, subjects that will be treated below.

This section will investigate Shaykh Ahmad Tijani's relationship to the Shari'a, the Prophetic Sunna and its external implications, and the tradition of jurisprudence *(fiqh)* that developed to interpret the Shari'a. The essential question for this latter subject is the Shaykh's views on scholarly interpretation *(ijtihad)*. The object of this section is not only to examine Shaykh Ahmad Tijani's affinity to the tradition of Islamic scholarship but to illustrate how Islam's mystical tradition might in some cases add to the discourse within Islam concerning the Law. As a final note, I will test the conclusions of previous writers such as Abun-Nasr and El Adnani as to the order's alleged departure from what they define as Islamic orthodoxy. A useful vantage point from which to view this latter question is the controversy over the Shaykh's ideas of the relationship of the Qur'an and the prayer upon the Prophet, called *Salat al-Fatih*.

It is clear from the primary sources containing Shaykh Ahmad Tijani's ideas and behavior that he possessed a profound respect for the legal value of the Qur'an and Sunna of the Prophet and his companions, as well as (though to a lesser extent) for the inherited tradition of scholarly interpretation of these sources. As was shown earlier, he was trained in the sciences of the Qur'an and Hadith and prior to his becoming a *shaykh al-tarbiyya* (of spiritual instruction), he spent most of his time during his travels teaching Qur'anic *tafsir* (interpretation) and Hadith. The *Jawahir al-Ma'ani* itself provides evidence of this emphasis, with frequent reference to Qur'an and Hadith throughout the work. Of 246 pages in the *Jawahir*'s 2001 Cairo edition, fifty-four are concerned specifically with explanation of certain verses of the Qur'an, twenty comments only on Hadith, while another ten are concerned with specific questions of *fiqh*. It seems many of Shaykh Tijani's students were attracted to him for his knowledge of the traditional Islamic sciences, even if they did not always stay long enough to receive initiation into his path. The celebrated *Tariqa Muhammadiyya* shaykh Muhammad al-Sanusi (1787-1859) testified,

> *I learned from him [Tijani], and I took the Qur'an from him, and he told me that he had taken it from the Prophet (may God bless him and grant him peace), asleep and awake. And he excelled in following his, may God bless him and grant him peace, example in all actions, and he honored me by letting me take the Qur'an from him, by this noble sanad, after he had taken it from him [the Prophet].[223]*

In his article, "Lumieres sur la Tijaniyya et les Tijan," the Senegalese Shaykh Ibrahim Niasse (d. 1975) quotes the statements of several notable scholars from Morocco, Tunisia and Egypt more or less contemporary to Shaykh Ahmad Tijani (but who were not known to have formerly entered the order) attesting to the level of his erudition.[224] As we have seen, his

---

223   Ahmad al-Sharif (grandson of al-Sanusi), Al-Anwar al-qudsiya fi muqaddimat al- tariqa al-Sanusiya, quoted in Knut S. Vikor, Sufi and Scholar on the Desert Edge, Muhammad b. Ali al-Sanusi and his Brotherhood (London: C. Hurst & Co., 1995), pp. 59-60.
224   Shaykh Ibrahim Niasse, "Lumieres sur la Tijaniyya et les Tijan," chapter entitled, "Elonges des Savants a l'endroit de Ahmad al-Tijani."

early circle of followers contained many distinguished *faqihs*, such as Ibrahim Riyahi, Muhammad al-Hafiz of Mauritania and Ibn Mishry of Algeria. Later Tijanis have been no less energetic in the field of Islamic law, as evidenced by the activities of such men as the Moroccan jurist and traditionalist Muhammad al-'Arabi al-Sa'ih (d. 1892), the Mauritanian scholar Ahmad al-Shinqiti (d. 1913), the Marakeshi Qadi Ahmad Sukayrij (d. 1949), Shaykh Ibrahim Niasse (who in 1963 received, for his Islamic scholarship and efforts to spread Islam, the title "Shaykh al-Islam" from the Azhar), the Egyptian scholar Muhammad al-Hafiz (d. 1978) and the present-day Mufti of Albania, Hafiz Sabri Cocki. With the spread of the Tijaniyya in places like West Africa, the order has sometimes become more famous for its Islamic scholarship than anything else.[225]

Shaykh Ahmad Tijani himself provides the model for the respect for the Shari'a many of his later followers would come to represent. When asked if false statements would be attributed to him after his death, he replied in the affirmative and urged his followers to use the criterion of the Shari'a to determine the truth: "If you hear anything attributed to me, weigh it on the scale of the Shari'a. If it conforms, accept it, otherwise reject it."[226] Ali Harazem al-Barada writes about his Shaykh, "We find him stem (*shadid*) concerning the religious obligations ... and he often says, 'The best of remembrances (*adhkar*) is the [servant's] remembrance of Allah at the command of his Lord and His prohibition.'"[227] He demanded of his disciples that saintly miracles be kept hidden and elaborated that "An act of righteousness is better than a thousand miraculous

---

225   Barbara Callaway and Lucy Creevey, The Heritage of Islam, Women, Religion and Politics in West Africa (Boulder: Lynne Rienner Publishers, Inc., 1994), p. 46.
226   Ifadat al-Ahmadiyya, p. 12. See also Shaykh Hassan Cisse, Translation and Commentary of the Spirit of Good Morals by Shaykh of Islam Shaykh Ibrahim Niasse (Michigan: A.A.I.I., 1998), pp. 12-13.
227   Jawahir, p. 35.

feats."[228] He was reportedly particular about the performance of the canonical prayer, emphasizing that it should be made in congregation and at its proper time, saying, "No work is better than prayer *(salat)* in its proper time."[229]

According to the *Jawahir,* he did not neglect the external sciences and his knowledge in this area included the theology of God's oneness *(tawhid),* Qur'anic interpretation *(tafsir),* Prophetic traditions *(Hadith)* and biography *(sira),* and other traditional sciences such as grammar and poetry; in fact sharing with the *'ulama* "the entirety of their knowledge."[230] But, as is illustrated from al-Sanusi's statement about Shaykh Tijani's knowledge of the Qur'an, it seems that he did not make a great distinction between esoteric and external knowledge, holding that the "external sciences return in their entirety" to the reality of the esoteric sciences.[231] Specifically, the study of the Qur'an and Hadith, which helps to instill the fear of Allah, serve to separate the aspirant from the frivolity of the material world *(dunya),* thereby allowing him to behave "as if he is seeing the afterlife between his hands."[232] The inner state of the worshipper before his Lord should be one of utmost sincerity and purity "in order to accomplish an act of pure adoration and satisfaction of Divine laws."[233] The contemporary Senegalese Tijani Shaykh Hassan Cisse explains in this regard the place of the Shari'a within the real knowledge of God *(ma'arifa):*

> *The importance of this knowledge [Shari'a] is that it is used to service and maintain the Ma'arifa (reality, beauty and magnificence) of Allah already acquired. It is a means of revisiting Allah through primary worship like prayer, fasting, alms giving and pilgrimage, and second-*

228   Benabdellah, La Tijania, p. 75.
229   Jawahir, pp. 59, 36.
230   Jawahir, p. 40.
231   Jawahir, p. 40.
232   Jawahir, p. 40
233

*ary worship like marriage/divorce, commerce/econom-
ics, etc.[234]*

It is clear that Shaykh Tijani held the classic Sufi opinion of the essential link between the Shari'a and the esoteric reality (*Haqiqa*). "It is incumbent on the truthful person," he said, "to immerse himself in the esoteric reality *(Haqiqa)* while working with the external Shari'a, keeping to the regulations, and that is the straight path in following the Messenger."[235]

* * *

Consonant with the *Tariqa Muhammadiyya* emphasis, Shaykh Ahmad Tijani laid much stress on following the Sunna of the Prophet. According to the *Jawahir*, he exerted himself to do exactly what the Prophet did, saying, "All the good is in following the Sunna, and all evil is in differing from it."[236] His love of the Prophet extended to the *Sahaba* (companions) and the *Ahl al-Bayt* (the Prophet's family). In what might be considered a defense of the then established Sunni orthodoxy, the *Jawahir* details the merit of different companions of the Prophet[237] and says the *Sahaba* who spread the religion of Is-

---

234   Shaykh Hassan Cisse, Spirit of Good Morals of Shaykh Ibrahim Niasse, p. 17.

235   Jawahir, p. 51. This statement is reminiscent of Imam Malik's famous diction, related by Shaykh Hassan Cisse, "He who practices Sufism (tassawuf) without understanding and observing the Fiqh (law) corrupts his faith, while he who understands and observes Fiqh without practicing Sufism corrupts himself. But he who combines the two has indeed proven to be true." See Shaykh Hassan Cisse, Spirit of Good Morals by Shaykh Ibrahim Niasse, p. 23.

236   Jawahir, p. 36.

237   Jawahir, p. 84. Shaykh Tijani, not inconsistent with other Sunni, especially Sufi, scholars, especially loved Ali ibn Abi Talib, honoring him as the "Door to the city of knowledge." Ali's special merit was his esoteric knowledge; Umar, his knowledge of the Shari'a and Abu Bakr the strength of his faith.

lam have a rank superior to all succeeding generations since they had the benefit of all prayers and good actions of the Muslims who came after them.[238]

The academic definition of the *Tariqa Muhammadiyya* suggests that such an emphasis on the Sunna might occasion the saint to speak out about the excesses of popular Sufism. It is difficult, however, to find instances of Shaykh Ahmad Tijani actually speaking against any of the other Sufi orders or the practices of their followers. But certainly his relationship to Mawlay Sulayman at a time when the latter was campaigning against some of the excesses taking place at the *mawlid* celebrations of certain zawiyas involves the Shaykh in these sorts of reforms as well. The Tijaniyya's emphasis that *ziyara* (visitation) should only be made to the graves of the Prophet, his companions or other Tijanis also can be perceived as a de-emphasis of the *ziyara* tradition so prevalent in popular Sufism, especially in the Maghreb.

The form of congregational *dhikr* adopted by Shaykh Ahmad Tijani may be one of the more sober of any Sufi order. Tijanis sit on the floor facing each other in a rectangle shape and recite their litanies in a measured fashion. There is no dancing, musical instrumµents, heavy breathing or any of the other practices some reformers have considered reprehensible in the performance of *dhikr*. Later Tijani scholars, such as al-'Arabi ibn Sa'ih and Ahmad al-Sukayrij, would in fact voice this sobriety in objection to excessive movement or melody in the *hadra* (congregational *dhikr*). In 1919, several prominent Tijani leaders gathered in Fes to produce a document stating in part, "reading the *hailalah* (the *hadra*) plainly is the form which accords with the *Shari 'a* and the Sufi way."[239]

Although musical instruments are not used in any of the formal Tijani *dhikrs,* the Shaykh was said to have permitted the

---

238   Jawahir, p. 59.
239   Abun-Nasr, The Tijaniyya, pp. 54-55.

use of such instruments for the more informal tradition of poetry recitation and *Sama,* he was known to himself occasionally appreciate the playing of a famous Moroccan *'uwd* (lute) musician.[240] Although musical instruments in *dhikr* gatherings seem rarely in use among Tijanis today, in Senegal the Tijanis are possessed of a quite lively, if informal, *Sama'* tradition even if the formal *hadra* in the mosque remains quite sober.[241] In any case, Tijani practice in regards to the performance of formal *dhikr* should not necessarily be seen as a reaction to the practices of other Sufi orders. Tijanis largely seem tolerant of the practices of other orders despite an obvious divergence in ritual. In this regard, Shaykh Hassan Cisse relates that when he first saw Sufis dancing during their *dhikr* in the Hussein mosque in Cairo, he did not have a good feeling in his heart. However, that night he dreamed of his own grandfather and shaykh, Shaykh Ibrahim Niasse, performing *raks* (Sufi dance) in a similar fashion. Shaykh Hassan has thereafter avoided criticizing the practice.[242]

The Tijaniyya, then, has maintained respect for other Sufi traditions despite the divergence from Tijani practice. It seems likely this tolerance was not the result of any timidity on the part of Tijani scholars, but stemmed from Shaykh Ahmad Tijani's own opinion that all the Sufi orders originated and returned to the Prophet himself. Still the lack of public criticism does not entail a blanket acceptance for all the practices associated with popular Sufism. In this area, the general sobriety of Tijani practice is itself an important commentary of the Tijaniyya's relationship to other forms of Sufism.

It is difficult to ascertain whether the emphasis on the Sunna of the Prophet and his companions was a result of what is thought to have been a general increase in interest in Hadith

---

240   Benabdellah, La Tijania, p. 104.
241   Observations from field work in Medina Baye, Senegal, 1997-2003.
242   Interview with Shaykh Hassan Cisse, Fes, March, 2003.

studies in the eighteenth-century Muslim world, as some have suggested,[243] or just came from the Shaykh's feeling of personal proximity to the Prophet. Certainly, during his earlier visits to Fes during the reign of Mawlay Abdullah (1757-1789), he would have benefited from the Sultan's promotion of a more involved study of Hadith, as part of a program to shift emphasis from later scholarly commentaries to primary sources.[244] He also would have inherited from his Khalwati teachers their stress of the Sufi's need to obey the external elements of the Sunna.[245] But love for the Prophet, as both an external and internal model, was prevalent enough throughout the history of Sufism[246] that it is not necessary to attribute Shaykh Ahmad Tijani's accent on the Sunna to any specific source.

---

243   John Voll, Islam, Continuity and Change in the Modem World (Boulder: Westview, 1982), p. 54.

244   Mansour, Mawlay Sulayman, p. 133.

245   Radtke, "Sufism in the 18th Century," p. 332.

246   Schimmel, And Muhammad is His Messenger, pp. 24-55.

Involvement in the world

Before examining the critical issue of the Shaykh's concept of *ijtihad* and his opinion of the *fuqaha* (*faqihs*, legal scholars), it is first of interest to see how his conception of following the Qur'an and the Sunna in an external sense played itself out more generally than in just his perspective on *fiqh* (jurisprudence). The Shari'a is of course conceived by Muslims as a broad set of ethical codes that extend to all aspects of life, not just those with a legal value. Despite the Shaykh's reported great love of solitary *dhikr*,[247] he thus laid much emphasis on general involvement in the world.

Of particular curiosity is his conception of wealth and its relationship to spiritual attainment. The *Jawahir* reports that many of his followers would come to him for a whole range of advice besides just spiritual matters, including advice about business affairs. For each person, including those concerned with matters of livelihood, the Shaykh "directs him to his advantage ... and to the success of his condition and prosperity in his wealth; and his desires meet with success and he obtains

---

247   Jawahir, p. 36, 41.

his needs."[248] The emphasis on success in worldly affairs was not only so that his followers would be thereby more thankful to God,[249] but so that they would have the benefit of giving charity. Although he once urged a rich follower not to give up all his money in order that his faith in God remain safeguarded,[250] he himself was reportedly extravagant in "spending in the cause of Allah and feeding the poor for the sake of Allah's Countenance."[251] That he "gave great gifts the like not seen by people" was considered one of his miracles, since he had been "guaranteed by the Prophet that he would have complete wealth without end."[252] Perhaps because of this, he "gave as if he did not fear poverty, neither desiring increase (in his wealth) nor ostentation," declaring that "the money belongs to God."[253] Having money and giving it in God's cause was one of the best ways to attain God's favor, even to the extent that "giving is better than many [extra] prayers or lofty supplications."[254]

> For they are the generous and open-handed ones of creation that are on the [path of] truth, and there is no grace (fadl) except their graces, and no favor except their favors; when from the Source of Bounty they spend and by the downpour of His flood they pour out, and they do not see possession or awarding, and no renunciation (tark).[255]

This emphasis on wealth and generosity seems to indicate a clear attempt to implement the Sunna of the Prophet, concerning giving in the cause of God, in a very tangible manner.

---

248   Jawahir, p. 31.
249   Abun-Nasr, The Tijaniyya, pp. 46-47.
250   Jawahir and Kashf al-Hijab, cited in Abun-Nasr, The Tijaniyya, p. 46.
251   Jawahir, p. 41.
252   Jawahir, p. 42.
253   Jawahir, p. 41. The Jawahir reports that often the Shaykh would give in secret so the benefactor would thank God instead of him.
254   Jawahir, p. 42.
255   Jawahir, p. 41.

It must be kept in mind that some Sufi orders at this time, such as the newly established Darqawiyya order, were known for their complete renunciation of worldly goods and their consequent alleged tendency to wander the countryside depending on the donations of the people.[256] In contrast, Shaykh Ahmad Tijani urged his followers to have a job and not to spend all their time withdrawn into the zawiya.[257] The Shaykh's concept of the Sunna of the Prophet and the Sufi's need to emulate this ideal model in both its external and internal attributes certainly contributed to his tendency to remain involved in society at its most tangible and pragmatic level: at the level of money and the basic needs of its members.

Still Shaykh Ahmad Tijani spoke of the concept of the *Faqir,* a word literally meaning "the poor one" often applied to a Sufi disciple, but generally applied the notion of poverty to the state of the aspirant's heart before God instead of material renunciation.[258] The state of complete submission to God required the aspirant to submit both his internal and external condition to Divine dictates, namely the Qur'an and Sunna of the Prophet. For this reason, the heart should not be attached to the *dunya* even while living within it. Ali Harazem al-Barada remarks in this regard, how people in the Shaykh's presence would forget about the material world and be inspired with the remembrance of God.[259] The necessary qualities of the aspirant for living in the *dunya* in a state of remembrance despite its corruption were sincerity and truthfulness, especially with regard to intention. In support of this exigency, the *Jawahir* reports how the Shaykh would refuse gifts brought to him if he

---

256   Mansour, Mawlay Sulayman, pp. 167-170. It seems that one of Mawlay al-'Arabi al-Darqawi's successors, Muhammad al-Haruq, himself an 'Alim and townsperson, would later soften the Darqawi stance on renunciation.
257   Benabdellah, La Tijania, p. 64.
258   Jawahir, p. 163.
259   Jawahir, pp. 46-47.

perceived the intention behind them to be a bribe in exchange for some favor.[260]

Relations with people in the *dunya* could nonetheless bring the aspirant closer to God, and Shaykh Ahmad Tijani stressed the link between the rights of one's brothers in religion and the rights of God.[261] In one letter to his followers, the Shaykh urges them to be truthful among the people and to ignore the evil of others.[262] He urged the showing of mercy to others as a means to incur the mercy of God and His angels, and once said that one should forgive another for acting wrongly if they were doing what was within God's decree.[263] This emphasis on manners (*adab*) of course has a long tradition in Sufi writings and obviously has its basis in the Sunna itself. Indeed the *Jawahir* explains the reason for the love the Shaykh would inspire among those who met him by citing a hadith about the relationship between God's love for an elect servant and the love the creation will necessarily have for him as well.[264]

---

260   Jawahir, pp. 45-46.
261   Jawahir, p. 38.
262   Jawahir, p. 191.
263   Jawahir, p. 43.
264   Jawahir, p. 38.

Ijtihad and the Islamic legal tradition (Fiqh and the Madhhab)

If Shaykh Ahmad Tijani's attempts to implement the Sunna al-
lowed him to de-emphasize certain trends of traditional Sufi
practices such as material renunciation, it also permitted him
a degree of transcendence of the tradition of Islamic jurisprudence (*fiqh*) and its schools (*madhhab*). According to Professor Muhammad Serag and others, the distinction between the
Shari'a and *Fiqh* is often forgotten; the former being the Divine Law contained in the Qur'an and Sunna while the latter
comprising the tradition of legal interpretations of these fundamental sources.[265] Even if Shaykh Ahmad Tijani maintained
the importance of the *Shari'a*, he and the Tijani scholars who
followed him have not always been so supportive of the tradition of blind trust (*taqlid*) given to the *Fuqaha*. This defossil-
ization of the Islamic legal tradition is manifested for Tijanis
in the permissibility for scholarly *ijtihad* by one versed in both
the external and esoteric sciences. While such a perspective

---

265   Muhammad Serag, lecture at the American University in Cairo,
March, 2001.

cannot exactly be called distinctive to the Tijaniyya, especially within the tradition of scholarly Sufism, it is nonetheless worthy of mention in order to demonstrate the order's simultaneous respect for and challenge of the Islamic legal tradition.

This discussion of the Tijani conception of *ijtihad* runs the obvious risk of assuming Tijani scholarship in this area has been exempt from the process of historical development and change. However, the opinions of later Tijani scholars are nonetheless included alongside Shaykh Ahmad Tijani's own statements, sometimes even as representative of what the Shaykh himself seems to be implying in this area. This is justified by the fact that later elaborations often seem the natural explanation of the Shaykh's own statements, and simply because his words, sometimes possessed of subtle or vague implications, often require such explanation. It is not presumed that these later elaborations represent the definitive opinion of Shaykh Ahmad Tijani himself, only that they are a better approximation than we, separated by cultural and temporal distance, might ourselves offer.

In general, Shaykh Ahmad Tijani and the Tijaniyya do not seem to go so far as Ahmad ibn Idris in completely rejecting the tradition of the *madhhab* and the *faqih's* tendency towards rational thought in the process of *Ijtihad*. [266] Where Ahmad ibn Idris says the primary qualification for the *mujtahid* is fear of God, Shaykh Ahmad Tijani lists a rather traditional set of qualifications, including knowledge of the Qur'an and the Sunna, the texts and precedents of interpretation surrounding them, the tradition of how decisions are arrived at *(usul al-fiqh)* and the knowledge of how a new circumstance relates to a precedent. [267] In his own answers to specific legal questions,

266   Ahmad ibn Idris, "Epistle in Refutation of the Adherents of Individual Opinion," in Radtke, O'Kane, Vikor and O'Fahey, The Exoteric Ahmad Ibn Idris: A Sufi's Critique o f the Madhahib and the Wahhabis (Lieden: Brill, 2000), pp. 47-144.
267   Jawahir, p. 214.

such as concerning women and marriage, the rights of parents, divorce, fasting, alms giving, etc., the Shaykh demonstrates his training in and basic acceptance of the classical tradition of jurisprudence, quoting from the Qur'an, Hadith and then scholarly works such as the *Mukhtasar* to arrive at conclusions.[268] The Shaykh also defends the tradition that a scholar who gives *ijtihad* will receive two rewards if he is correct and one reward if he is wrong.[269]

Nevertheless, in what might be considered a conservative conception of the subject, at least by modem standards, he limits the activity of *ijtihad* by the classical understanding that scholarly reasoning should only be engaged in the absence of a clear text. If a new occurrence presents itself that has never been ruled on before, the *mujtahid* is perfectly justified in giving his opinion. In this regard, the Shaykh emphasizes an understanding of the reason or context *('ilia)* behind a ruling so that the principal of a previous ruling from the Qur'an and Sunna can be extended to a new circumstance.[270] While Tijanis do not miss the opportunity to quote the verse from the Qur'an, "So fear Allah; for it is Allah that teaches you,"[271] rational thought in the process of arriving at legal decisions, although admittedly subject to error, is granted limited endorsement by the likes of al-Hajj Umar al-Futi (d. 1865),[272] the student of Shaykh Tijani's disciple Muhammad al-Ghali and who was the author of an essential book on Tijani doctrine, the *Kitab al-Rima,* and also the primary propogator of the Tijani-yya in nineteenth-century West Africa.

Shaykh Ahmad Tijani's conception of the *mujtahid* reveals a deep respect for the classically trained scholar. Indeed, he

---

268 Jawahir, pp. 204-213.

269 Jawahir, p. 213.

270 Jawahir, pp. 213-214.

271 Qur'an, 2:282. See Shaykh Hassan Cisse, Spirit of Good Morals, p. 20.

272 Kitab al-Rimah, cited in Radtke, "Ijtihad and Neo-Sufism," p. 917.

once advised his disciples, "Honor the *'ulama* in as much as they are the bearers of the Law."[273] Later Tijani tradition has maintained this high regard for the *'ulama,* and Shaykh Hassan Cisse quotes the well-known adage in this regard that, "Whoever emulates a scholar [properly trained in the Islamic sciences] meets Allah safely."[274] Neither does the Tijaniyya contain any conclusive rejection of the *madhhab.* Shaykh Ahmad Tijani himself practiced Maliki *fiqh* along with the rest of his contemporaries in Morocco and North and West Africa in general. Al-Hajj 'Umar al-Futi advises the Tijani disciple to follow one *madhhab,* but only does not conceive this allegiance as the basis for sectarian difference as the scholar should be able to recognize the value of the other schools. There are three types of scholar, according to al-Hajj 'Umar, of which the last is best: one who follows blindly (*taqlid*) one *madhhab,* one who rejects everything in the four schools, and one who follows one *madhhab* but does not conceive his school as possessing an absolute monopoly on the truth.[275] Shaykh Hassan Cisse holds that a disciple of the Tijaniyya can be a member of any of the *madhhabs,* since "*tariqa* has nothing to do with the *madhhab.*"[276]

However, this does not mean Shaykh Ahmad Tijani and later Tijani scholars considered the *fuqaha* and the tradition of the *madhhab* exempt from censure, or that there was in fact any such thing as the "closing of the gates of *ijtihad* (personal reasoning)."[277] According to al-Hajj 'Umar,

---

273   Jawahir al-Ma'ani, cited in Jacques Berque, L'interieur du Maghreb XV-XIX siecle (Poitiers/Liguge: Editions Gallimard, 1978), p. 261.

274   Cisse, Spirit of Good Morals, p. 27. This statement should not be interpreted as an endorsement of the scholar's need for taqlid of one madhhab, rather it concerns one who does not possess the necessary qualifications of a scholar, which would include knowledge of both the external and the esoteric sciences.

275   Kitab al-Rimah, cited in Radtke, "Ijtihad and Neo-Sufism," p. 917.

276   Interview with Shaykh Hassan Cisse, Medina Kaolack, Senegal, August, 2001.

277   This famous event, believed to have happened in the tenth century C.E. after the last of the four great Imams (Ahmad Ibn Hanbal), dominated

God did not make it obligatory for anyone to adhere [exclusively] to a specific madhhab of the mujtahidin .. [for] every imam of this community – may God be pleased with them all – has renounced any claim that men must necessarily follow him exclusively in every religious matter since [the imams] know that unqualified fidelity is due only to him who is guarded from error.[278]

While the *Jawahir* does not contain any such decisive rejection of the *madhhab* as al-Futi's above statement implies, Shaykh Ahmad Tijani is himself clear that none of the *mujtahids* are protected from error. *Ijtihad* is only to be engaged in with the absence of a clear ruling from the Qur'an or Sunna, so *ijtihad* is practiced under circumstances where no *mujtahid* is able to claim impeccability. It is thus strictly prohibited *(haram)* for him to denounce the perceived mistakes of other scholars.[279] However, if the Shaykh respected the idea of the scholar in the ideal sense, he believed that the Muslim community was becoming largely bereft of true scholars, and he cites the following tradition in this regard:

Allah will not roll up knowledge by withdrawing it from people but will put it out of reach through the death of divines [scholars] with the result that when there are no divines people will adopt ignorant ones as their leaders and will ask them for guidance and they will render their opinions without knowledge. They will be astray themselves and will lead others astray.[280]

---

medieval Islamic scholarship and was thought to require the taqlid (blind following) of one of the four schools: Hanafi, Maliki, Shafi'i or Hanbali.

278   Kitab al-Rimah, cited in John Hunwick, "An Introduction to the Tijani Path: Being an Annotated Translation of the Chapter Headings of the Kitab al-Rimah of Al-Hajj 'Umar," in Islam et Societes au Sud du Sahara (no. 6, 1992), p. 25.

279   Jawahir, p. 214.

280   Jawahir, p. 214. Hadith related by Abdullah ibn Amr ibn 'As and contained in Bukhari and Muslim. The translation is from Imam Nawawi, Riyad al-Salihin (trans. Muhammad Zafrulla Khan, Gardens o f the Righteous.

From this opinion al-Hajj 'Umar no doubt draws justification for his description of his own mission as "endeavoring to destroy what the innovators and the venal scholars had invented, and presenting the Prophet's merits to the people."[281] What seems to be warned against is not the effort to arrive at a correct decision, but only such an effort by unqualified scholars and the tendency towards the practice of *takfir* (excommunication) sometimes present among the *fuqaha*. Al-Hajj 'Umar explains, citing the famous Egyptian scholar Sha'rani, "The Companions disagreed one with the other, and they are equal. Not one Companion was excluded from the Community by the others."[282] The author of the *Rimah* continues further,

> *Al-Tabarani has informed us that the Prophet said, "Allah has three hundred and thirteen ways [i.e., to the Truth]. Whosoever meets Allah through one of these ways, Allah will grant him a place in Paradise." If you were actually informed about all these ways, my friend, and then discovered a [legal] rule contrary to them then you would be in a position to object to them. Otherwise, acceptance [of an unfamiliar way] is better for you, and is to be preferred, since it is impossible to encounter someone who is informed on all three hundred and thirteen ways.*[283]

Such an argument clearly could, in the context of modernist polemic, have a bearing on the idea of the Muslim community's transnational and trans-ideological unity. Differences in legal interpretation should not cloud the common attachment of all Muslims to the basic Shari'a, which should serve as a source of unity rather than exclusion. The Senegalese Tijani

New York: Olive Branch Press, 1975), p. 233.

281   Kitab al-Rimah, cited in John Ralph Willis, The Passion o f al-Hajj 'Umar: An Essay into the Nature o f Charisma in Islam (London: Frank Cass, 1989), p. 153.

282   Kitab al-Rimah, cited in John Ralph Willis, The Passion o f al-Hajj 'Umar, p. 155

283   Kitab al-Rimah, cited in Willis, Passion of al-Hajj 'Umar, pp. 90-91.

Shaykh Ibrahim Niasse (d. 1975) does indeed take such a line. He quotes the Qur'an, "And hold fast, all together, by the rope which Allah (stretches out for you), and be not divided among yourselves,"[284] in urging Muslims to recognize the "immense treasure" of their common bond.[285] The underlying precept seems to be that true knowledge of the Shari'a lends itself to tolerance and compassion for the Muslim community rather than exclusion on the basis of petty differences, this former being the perceived practice of the Prophet.[286]

In contrast to the true scholar's complete understanding of the essential sources of the Shari'a, most of the contemporary *Fuqaha*, according to Shaykh Ahmad Tijani, are limited in their rulings because theirs is the activity of the *nafs* (ego or lower self). This opinion among Sufis dates back at least to Hakim al-Tirmidhi.[287] Since the *Fuqaha* understand the Law from the perspective of the *nafs*, their rules, says Shaykh Ahmad Tijani, can sometimes be in error because, "They allow themselves to be impressed by the qualities pertaining to their eyes [which are] inherent to beings, things and situations."[288] For this reason, the books of *fiqh* are not infallible, and sometimes contain clear errors.[289] Thus, while the Shaykh advised his disciples to respect the *Fuqaha*, as mentioned above, he also warned them, "but abstain from frequenting them so long as they allow themselves to be dominated by their own selves (*nafs*)."[290]

284   Qur'an, 3:103.
285   Shaykh Ibrahim Niasse, "The Eternal Islam," in Abul Hakim Halim ed., Shaykh al-Islam al-Hajj Ibrahim Niasse, Selected Writings (Detroit: A.A.I.I., 2000), p. 22.
286   Speaking of his efforts to show people the "good path" of the Prophet, Shaykh Ibrahim Niasse once said, "You will not find anybody who loves Muslims more than I." See Muhammad al-Amin, "Cheikh Ibrahima, un etre predestine," in Le Regional (Dakar, 7 August 1995), p. 3.
287   Radtke, "Ijtihad and Neo-Sufism," p. 912.
288   Jawahir, cited in Berque, L 'interieur du Maghreb, p. 261.
289   Jawahir, cited in Berque, L 'interieur du Maghreb, p. 261.
290   Jawahir, cited in Berque, L 'interieur du Maghreb, p. 261.

Shaykh Tijani's emphasis on difference (*ikhtilaj*) in scholarly opinion was interpreted by later Tijani scholars as directed towards providing space for the interpretations of the *Wali* (saint), who possesses a privileged relationship to the Shari'a. Chapter six of the al-Hajj 'Umar's *Rimah* is thus concerned with, "Warning them [the *Fuqaha*] against and deterring them from denouncing and showing enmity towards any of our lords, the Friends of God, and informing them that [such behavior] is the essence of perdition in this world and the next."[291] The *Wali* is not limited in his insight to only esoteric affairs, for he is the true inheritor of the Prophet. As Rachida Chih has remarked of the eighteenth-century conception of the saint in her study of the Khalwatiyya order around Muhammad al-Hifni, "The saints are the inheritors of the Prophets chosen by God to renew the faith among the believers and to guide them to the straight path: giving life to the path in a period of decline is their principal function."[292]

For Shaykh Ahmad Tijani, this role of the *Wali*, who is blessed with hidden knowledge, obligates him to speak out concerning matters of the Shari'a.[293] This idea was of course not limited to the Shaykh, however, and Abd al-Aziz al-Dabbagh made similar claims: "The Wali, to whom Allah unraveled the Divine Essence, does not limit himself to one *madhhab* ... because he is able to revive the Shari'a. And why not if the Prophet does not absent himself from him for one moment?"[294] For Shaykh Ahmad Tijani, the pure state of the *Wali* and (most importantly) the Divine grace bestowed on him, have combined to allow

---

291   Kitab al-Rimah, cited in Hunwick, "Introduction to the Tijani Path," p. 25.

292   Chih, "Les debuts d'une tariqa," p. 144. Chih's cites al-Makki, al-Hifni's biographer, in this statement.

293   Radtke, "Sufism in the 18th Century," p. 336. Radtke cites one of Shaykh Tijani's fatwas from the Jawahir al-Ma 'ani in support of this observation.

294   Kitab al-Ibriz, cited in Kitab al-Rimah, cited in Willis, Passion o f al-Hajj 'Umar, p. 156.

him to perceive the inner meanings of the Law and the totality of the Divine sciences. This process is essentially non-rational and consists of the descent of knowledge from God to the "internal soul" of the *Wali*, granting him the "eye of discernment."

> *He who perceives through the eye of discernment is a knower of truths and of hidden meanings. No outward forms remain with one who has perceived with the eye of discernment. Nor is there any suffering connected with it; one is relieved of the difficulty of thought. With the arrival of these revelations in his inner soul, one masters the Divine sciences, and the sciences of the secrets of internal (hidden) meanings and of that which is related to the hereafter, and of direct knowledge of the unity of existence and the denial of anything that might be equated with God. And the secrets of tawhid and of gnosis appear to him.*[295]

Such inner knowledge will not, however, contradict the external Shari'a, and the inner revelations mentioned above are clearly not to be equated with the revelation brought by Muhammad. Shaykh Ahmad Tijani clarified that he "had not come to bring a [new] Law, but a [means of] drawing near."[296] Shaykh Hassan Cisse elaborates on the *Wali*'s relationship to the Law by saying, "A *Wali* will not bring a new revelation, but he can bring a new understanding."[297] Moreover such an inner knowledge does not by itself grant the *Wali* free license in *ijtihad*, insists al-Hajj 'Umar, for, in order to reject the established opinion of a *madhhab*, he must possess complete knowledge of the Qur'an and Sunna together with the tradition of law and legal judgements.[298] Such an opinion, as was demonstrated

---

295   Jawahir, cited in Louis Brenner, West African Sufi: The Religious Heritage and Spiritual Search of Cemo Bokar Saalif Taal (London: C. Hurst & Co., 1984), pp. 105-106.

296   Jawahir, cited in Berque, L 'interieur du Maghreb, p. 250.

297   Interview with Shaykh Hassan Cisse, Medina Kaolack, Senegal, August, 2001.

298   Kitab al-Rimah, cited in Radtke, "Ijtihad and Neo-Sufism," p. 918.

above, was apparently the same held by Shaykh Ahmad Tijani himself and one that was followed in his own decisions on questions of legal interpretation.[299]

According to the Shaykh, the rare scholar whom God has blessed with both external and esoteric knowledge is the only true interpreter of the Shari'a. Thus the true scholar is one in whom God has combined proclivity towards striving, ability to memorize external knowledge and to whom He has given a "Divine light." This sort of scholar has such comprehensive knowledge of the Shari'a that if the whole of the Divine Law were to be completely forgotten, it would be possible to recreate it from his knowledge.[300] This sort of valorization of the scholar ideal is reminiscent of other Sufi theorists such as Najm al-din Razi (d. 654/1256) of the Kubrawiyya, who writes:

> Scholars fall into three groups: those that have outer knowledge; those that have inner knowledge; and those that have both outer and inner knowledge, which is a rarity. If there are five people belonging to this last group in the world in each age, it is a large number. Indeed, the blessedness of one of them will embrace the whole world, from east to west: He will be the pole of his age, and the people will seek refuge in his high fortune and take shelter in his lofty aspiration … It is in truth to these scholars that belong the heirs of the prophets, upon whom be peace, for they have received the legacy of both outer and inner knowledge. "The scholars are the heirs of the Prophets."[301]

This idea was no doubt current among eighteenth-century Sufism as well. What is of interest to us here is the notion that

---

299   See examples of the Shaykh's ruling on legal issues, Jawahir, pp. 204-214.

300   Jawahir, p. 214.

301   Najm al-din al-Razi, The Path of God's Bondsman from Origin to Return (trans. Hamid Algar, New York: Caravan Books, 1982), pp. 447-448.

the *Wali* or *Qutb's* position as a scholar, which included his privileged relationship to the Shari'a, was one of the foundations for any election to the highest spiritual states. About the true scholar, Shaykh Ahmad Tijani explains,

Allah gives him the power of Divine light, and if a thousand issues of the time were exposed to him, each with no text concerning it, he would establish every issue on its [relevant] text... if the earth were to lose this person, then the allegation or proof (*hujja*) of Allah would fall on His creation. However, this is not the case except for the completed one (*fard*) ... [whom] Allah has supported by His favor (*fadl*).[302]

It is here that traditional Sufism as represented by Shaykh Ahmad Tijani can be said to contain its real respect for the Shari'a. Knowledge of the Divine Law is an integral component of spiritual perfection. It is also the source for divergence between what Sufis would consider a true understanding of the Shari'a and the opinions of the *Fuqaha* who remained dominated by their egos. Interpretation of Divine Law was a weighty matter that should not be left to "venal scholars" but should be reserved for those to whom God had given Divine light or the "eye of discernment" by which they could perceive the true meanings of the Law.

* * *

To summarize then, the Tijani consensus on the Shari'a seems to be that it is, in its larger definition as the Qur'an and Sunna, a guide for all actions of the Sufi. Popular Sufism can thus be subjected to criticism by scholarly Sufis themselves, whose mysticism emerges out of the Shari'a instead of in opposition to it. In practice, there are few instances of Shaykh Ahmad Tijani actually criticizing the behavior of other Sufi

---

302   Jawahir, p. 214.

orders, but his own restriction of the *ziyara* tradition, general emphasis on sobriety in mysticism and complicity with Mawlay Sulayman during the latter's very obvious campaign against popular Sufism, may be considered an endorsement of the *Tariqa Muhammadiyya* tendency to attempt to reform certain popular practices on the basis of the Sunna. Shaykh Ahmad Tijani's order can thus be considered one of the "orthodox" orders, even though Tijani tradition does not itself record any irreconcilable differences between itself and the larger Sufi tradition which some might charge with harboring certain "unorthodox" practices.

Aside from the Qur'an and the Sunna, or the Shari'a proper, the heritage of legal interpretation is likewise of value, although it is not infallible. It is only the people of both external and esoteric knowledge who have comprehensive knowledge of the Shari'a, and they have a right to *ijtihad* that is not limited by the *madhhab*. Nevertheless, the *Fuqaha* should not be overly belittled or abandoned; only they should take care not to make exclusionist statements, to criticize those who have more knowledge than they do or to make *ijtihad* without themselves possessing the proper knowledge. Al-Hajj 'Umar, himself reacting to what he saw as the entrenchment, elitism and self-interested nature of many of the West African *'ulama* at the time, wrote that the *Fuqaha* should "be wary of comprehensive condemnation and should confine themselves to matters which are explicitly [deemed] obligatory or forbidden by the Book, the Sunna and the consensus of the community."

The Qur'an and Salat al-Fatih

Given Shaykh Ahmad Tijani's largely conservative conception of the Shari'a, it is necessary to delve further to investigate the source of the claims of his unorthodoxy. Most often quoted in this regard is the statement in the *Jawahir al-Ma'ani* that one recitation of the prayer on the Prophet called *Salat al-Fatih* (prayer of the opening) is equivalent to reading the Qur'an six thousand times.[303] The argument of course is that the Qur'an, being the word of God, is better than any prayer created by men.[304] Aside from the point that Tijanis believe the *Salat al-Fatih* itself to be of Divine origin, it seems evident from the *Jawahir* that the above statement attributed to Shaykh Tijani was taken quite out of context. Put back into context, the statement provides little basis for the charges of unorthodoxy for which it has so often been charged with. It is also possible, as some later Tijanis have suggested, that the statement was itself mistakenly transcribed in the first place.

It is important to contextualize the above statement concerning *Salat al-Fatih* with Shaykh Ahmad Tijani's own per-

---

303   Jawahir, p. 57.
304   Jean-Louis Triaud, "La Tijaniyya, voie infaillible," p. 180.

spective on the Qur'an from the *Jawahir*. In general, it is apparent that many of the Shaykh's statements recorded in the *Jawahir* are concerned with elaborating on the bounty of Allah connected with the specific rewards for the recitation of certain prayers or verses of the Qur'an. He says, for example, that each letter of the Qur'an contains the reward of all the other prayers of the creation.[305] There are certain chapters, such as *al-Fatiha* (the Opening), *al-Qadr* (the Night of Power) and *al-Ikhlas* (Pure Faith), to which he gives special weight, often quoting Hadith.[306] Reading *Surat al-Ikhlas* 100,000 times, for example, will protect a person from Hell-fire.[307] Even though known Hadith are often cited, he emphasizes that this knowledge of the great benefit of certain verses is gained directly from the Prophet in waking vision. He does not limit himself to speaking of the benefit of the Qur'an, but also elaborates on the reward for repeating the Muslim testimony of faith (*Shahada*), the canonical prayer, the night prayer, *dhikr,* fasting, charity, etc.[308]

He is also concerned with the benefits of offering prayer on the Prophet, which he declares to be the best form of *nafila* (superogatory worship).[309] He explains further that,

As for he who perseveres in the prayer on the Prophet, may Allah's blessing and peace be upon him, even if he is attributed all the faults committed by all the inhabitants of the earth, while adding to them without end, from the creation of the

---

305   Jawahir, p. 62.

306   Jawahir, pp. 62-63.

307   Jawahir, p. 143.

308   Jawahir, pp. 62-63, 41-42.

309   Jawahir, p. 64. This is reminiscent of some Hadith, such as that reported by Ibn Mas'ud and contained in al-Tirmidhi, "The nearest people to me on the Day of Rising will be those who have said the most prayers on me," or that reported by Ubayy ibn Ka'b and contained in al-Tirmidhi where the Prophet urges Ubayy to spend all of his extra prayer time sending blessing upon him. See Qadi Iyad ibn Musa, Ash-Shifa (trans. Aisha Bewley, Muhammad Messenger of Allah, Granada: Medinah Press, 1991), pp. 259-260.

world until its ending, Allah - may He be praised and exalted will forgive him these faults in the ocean of His forgiveness and grace (fadl).[310]

He is especially keen to enumerate, based on what the Prophet had told him, the benefits of Salat al-Fatih. It was revealed on a sheet of light to Muhammad al-Bakri (d. 1545) during a retreat inside the Kaba in search of the best way to send blessing on the Prophet, this prayer is "equivalent to that of the recitation of all prayers of glorification to God (tasbih) that have ever been said in the universe, all Sufi prayers or remembrance of God (dhikr), every invocation (du'a) long or short.. "[311] The text of the prayer is as follows:

> O Allah, bless our master Muhammad, who opened what was closed, who sealed what had gone before; the helper of Truth by the Truth, the guide to Your straight path, and on his family, may this prayer be equal to his immense position and grandeur.[312]

The value of the prayer seems largely based on its believed Divine origin and because of its description of the Haqiqa Muhammadiyya, the light by which God "opened," or brought the creation from non-existence into being.[313] Nevertheless, despite the prayer's great value, Shaykh Ahmad Tijani makes clear it is not meant to take the place of the Qur'an. Salat al-Fatih is a superogatory act, while the reading of the Qur'an is obligatory. To leave reading of the Qur'an, being the basis of

---

310   Jawahir, cited in Triaud, "La Tijaniyya, voie infaillible," p. 180.

311   Jawahir, p. 57.

312   As has been noted by Tijanis, the text of this prayer is very similar to a prayer on the Prophet written by Ali ibn Abi. Talib. See Sheikh Abubakar Abayawo, Toriqat Tijaniyat: the way of Allah and His Messenger from the Holy Qur'an and the traditions of the Prophet (S.A.W.) (Ilorin, Nigeria, unknown date), pp. 42-43. Shaykh Abayawo quotes from Ibn Kathir, Tafsir, v. iii, p. 510.

313   Jawahir, p. 60; Kitab al-Jami', b. I, p. 41.

141

the Shari'a, is to incur the wrath of God, while *Salat al-Fatih* can be left or taken as the person desires.[314] The relationship is further contextualized by Shaykh Ahmad Tijani's description of the benefit of saying Allah's greatest name. Reciting this name once is equal to one recital of the Qur'an's opening chapter (*al-Fatiha*), one whole reading of the Qur'an or saying *Salat al-Fatih* 6,000 times.[315.] By implication, as many later Tijanis have pointed out,[316] reciting the *Fatiha* or the entirety of the Qur'an is 6,000 times greater than *Salat al-Fatih*.

Later Tijanis have offered a further explanation of how the statement of the worth of the *Salat al-Fatih* over the Qur'an came to be in the *Jawahir al-Ma'ani* in the first place. According to Shaykh Hassan Cisse, Shaykh Ibrahim Niasse had proposed that what was meant, was six thousand *khatms* (seal or completions). The scribe had understood this to mean a completion of the Qur'an, but in reality the statement was to be understood in the context of the people of Fes at the time, who used to boast of the number of *khatms* of the popular prayer on the Prophet called *Dala'il Khairat,* they had finished.

In any case, insists Shaykh Hassan, it is true there is nothing better than the Qur'an, but in terms of the fault-filled servant of God, it is sometimes better for him to say any form of prayer on the Prophet than to read the Qur'an. This is because the Qur'an, according to Hadith, can be cursing its reader if he is not obeying its dictates not to fornicate, steal, lie, gossip, backbite, etc., whereas there is no such Hadith that a person can be sending a prayer on the Prophet and it cursing him. To the contrary, one Hadith states that Allah is sending ten prayers on the person for every one he is sending on the Prophet.[317] A

---

314   Jawahir, p. 59.

315   Jawahir, p. 32.

316   Interview with Abdelaziz Benabdellah, Rabat, Morocco, October, 2002.

317   Interview with Shaykh Hassan Cisse, Medina Kaolack, Senegal, November 2002, and February 2003.

142

similar opinion was in fact expressed by Shaykh Ahmad Tijani himself, who described two classes of readers of the Qur'an, one who acted upon what they read and another who did not. For the former, the Qur'an was the best for them, for the latter, prayer upon the Prophet was more beneficial.[318]

The issue of *Salat al-Fatih* and the Qur'an has been one of the most contentious, though not the only, issues raised by detractors of the Tijaniyya. But, as with the other major derogation, concerning the issue of salvation (to be discussed later in chapter five), the accusation against the Tijaniyya in this regard suffers from the common polemicist tendency to quote one's enemies out of context instead of examining the ideas and actions of Tijani scholars themselves. Shaykh Ahmad Tijani hiimself urged his disciples to read two *hizbs* (l/30th) of the Qur'an every day.[319] The Shaykh's companion, Ibrahim Riyahi, reportedly used to require Tijanis to read a similar amount.[320] Shaykh Ibrahim Niasse used to ask his disciples to also read two *hizbs* of the Qur'an a day, and he himself used to recite the whole Qur'an twice every week, once while reading and once from memory.[321]

---

318   Kitab al-Jami', b. I, pp. 50-51.
319   Ifadat al-Ahmadiyya, p. 28. See also Shaykh Ibrahim Niasse, Kashf al- 'Ilbas, pp. 84-85, for a discussion of Shaykh Ahmad Tijani's great respect for the Qur'an.
320   Benabdellah, La Tijania, p. 45.
321   Shaykh Ibrahim Niasse, "Lumieres sur la Tijaniyya," p. 5. Also interview with Shaykh Hassan Cisse, Medina Kaolack, Senegal, August, 1997.

Chapter IV

Shaykh Ahmad Tijani and the Sufism of his time

In order to trace the development of the *Tariqa Muhammad-iyya* phenomenon, the late eighteenth-century Sufi reformers such as Shaykh Ahmad Tijani must be situated within the context of the larger tradition of Sufism. The particular ideas with which the Shaykh has come to be associated were not of his own origination, even if the way he combined them in one doctrine of God's bounty or grace inseparably linked to the *Tariqa Muhammadiyya* and the Muhammadan saints, was unique. It is thus important to examine the specific influences that his early affiliation with the Sufism of his time could have had on the later development of his thought and practice.

One can assuredly cite the general atmosphere of Islamic mysticism, and eighteenth-century Maghrebi Sufism in particular, which provided the background to the Shaykh's emergence. The *Jawahir al-Ma'ani* contains reference to many of these traditions. With regards to the period of earlier Sufism, most of the seminal Sufis of the past are referred to, such as

Abu Yazid Bistami (d. 875),[322] Abu al-Qasim al-Junayd (d. 910),[323] 'Abd al-Karim al-Qushayri (d. 1074),[324] Abu Hamid al-Ghazali (d. 11 ll),[325] Abd al-Qadir al-Jilani (d. 1166),[326] Abu Madyan (d. 1198),[327] Abd al-Salam ibn Mashish (d. 1228),[328], Ibn al-'Arabi al-Hatimi (d. 1240)[329] and Abu Hasan al-Shadhili

---

322   Bistami, of Khurasan (Iran), was renowned for his asceticism and affirmation of the Shari'a (Michael Sells, Early Islamic Mysticism (New York: Paulist Press, 1996), p. 23).

323   Al-Junayd, "perhaps the most famous of the early Sufis within Islam," was from Baghdad and was instrumental in articulating the idea of the annihilation of the nafs in God (Sells, Early Islamic Mysticism, pp. 21-22). It might be recalled that Shaykh Tijani's silsilah back to the Prophet through the Khalwatiyya passes through Junayd.

324   Al-Qushayri is known for his Qur'anic commentary and his compendium of the thought of the early period of Sufism, perhaps the most important idea being that of passing away from the self (Sells, Early Islamic Mysticism, p. 24).

325   The famous jurist and mystic of Baghdad, al-Ghazali is sometimes credited with reconciling Sufism to the Fuqaha through his work Ihya 'ulum al-din (the Revival of the Religious Sciences).

326   The founder of the Qadiriyya order, Shaykh Abd al-Qadir of Baghdad situated Sufism firmly within the Shari'a and was considered the Qutb (pole) of all the saints before him. See Khaliq Nizami, "The Qadiriyyah Order," in Nasr ed., Islamic Spirituality, Manifestations (New York: Crossroad, 1991), pp. 6-25.

327   The Andalusian mystic, Abu Madyan Shu'ayb, known as the succor (ghawth) of his time. His brand of orthodox mysticism had influence on both Ibn al-'Arabi (Claude Addas, Ibn 'Arabi ou La quete du Soufre Rouge (Paris: Gallimard, 1989), p. 66) and al-Shadhili. He was reportedly also a student of Abd al-Qadir al-Jilani. See Vincent Cornell, The Way of Abu Madyan (Cambridge: Islamic Texts Society, 1996), pp. 14-16.

328   Known as the "Pole of the West," Ibn Mashish, of Tetuan, Morocco, was the teacher of Abu Hassan al-Shadhili (Victor Danner, "The Shadhiliyyah and North African Sufism," in Islamic Spirituality, p. 28).

329   Referred to in the Jawahir as the Shaykh al-Akbar (the Greatest Master), the Andalusian-born saint was a prolific writer and important explicator o f such ideas as the Haqiqa Muhammadiyya, Insan al-Kamil (perfect man) and the Khatm al-Awliya' (seal of the saints). See Michel Chodkiewicz, Seal o f the Saints.

(d. 1258).[330] Shaykh Ahmad Tijani was known for his ability to tell his followers about the past saints of God, their *maqam* (rank), condition, states, realizations and "what Allah had reserved for each one of them from the special [knowledge]," from the time of the Prophet until his own, "as if he was the contemporary to every one whom he describes."[331] He had particular reverence for Abd al-Qadir al-Jilani and Ibn 'Arabi al-Hatimi, concerning whom the Prophet informed him held a rank superior to all the other saints before the Shaykh himself.[332] But he encouraged his followers to honor all the past saints in general.

> We do not jest about the sanctity of our masters, the saints, nor do we hold their glorification lightly. Therefore glorify the sanctity of the saints; both the living and the dead, for he who glorifies their sanctity will have his own sanctity glorified by God. Whoever despises them, God will humiliate him and be angry with him. Do not take the glorification of the saints lightly.[333]

Later Tijani scholars have taken the Shaykh's advice, and many of their works can be considered veritable compendiums of Sufi thought. Al-Hajj 'Umar's *Kitab al-Rimah* contains about 650 quotations, most of them from earlier Sufi saints.[334] Likewise Muhammad al-'Arabi ibn Sa'ih's *Bughyat al-Mustafid*

---

330   Eponym for the Shadhiliyya order, Abu Hassan was from Morocco but died in Egypt. Among his many miracles was the composition of his famous Ahzab (s. hizb, litany), which were dictated to him by the Prophet in visions (Danner, "The Shadhiliyya," p. 29). Of the famous Hizb al-Bahr, the Prophet told him to "guard it well, for it contains the greatest name of God" (Ibn al-Sabbagh, Durrat al-Asrar wa Tuhfat al-Abrar (trans. Elmer Douglas, The Mystical Teachings of al-Shadhili. Albany: SUNY Press, 1993), p. 75.
331   Jawahir, p. 31.
332   Kitab al-Jami', b. I, p. 17.
333   Letter of Shaykh Ahmad Tijani to his followers contained in Jawahir al-Ma 'ani, quoted in Muhammad S. Umar, "Sufism and its Opponents in Nigeria," in Radtke and De Long ed.s, Islamic Mysticism Contested, p. 365.
334   Bemd Radtke, "Ibriziana," p. 156.

has been described as "a compendium ... clear and exhaustive, a structural foundation of mystic thought."[335] Shaykh Ibrahim Niasse's *Kashf al-ilbas* also displays a remarkable familiarity with the important works and authors of the Sufi tradition prior to the Tijaniyya.[336] Beginning with Shaykh Ahmad Tijani himself, the Tijani tradition makes use of the past Sufi tradition to explain key concepts in the Sufi path, such as the passing away of the self, *ma'arifa* or knowledge of God, the nature of the *'Arif billah* (gnostic), the *Haqiqa Muhammadiyya*, sainthood and the necessity of having a shaykh.

The emergence of the Tijaniyya should also be understood against the backdrop of the eighteenth-century Sufism with which it emerged. One of the most important figures in this context is the Fassi, 'Abd al-'Aziz al-Dabbagh (d. 1719), the subject of Ahmad al-Lamati al-Sijilmasi's (d. 1742) important book, *al-Ibriz min kalam sayyidi al-ghawth 'Abd al-'Aziz.* The *Jawahir* makes reference to the *Ibriz,* although there is no known link of direct transmission from al-Dabbagh to Shaykh Ahmad Tijani as there is for Ahmad ibn Idris.[337] However, the book had a wide circulation and is relevant to describing the emergence of the Tijaniyya, given its emphasis of the idea of the *Tariqa Muhammadiyya* and the phenomenon of the waking vision of the Prophet.[338]

---

335   Benabdellah, Le Soufisme AJro-Maghrebin aux XIXe et XXe Siecles (Rabat: Media Strategie, 1995), p. 9.

336   This in contradiction to Chodkiewicz's mistaken belief that Shaykh Ibrahim did not possess any first hand knowledge of thinkers such as Ibn 'Arabi (Chodkiewicz, Ocean without Shore, pp. 10-11). The Kashf al- 'Ilbas contains specific references to works such as the Futuhat al-Makkiya.

337   This through 'Abd al-Wahhab al-Tazi, a student of al-Dabbagh who became one of Ibn Idris's most important teachers. See R.S. O'Fahey, Enigmatic Saint, Ahmad Ibn Idris and the Idrisi Tradition (London: Hurst & Co, 1990), pp. 38-41.

338   See Radtke, "Ibriziana."

Prior Tariqa affiliations

Shaykh Ahmad Tijani's specific *tariqa* affiliations prior to his grand illumination also shed light on the possible source of some of his ideas. Certainly, the most important of these was the Khalwati tradition centered around Mustafa Bakri, Muhammad al-Hifni, Mahmud al-Kurdi and Muhammad al-Samman. Most of the essential elements of Shaykh Ahmad Tijani's thought can be found among his earlier Khalwati contacts, such as *Tariqa Muhammadiyya* nomenclature, emphasis of the Shari'a, a tendency towards reform of popular Sufism, the progression of the *nafs, Haqiqa Muhammadiyya,* exclusive affiliation to one's shaykh and the waking vision of the Prophet.

However, the Shaykh also had direct contact with the Maghrebi Sufism of his time through his connection with the Nasiriyya, the Wazzaniyya, the Zarruqiyya and the Jazuliyya. The Nasiriyya, as might be recalled, was the likely the dominant order in the Shaykh's native town of 'Ain Madi prior to the rise of the Tijaniyya, so he would have had contact with it even before his formal initiation into the order during one of his early visits to Fes. The Nasiriyya is a Shadhiliyya offshoot founded in the seventeenth century by Muhammad Ibn Nasir (d. 1674). Ibn Nasir was famous for his scholarship and had simplified the Shadhili *wird* (litany). He was also critical of some of the practices of popular Sufism.[339]

One of Shaykh Ahmad Tijani's first teachers in Fes was Mawlay al-Tayyib (d. 1180/1767), the head of the Wazzaniyya order at that time. Although the *Jawahir* states that he refused an invitation to instruct others on al-Tayyib's behalf, desiring instead to first purify his own *nafs*,[340] El Adnani has emphasized the similarities between many ideas present among the Wazzaniyya at that time and the later emergence of the Tijaniyya.[341] In scribing the *Jawahir*, Ali Harazem al-Barada, himself a prior member of the Wazzaniyya order, copied the introduction of a Wazzani book, the *Kitab al-Maqsad* (concerning the sainthood of Ibn Mu'an). The first Wazzani zawiya was founded in Morocco by 'Abd Allah Ibn Ibrahim (d. 1678) reportedly by inspiration of the Prophet in a waking vision.[342] Ibn Ibrahim was himself a prior member of the Jazuliyya and, according to Muhammad Mansour, "On a doctrinal level, there was hardly any difference between the Wazzanis and the other Shadhili *tariqas*."[343]

Shaykh Ahmad Tijani had direct contact with another Shadhili offshoot, that of Ahmad Zarruq (d. 1493), but his obtainment of permission to recite Zarruq's *wazhifa* from Muhammad al-Samman in Medina[344] demonstrates his knowledge of the great Shadhili scholar, who stressed the balance between the Shari'a and *tariqa* and Sufism's accordance to the Law.[345] Similarly, the Shaykh had received (also from al-Samman) the *Dala'il Khairat* of the Marakeshi Imam al-Jazuli (d. 1470)[346]

---

339   Mansour, Mawlay Sulayman, p. 161.
340   Jawahir, p. 23.
341   Al-Adnani, "Reflexions sur la naissance de la Tijaniyya," pp. 28-32.
342   Al-Adnani, "Reflexions," p. 29.
343   Mansour, Mawlay Sulayman, p. 165.
344   Benabdellah, La Tijania, p. 116.
345   Danner, "The Shadhiliyyah and North African Sufism," p. 41.
346   Benabdellah, La Tijania, p. 116.

without any known initiation into the Jazuliyya. Nonetheless al-Jazuli's emphasis on love for the Prophet and sending blessing upon him, the saint's need to be involved in society and his role in channeling God's mercy to the creation[347] have clear parallels in Shaykh Ahmad Tijani's own thought.

The links between the Tijaniyya and the prior Sufi tradition extend beyond similarity of ideas to actual practice. This is mainly demonstrated through the continued use of the litanies of previous orders by Shaykh Ahmad Tijani himself. The prayers inherited from Ahmad Zarruq and al-Jazuli have already been mentioned, but the Shaykh also made use of the renowned *Ahzab* of al-Shadhili, as well as the *Dawr al-'Ala* (the highest stage) of Ibn 'Arabi, both of which were given to him by Muhammad al-Samman in Medina.[348] Likewise, he received permission for the *Musaba'at al-'Ashr* (the ten sevens) from Mahmud al-Kurdi, who himself had received it in a vision from Khidr.[349] Neither should it be forgotten that the famous *Salat al-Fatih* was itself previously revealed to the saint Muhammad al-Bakri in the sixteenth century.

Whatever the inherited nature of some litanies however, the Shaykh integrated them in the new *Tariqa Muhammadiyya* with a renewed purpose. According to the *Jawahir*, the Shaykh insisted, "I do not use any *Dhikr* except that the Prophet, God's blessing and peace be upon him, is arranging it for me in all its conditions and that he is prompting his companions to do it, especially *Salat al-Fatih* because of the great benefits that are attached to it."[350]

---

347   Vincent Cornell, Realm of the Saint, pp. 155-195.
348   Benabdellah, La Tijania, p. 115-116. Also, Imam Sayed, "Shaykh Ahmad Tijani,"
349   P-¹- Jawahir, p. 63.
350   Jawahir, p. 36.

The Tijaniyya within the ideology of earlier Sufism

Prior study of the Tijaniyya and its relationship to earlier Sufism has tended to concentrate on its supposed deviation from previous traditions. Thus, much attention is given to its ideas of soteriology or worldly involvement, without first examining its firm rooting within the earlier tradition of scholarly Sufism, indeed, what the bulk of a work like *Jawahir al-Ma'ani* has to say. Certainly, the historical development or elaboration of ideas over time is inevitable, and the Tijaniyya does indeed represent an important historical elaboration of both Islam and Sufism, but the reader of the *Jawahir* is nonetheless struck by the frequent reference to the earlier Sufi tradition. This emphasis cannot be forgotten if the historian is to maintain, as he should, the importance of how Tijanis see themselves as Sufis and members of a *Tariqa Muhammadiyya*.

As was the case with the Shaykh's conception of the Shari'a and *ijtihad,* so too the *Jawahir* is filled with rather traditional Sufi ideas of esoteric knowledge and its attainment. It thus refers to such established principals as Divine attraction (*jadhb*), drowning in the sea of reality, drinking from the eternal wine, etc. The *Jawahir* being a work concerned with the spiritual realization of Tijani disciples, a great portion of the book refers to the traditional Sufi notions of purification of the self *(nafs)*, knowledge of God *(Ma'arifa)* and human purpose. Shaykh Ahmad Tijani can however, sometimes be seen further developing or specifying these ideas, but usually he offers only minor clarifications to well established notions. The same might be said of his conception of the central element of the *Tariqa Muhammadiyya*'s esoteric component, the *Haqiqa Muhammadiyya* (Muhammadan Reality). The Shaykh's particular contribution to Sufi doctrine mostly seems to revolve around the endowment of God's grace *(fadl)*, inherent, he believed, in the *Tariqa Muhammadiyya*, with a historical purpose in a corrupt age.

This section thus aims at reconstructing Shaykh Ahmad Tijani's doctrine on three levels: first within the context of earlier Sufism, next within the context of the *Tariqa Muhammadiyya* and lastly, what might be said to be distinctive to his own order. This last includes discussion of the Shaykh's notions of sainthood and the *shaykh al-tarbiyya* (shaykh of spiritual education), not because they are particularly special to him, but because they are important developments on prior notions of the *Tariqa Muhammadiyya* and because they are essential in understanding how the aforementioned grace is distrubuted and attained.

Purification of the Self

Sufis have often emphasized a Hadith where the Prophet speaks of the *jihad al-akbar,* or the greatest holy war, as being the struggle to purify the *nafs* and bring it into submission with Divine ordinance. The word *nafs* possesses a range of meanings in the English language, from self or soul to ego or carnal self. The idea seems to be that the *nafs* is the unruly steed God has placed at the individual's disposal so that he may make the long journey back to the unity and peace of the Divine presence. In this conception, God's commands and guidance become a gift to the servant so that he may tame his *nafs* and thereby attain true felicity. Citing a well-known Sufi conception, the nineteenth-century Tijani khalifa in West Africa, al-Hajj 'Umar, writes,

> Beat it (the nafs) with the whip of the Book, bind it with the halter of reproach and judgement, set limits upon it with conscientious rebuke and reprimand, and place the saddle of firm intention upon it with the girth of determination. Then mount it with the profession of the Shari'a and ride it into the fields of Truth.[351]

---

351   Kitab al-Rimah, quoted in Brenner, West African Sufi, p. 114.

Since the state of the *nafs* is an essential component to the aspirant's ability to attain Divine knowledge, Sufis, citing different names by which the *nafs* is addressed in the Qur'an, very early on detailed different stages through which the *nafs* must pass. The Khalwati tradition familiar to Shaykh Ahmad Tijani possessed one of the most detailed descriptions of these stages, enumerating seven states of the *nafs*, each one corresponding to a different name of God into which the aspirant was initiated in order to transcend a particular stage. The first stage, the self commanding to evil *(nafs al-ammara)*, was passed by affirming the Oneness of God saying *la ilaha illallah.* The other stages, in succession, were: the self blaming self *(nafs al-lawwama)*, corresponding to the name Allah; the inspired self *(nafs al- mulhama)*, linked to the name *Huwa* (He); the self at peace *(nafs al- mutma'inna)*, arrived at through the name *Haqq* (the Truth); the self at pleasure with God *(nafs al-radiyya)*, going with the name *Hayy* (the Living); the self with whom God is pleased *(nafs al-mardiyya)*, linked to the name *Qayyum* (the Self-Subsisting); and the perfected self *(nafs al-kamila)*, corresponding to the name *Qahhar* (the Dominator).[352] This system may possibly have been one of the subjects dealt with at the time of Shaykh Ahmad Tijani's initiation at the hands of the Khalwati Shaykh Muhammad al-Samman, who "informed him [Shaykh Tijani] of the names."[353] In any case, the Shaykh adopted the Khalwati version, but following his illumination added a final stage, the hidden self *(nafs al-ikhfa ')*.[354] It is tempting to wonder if the corresponding name to this stage was the same secret and greatest name of God given to the Shaykh by the Prophet in a vision, a name only given by the Prophet among his companions to 'Ali ibn Abi Talib and corresponding to the station of *Qutbaniyya* (Polehood).[355]

---

352   This scheme was reportedly elaborated by Mustafa al-Bakri.' See Rachida Chih, "Les débuts d'une tariqa,"..p. 143.

353   Jawahir, p. 25.

354   Jawahir, cited in Radtke, "Sufism in the 18th Century," pp. 348-349.

355   Jawahir, p. 37.

Shaykh Ahmad Tijani's conception of the purified *nafs*, prepared for the reception of Divine knowledge, differs little from classic Sufi conceptions. The idea that the selfs desires should be broken so that nothing remains but the will of God is easily traceable in the origins of the Islamic message. Indeed, the Shaykh cites a Hadith Qudsi in support of the notion, where God says, "O son of Adam, you want and I want ... [but] nothing is existing except what I want."[356] He likewise quotes Junayd's description of the purified selfs translucence to God's command, "The color of water is the color of its container."[357] Thus, the Shaykh urged the aspirant to be firm "in the purpose of cutting [himself] off from all things except Allah, may He be glorified and exalted, so that he is not consoled by anything except His grace and beneficence."[358] Ali Harazem al-Barada elaborates about the Shaykh,

> He never had a desire except what Allah determined and desired ... he does not like scheming with Allah or [personal] choice, and he said, "There is no action better than that which He who acts has done, and there is no decision better than that which He who decides has decided."[359]

This state of complete submission to God can only be achieved through the annihilation of the self, for, "The knowledgeable person of God is spiritually extinguished, crushed and annihilated by the Splendor of the Being."[360] At such a state the servant will realize that, "It is not necessary for the slave to know except for his Master, and to see except for His [attributes of] beneficence and mercy."[361] Actions themselves become a remembrance of God, where "the principal and end of

---

356   Jawahir, p. 50.
357   Jawahir, p. 30.
358   Jawahir, p. 44.
359
360   Jawahir, quoted in Benabdellah, La Tijania, p. 115.
361   Jawahir, p. 50.

every action is the attachment of the heart to God and [having] faith in Him, in the general as in the particular."[362] Shaykh Ahmad Tijani explains further,

The disciple must strive towards these two goals:

[First] to prefer God over everything else. God must be for him the principal and the end of his desires so that not one single instant of his life be dedicated to another, because to look to another is to find self-interest or squandering. [And second] to devote himself completely to God, free from all bonds, completely and mysteriously united to Him in body, soul, spirit and heart, in such a manner that not one particle of the being is a stranger to God. The disciple will give himself over completely to this goal, detached from all passion. Like this, he will stand before God, in the total renunciation of his whole being, in order to accomplish an act of pure adoration and satisfaction of divine laws, without expecting the slightest advantage. He will not despair of the mercy of God nor will he err in pride in believing himself full of good qualities.[363]

This last sentence is of interest for its emphasis that for the self to attain Divine union, it must realize that everything, even its own ability to worship God, comes from God.[364] The

---

362   Jawahir, quoted in Amadou Samb, Introduction a la Tariqah Tidjaniyya, p. 88.

363   Jawahir, quoted in Samb, Tariqah Tidjaniyya, p. 89.

364   As Qushayri said, "The strongest determination of the ego-self and the most difficult to overcome is the delusion that it contains something good or that it deserves some status. This is considered a secret form of idolatry" (Sells, Early Islamic Mysticism, p. 148). Hakim al-Tirmidhi expresses a similar sentiment, "Really I am amazed at their ignorance when they postulate that reaching God is a recompense for the servant's efforts ... Indeed, has anyone reached God other than by the means of God? But they claim that they have reached Him by the efforts of their carnal souls. By God, what liars are they! No one who has reached God ever did so other than by the means of God" (Ratke and O'Kane, The Concept of Sainthood in Early Islamic Mysticism: Two works by al-Hakim al-Tirmidhi (Great Britain: Curzon Press, 1996), p. 171).

idea of the self's inability to worship God as He deserves except through His grace is important in understanding Shaykh Ahmad Tijani's conception of God's grace or favor *(fadl)* and the path of giving thanks *(shukr)*, ideas to be revisited later.

Knowledge of God and Human Purpose

Shaykh Ahmad Tijani's conception of the *nafs* and its purification also provides valuable insight into his conception of human nature and its essential relationship to the Creator. Each human being is possessed of both a hidden and an external nature, neither of which recognizes the other. This duality is the reason for most people's ignorance of their essential nature, but it is also the reason for the ability of the gnostic to both love God and to give to the material creation its rights. However, it is the unseen aspect of the human being that defines his essential nature, since it defines his ability to know God.

> *The spirit (ruh) of every human being has been created initially endowed with a conscience and a perfect knowledge of God. An intense degradation then follows, by biological contact with the corporal substance; and this soul becomes ignorant, losing its original memory.*[365]

---

365   Jawahir, p. 148. See also Benabdellah, La Tijania, p. 109, and Radtke, "Sufism in the 18th Century," pp. 348-349.

However, since the quintessential *ruh* is created from the Light of God,[366] the human's essential nature is never fully clouded, and even wrongdoers cannot escape the reality of God's existence, but "recognize God introspectively in themselves."[367] As al-Hajj 'Umar explains, "Each human being or *jinn* possesses a luminous body, linked to his biological substance by a ray of light; it is this invisible body that adores God."[368] This spiritual or luminous nature of the human being, which can only be perceived once the *nafs* has been purified, is what defines the real honor of human creation, that of being the *khalifa* (deputy) of God. For as *khalifat-Allah*, he is "capable of carrying the burden of the secret,"[369] that he is a locus of Divine manifestation.

> As for the spiritual counterpart [of the human], its intrinsic reality is symbolized by the words of the Messenger of God, "God has created man in His image." This is a subtle allusion to the state of man, as well as his perfectibility in relation to the presence of Divine Beauty, comprising the secrets of the Being. This is what Imam Ibn 'Arabi defines in his Futuhat al-Makkiya, in saying that the Adamic being is either an image of the presence of God, or the symbol of His names [370]

The *ruh* of each human, endowed with the secrets of its Creator, existed for thousands of years with its Lord before the creation, and even after the creation, does not stop worshipping God, whether its fate is to be rewarded with Paradise or to be punished in Hellfire.[371] The *ruh* is itself measured 980,000 years long and the same wide, though less in the case of an unknowledgable person of God or the disbeliever. Before the ma-

---

366   Jawahir, p. 148.
367   Jawahir, quoted in Benabdellah, La Tijania, p. 109
368   Kitab al-Rimah, quoted in Benabdellah, La Tijania, p. 108.
369   Kitab al-Rimah, quoted in Brenner, West African Sufi, p. 113;
370   Jawahir, p. 150. See also Benabdellah, La Tijania, pp. 108-109
371   Kitab al-Jami b. I, p. 100.

terial creation, each *ruh* was carressed and molded "in the lap of the *Haqq* (Truth, Real)." With the material creation-and the separation of the *ruh* from the Divine presence, God warned it that He had not created it to desire itself, but "to show in you the secret of Our Oneness." And then out of it God created the particles of the world, and the *ruh* was married with the material body. This partition caused the *ruh* a period of "intense crying until there became great seas brimming over." The people of illumination sense the original state of their souls, and long to return to the lap of the Real, a state possessed of a special "blessing and taste that cannot be [self] fashioned." But, "as for he who is veiled from the original state of the souls (*ruhs*), he has forgotten Him."[372]

The *ruh* might define the essential potential of the human being in terms of knowledge of God, but it does not by itself define humanity. The Shaykh admitted to once holding the idea, together with the rest of the savants, that it was the *ruh* that was the reality of the human being. He said he was later informed by Divine inspiration that in fact the human was defined by the resultant combination from the marriage of the *ruh* with the body, and that it is the "realization (*idrak*) of their mixture" that characterizes humanity.[373] Moreover, by themselves it is impossible for either the *ruh* or the body not to be in constant praise and remembrance of its Creator. Ibn Mishry questioned the Shaykh how, in this case, were to be explained the descriptions in the Qur'an of the punishment or reward of the spirit and the body by Paradise or Hellfire. The Shaykh replied that it is because of their proximity to the realization (*idrak*) of the human, since essential human realization was created by their combination.

If the human being was defined by his *ruh*, the Shaykh reasons, then all humans would possess the intrinsic knowl-

---

372   Kitab al-Jami', b. I, pp. 101-102.
373   Ibid., pp. 100-101.

edge contained in their *ruh,* but in most cases the knowledge hidden in the *ruh* cannot be grasped. If the human being has knowledge, it is because he has sensed the secret knowledge carried by his *ruh,* and it is this process that the Shaykh calls the "realization" that defines human existence. When the spirit leaves the body at death, usually the realization departs from both spirit and body, except for God's most select. Both the bodies and the spirits of these saints retain the realization, which is why their bodies are physically preserved to continue praying to God after death.[374] It is in such a context that is understood the saying of the Prophet that God would return his spirit to his body to return the greetings of those who send prayers upon him.[375] The implication is that the spirit of the individual who has attained realization is active even after its separation from the body.

Elsewhere Shaykh Ahmad Tijani insists that it is the individual's ability to realize the knowledge of God's Essence *(dhat)* that defines his humanity. To understand such a conception, one must return to earlier Sufi ideas concerning the division of different types of knowledge of God. Al-Ghazali, for example, detailed three classes of knowledge: knowledge of God's Works, knowledge of God's Attributes or Names, and knowledge of God's Essence.[376] Each sort of knowledge is in fact a stage in the individual's progress towards full knowledge of God, but it is the last stage that defines the true knowledge or *ma'arifa* of which only the human being is worthy. According to Shaykh Ahmad Tijani,

---

374   Since early Islam, Islamic literature has contained descriptions of the preserved state of saints and martyrs in their graves.
375   Kitab al-Jami', b. I, pp. 100-101. This act of returning does not mean, the Shaykh warns, that either the Prophet's body or spirit has lost its realization with death, the statement simply is meant as an expression of honor for the one sending prayers on the Prophet.
376   Abu Hamid al-Ghazali, Jawahir al-Qur'an (trans. Muhammad Abdual Quasem, Malaysia, 1997).

> *The saints of the Jinn revolve around the Divine Act, of the secret of the Act and its light. The Ruhanis (spirits or lesser angels) turn around the Name, its secret and its light. As for the Angels, their axis is the Attributes and their secret. Finally, for the Adamic being, his pivot is the Essence, its secret and light. The first degree, that of the Jinns, is the initial stage of departure, for the coming of unveiling (kashf), before the attaining of the last three stages.[377]*

Consonant with the classic Sufi conception of God's presence, Shaykh Ahmad Tijani rejects the opinion that God only exists in this world in knowledge, maintaining that He is present in Essence as well as in His attribute of knowledge.[378] As such, the pure servant is able to experience the knowledge of God in this life as well as the next. This knowledge or *Maarifa*, sometimes described as "the science of reality in non-existence,"[379] is basically non-rational, meaning that its reality cannot be communicated except through the individual's own experience. When asked to describe *Maarifa*, the Shaykh replied simply that it is when "Allah takes the servant, and he does not know origin or separation, neither reason or rationale."[380] Elsewhere he elaborates,

> *Indeed, at the presence of the Simple Essence (al- dhat al-sadhij) is a sea of blindness and effacement. There is no thinking in it, no description, no name, no cause and no effect, no variation and no illusion, no quantity and no quality (la kam wa la kayf), no specification and no particularity.[381]*

377   Jawahir, quoted in Benabdellah, La Tijania, p. 108.
378   Jawahir, pp. 99-100.
379   Cisse, Spirit of Good Morals, p. 48.
380   Jawahir, p. 161.
381   Jawahir, p. 220.

Shaykh Ibrahim Niasse took particular interest in the notion of *Ma'arifa* and the necessity of its attainment during this life.

> Whoever does not attain the knowledge of the Merciful (Allah), his life has been in ruin for all time spent. I created these creations (Allah said) to worship Me, "To worship Me" meaning "To know Me". Do not lessen your effort in acquiring the knowledge (of Allah); then you shall be astonished by the closeness of the Most Merciful. He is manifest in everything, upon everything, and by everything, before it and yet after it, forever.[382]

This last statement is reminiscent of the much disputed idea of the Oneness of Being *(wahdat al-wujud)*, first named such by Ibn 'Arabi and energetically rejected by some since the time of Ibn Taymiyya. One of the elements of the Neo-Sufi consensus is that the reformist orders such as the Tijaniyya themselves rejected this idea of Ibn 'Arabi. Such an assumption cannot be said to apply to Shaykh Ahmad Tijani, as there is no evidence of it applying to Ahmad ibn Idris.[383] Shaykh Tijani himself specifically elaborates on the topic in the *Kitab al-Jami'* through a number of parables. His first example is to reduce the concept to the level of the human microcosm and its unity, where different parts of the body possess different functions and have different degrees of honor but nonetheless are created of the same material and form the same whole. [384] Another example of how the multiplicity of the creation can in fact be unified and pervaded by the same Being is that of the written word. Like "the flood from the Divine presence" which is unified but settles in different forms and descriptions, it is the same ink that pervades different letters, words and pictures, despite the

---

382   Spirit of Good Morals, verses 77-80.
383   R.S. O'Fahey and Bemd Radtke, "Neo-Sufism Reconsidered" in Der Islam, v.70, 1993.
384   Kitab al-Jami b. I, p. 98.

divergence in shape between letters, meaning between words and images between pictures. Every mark of the pen is in reality nothing but the ink to which it owes its existence.[385]

Tijani thought seems to have conceived the *'Arif billah* or gnostic as the quintessential human and Muslim. In this manner, the Tijani tradition can thus be seen as a reaffirmation of earlier Sufism's emphasis on attaining knowledge of God. Even if the Tijaniyya can be considered a later development in the history of Sufism, Shaykh Ahmad Tijani's notions of *Ma'arifa* clearly situate his path firmly within the tradition of Sufism and what he considered the essential Islamic message. No doubt, to emphasize the historical continuity of the path to knowledge of God, the Shaykh cites the *Ibriz* in articulating the necessary unity of all the gnostics.[386] Such an idea stresses the Muhammadan inheritance of the saint. Since Muhammad is "the well/source of Divine knowledge,"[387] the saints are unified by their close relationship to the Prophet. Shaykh Ibrahim Niasse elaborates on the unity of the *'Arifin* (gnostics) that it is they who are the real followers of the Prophet, and the sect guaranteed salvation referred to in the Hadith detailing how Muslims will be divided into seventy-three sects, of whom only one is saved, those who follow the way of the Prophet and his companions.[388]

---

385   Kitab al-Jami ', b. I, p. 99.
386   Kitab al-Jami', b. I, p. 96. See also, Shaykh Ibrahim Niasse, Kashf al-'Ilbas, p. 180.
387   Line from the well-known Tijani prayer on the Prophet, Jawharat al-Kamal.
388   Kashf al- 'Ilbas, p. 179.

The Tariqa Muhammadiyya And the Haqiqa Muhammadiyya

For Shaykh Ahmad Tijani, God bestows knowledge of Himself on the saints through their proximity to the Prophet Muhammad in both an external and spiritual sense. It is such a relationship of love between the Prophet and the saint that defines a saint's position. The true saint's path is thus that of the *Tariqa Muhammadiyya*, labelled as such since it permits him access to the transcendent guiding light of the Prophet, or the *Haqiqa Muhammadiyya*, where all "the veils between him [the saint] and the Prophet are lifted."[389] Shaykh Ahmad Tijani's notion of the *Tariqa Muhammadiyya* was thus intimately linked with the idea of the *Haqiqa Muhammadiyya*. It is through such a reality that the primary esoteric elements of the *Tariqa Muhammadiyya*, the waking vision of the Prophet and the concentration on the spiritual essence of the Prophet, are made possible.

It should not be forgotten that access to such an existence is also largely what permits the saint his ability to implement the external elements of *Tariqa Muhammadiyya*, namely the emphasis on the Sunna. Remember that Abd al-Aziz al-Dabbagh

---

389   Kitab al-Jami\b. I, p. 71.

defined the saint's ability to interpret the law on the basis of his capacity to see the Prophet in a waking state [390] The Egyptian Tijani scholar al-Hajj Muhsin Shalaby insists that it is the saint's direct contact with the spirit of the Prophet that makes him so keen to implement even the minutest detail of the Sunna.[391] It is thus the notion of the *Haqiqa Muhammadiyya*, which comprises one of the central elements to the *Tariqa Muhammadiyya* ideal.

To understand how the Prophet, a man who lived over a thousand years before his own time, could have had such an intense impact on Shaykh Ahmad Tijani, it is important to understand the latters' conception of the *Ruh Muhammadi* or the *Haqiqa Muhammadiyya*. The notion of Muhammad's transcendent luminescence dates at least to the time of Ibn 'Arabi, but likely much before, and even some hadith contain resonance of the idea.[392] The Shaykh's discussion of the subject mentions earlier conclusions from the likes of Abd al-Qadir al-Jilani, Abd al-Salam ibn Mashish and Ibn 'Arabi, and generally he seems to present an earlier Sufi opinion of the *Haqiqa Muhammadiyya* taken up by later formulators of the *Tariqa Muhammadiyya*. According to Shaykh Ahmad Tijani, "It is the first existent Allah the Most High brought into existence from the presence of the unseen, and there was not at the presence of Allah any from the existent creation that preceded it."[393] Before

---

390   Kitab al-lbriz, cited in Willis, Passion of al-Hajj 'Umar, p. 156.

391   Muhsin Shalaby, interview, Fes, Morocco, April, 2003.

392   See Schimmel, And Muhammad is His Messenger, pp. 130-132. Among the Hadith cited by Schimmel are found the following sayings of the Prophet, "I was a Prophet while Adam was still between water and clay" (Furuzanfar, Ahadith-I Mathnawi, no. 301); "The first thing that God created was my spirit" (Najm al-Razi, Path o f God's Bondsman); "But for your sake I would not have created the spheres" (Ahadith-i Mathnawi, no. 546); "Who has seen me, has seen the Truth" (Ahadith-I Mathnawi, no. 163, also in Bukhari and Muslim). According to Schimmel, the first to explain the idea o f the Haqiqa Muhammadiyya were Sahl al-Tustari and al-Hallaj.

393   Jawahir, p. 60.

the creation itself, God created the "honorable spirit *(ruh)*" of the Prophet, "and this is the *Haqiqa Muhammadiyya*."[394]

In what might be considered a further elaboration of the concept, Shaykh Ahmad Tijani also speaks of the Prophet's creation in different stages, of being clothed in the Light of God. After the creation of the Prophet's *ruh* and its endowment with Divine Light, God next dressed in light the Prophetic *'aql* (intelligence), then his heart, then his *nafs*, then his body. The positions of the *awliya* or saints differ in relation to the level of the Prophet's reality from which they derive their inspiration. Some of the saints realize the Prophet on the level of his *nafs*, some at his heart, some at his *'aql*, and some, the most elevated of the saints, understand the Prophet on the level of his *ruh*.[395]

The spirit of the Prophet is itself the *barzakh* (isthmus) between the material world and that of the unseen, the two worlds referred to in the Qur'an as two seas that do not meet but having between them a *barzakh*.[396] The Shaykh uses this same verse to describe the relationship between the material and spiritual natures of the human being,[397] and it is the Prophet who serves as the isthmus or bridge in both cases. To understand how the Prophet's *ruh* serves as the *barzakh* between the two worlds on both a macrocosmic and microcosmic level, the Shaykh is clearly assuming an understanding of the Prophetic *ruh* widespread in the Muslim world at least by the time of Abd al-Aziz al-Dabbagh and the *Kitab al-Ibriz*. According to the *Ibriz*, the Prophet's *nafs* or *dhat* (self/essence) had become completely dissolved into his *ruh*, itself the Light from God. As Radtke summarizes of the *Ibriz*,

> The Prophet has no partition between his dhat and ruh;
> they are joined together. The ruh lives within the Proph-

---

394   Jawahir, p. 61.
395   Jawahir, p. 61.
396   Jawahir, p. 84. The Shaykh cites the Qur'an, 55:19-20
397   Jawahir, p. 150.

*et's dhat the way love lives within a human being's soul,
namely it permeates the dhat completely. As a result, the
Prophet's dhat is endowed with a special power; it draws
upward to God and not, as is usual [with other beings],
downward to the earth and darkness. Due to the special
power of light that is active in the Prophet's dhat, he is
the intermediary between creation and God. On the one
hand, the divine lights pour down on the Prophet's dhat
uninterruptedly, while on the other hand his dhat passes
them on to God's creatures ... Furthermore, even after
his death, it is possible to perceive the Prophet as he is in
flesh and blood, in other words to perceive his dhat.*[398]

It is useful to situate Shaykh Ahmad Tijani's ideas on the
Prophet's *ruh* in such a context as the *Ibriz*, even if there was
no direct link of knowledge transmission between al-Dabbagh
and the Shaykh. Such a conception from the *Ibriz* adds insight
into what the latter meant by Muhammad's position as the *barzakh* and also helps to explain the relative ease with which
eighteenth-century Sufism accepted the idea of the waking
vision of the Prophet. Indeed, one of Shaykh Ahmad Tijani's
teachers, Muhammad al-Samman, said that, after the aspirant's immersion in the *dhat* of the Prophet,

> *He will then stand directly before your eyes. You will
> perceive him, speak to him, put questions to him and
> converse with him. He will give you answers, speak to
> you, and converse with you; in this way you will attain
> the rank of the Sahaba.*[399]

The above thoughts from the *Ibriz* thus help to contextualize
the Shaykh's almost casual reference to another of the *Tariqa
Muhammadiyya's* essential components, the form of spiritual
concentration on, or annihilation in, the Prophet. Given the

398   Radtke, "Sufism in the 18th Century," pp. 354-355.
399   Muhammad al-Samman, al-Futuhat al-ilahiyya fi al-tawajjuhat
al-ruhiyya, cited in Radtke, "Sufism in the 18th Century," p. 355.

conception of the Prophet's position as the *barzakh,* it is easy to conclude the efficacy of the "annihilation in the essence *(dhat)* of the Prophet," where the saint "does not see his own self, but only the essence *(dhat)* of the Prophet."[400]

In any case, it hardly needs to be stated given the above discussion of *Ma'arifa* or the knowledge of God, that the *Haqiqa Muhammadiyya* and the annihiliation in the Prophet are not the end in and of themselves. The purpose of the annihiliation in the Prophet was to inspire the aspirant to greater devotion towards God and love of the Prophet. In one prayer, Shaykh Ahmad Tijani used to entreat God concerning the Prophet,

> *Make him to us a spirit and the very secret of our worship. And make his love, to us a food aiding us to magnify him. And make our magnifying of him, life in our hearts by which I may arise and with its aid make mention [...] of his Lord.*[401]

The impression given by the *Jawahir* is that the *Haqiqa Muhammadiyya* represents what had become, by the eighteenth century, simply another element, albiet an important one, in the milieu of Sufi doctrines. The aspirant's realization of the essential reality of his Prophet was a stage in a continuum, which was situated between the knowledge of his shaykh and knowledge of God.[402] Rather than the *Haqiqa Muhammadiyya* being the only goal of the seeker and its attainment leading to an obviation of the other stages, as the Neo-Sufi

---

400   Kitab al-Jami', b. I, pp. 72-73. This is reminiscent of the well-known hadith where the Prophet says a Muslim has not attained true faith until he loves the Prophet more than his own self.

401   Shaykh Ahmad Tijani, al-Awrad al-ikhtiyariyya, quoted in Padwick, Muslim Devotions, p. 142.

402   Shaykh Hassan Cisse, Spirit of Good Morals, p. 23. Shaykh Hassan says, "The murid or disciple in reality seeks the countenance of Allah. This countenance of Allah has a gate which is the Prophet, the coutenance of the Prophet also has a gate which is the Shaykh."

consensus would have us believe of late eighteenth-century Sufism,[403] knowledge of the Prophet was intimately linked with the stages both above and below him, such that attaining such knowledge deepened the aspirant's knowledge of both God and his shaykh.[404]

403   Fazlur Rahman, Islam (London: Weidenfeld & Nicolson, 1966), p. 206.
404   Shaykh Hassan Cisse, interview, Medina Kaolack, Senegal, November, 2002.

Chapter V

Towards a Distinctive Tijani Sufi Doctrine

The previous chapter involved Shaykh Ahmad Tijani's ideological relationship to both the earlier tradition of Sufism and to the *Tariqa Muhammadiyya* emphasis present among many Sufis in the end of the eighteenth century. It is clear, then, that most of what the Shaykh had to say was firmly situated within prevalent Sufi principles. Nevertheless, this does not mean that he had nothing new to add to the discourse on Sufism. It is evident from the *Jawahir* that the Shaykh has very specific things to say about Divine grace *(fadl)* and the manner of its dispensation and attainment. Beside this topic, this section also considers his views on sainthood and the *shaykh al-tarbiyya* (guide of spiritual education), views which are not particularly distinctive, but which help to understand how the aforementioned grace is dispensed (through the saints) and attained (through the *shaykh al-tarbiyya*). This is followed by a discussion of the nature of Divine grace itself, and the implications in terms of historical distinction of its embodiment in the Tijaniyya order.

Sainthood

The *Haqiqa Muhammadiyya,* being the source of Divine flux in the universe, or "the flood from the Divine presence,"[405] was also important for Shaykh Ahmad Tijani's ideas concerning *wilaya* or sainthood. As was mentioned in the last chapter, sainthood was primarily defined for the Shaykh, as the saint's ability to receive this flux passing through the spirit of the Prophet to the creation.

Of course, such a reception assumed the saint's annihilation of his self in God. According to the Shaykh, this annihilation could exist on three different levels: a saint could be annihilated in God on the level of His Works, on the level of His Attributes or on the level of His Essence. The most elevated saints were of course those who had finished themselves in God's Essence and who worshipped Him for the reason of His Essence alone, and "not in order to obtain anything from Him."[406] Tijani tradition often emphasizes the hidden nature of the saint, who might exist in the world exactly as any other ordinary being. According to nineteenth-century Moroccan

---

405   Kitab al-Jami ', b. I, p. 99.
406   Jawahir, quoted in Berque, L 'interieur du Maghreb, pp. 255-266.

Tijani savant al-'Arabi ibn Sa'ih, the highest saint, the *Qutb,* behaves like a humble servant, accepting whatever God wills for him. His outward characteristics do not necessarily call attention to himself, and his position does not require him to fly or walk on water.[407] It is only through the aspirant's desire to reach God that the saint's true nature is revealed. Shaykh Ahmad Tijani was reported to have said in this regard, "Whoever loves me out of love for Allah and His Messenger is blessed, but whoever loves me for another reason, I am only an ordinary man."[408]

The saint's proximity to God was defined, for Shaykh Ahmad Tijani, by his proximity to the Prophet. At the highest stage of sainthood, the saint has removed all the veils between himself and the Prophet, such that he realizes the statement of Abu Abbas al-Mursi that if the Prophet were to disappear from him for a moment, he would cease to count himself among the Muslims.[409] All who have attained sainthood do so only through the intermediary of the Prophet, even if their words issuing from a state of absorption (*istighraq*) might lead the listener to believe the saint considers himself to have reached a stage never before attained. In fact, every saint is granted a private, special audience in the Divine presence, where he receives such favor, knowledge and secrets that he believes what has been given to him never was given to another before him, nor will ever be given to another after him.[410] However, this favor, and the statements that result from the saint's rapture in this state, do not in fact reflect on the reality of his own position. Thus the statements of 'Umar ibn al-Farid (d. 1234) or Ibrahim al-Dasuqi (d. 1285), for example, containing ecstatic utterances of the saint's unparalleled ascendence, have their source in the saint's "annihilation in the essence *(dhat)* of the

---

407   ³ Bughyat al-Mustafid, pp. 187-188.
408   ⁴ Kitab al-Rimah, quoted in Benabdellah, La Tijania, p. 117.
409   ⁵ Kitab al-Jami \ b. I, p. 71.
410   ⁶ Kitab al-Jami', b. I, p. 85.

Prophet." Such words thus reflect the reality of the Prophet, not the saint: "For who hears him, thinks he is refering to himself, however the reference is actually to the Prophet."[411]

Shaykh Hassan Cisse explains the relationship of the saint to the Prophet in a similar fashion. There are in fact, according to Shaykh Hassan, two types of saints: one of differentiation (*farq*), such as Muhammad al-Busiri (d. 1296), and one of collection (*jami'*), such as Ibn al-Farid. Busiri, who composed the famous *Burdah* poem in praise of the Prophet, was known to have said that every position is worthless except that in which is found the Prophet. Ibn Farid, on the other hand, wrote that he had plunged into the ocean of God's Reality, whereas the rest of creation had only dipped the edge, or that they had only drunk the leftover drops from his own draught. Both types of saints return to the Prophet, since Ibn Farid is annihilated in the *Haqiqa Muhammadiyya* and is speaking on the Prophet's behalf, according to Shaykh Hassan, and so both types are excellent.[412] In another interview, Shaykh Hassan emphasized the importance of the words of the Prophet in a waking vision to the saint in determining the reality of his position.[413]

For Shaykh Ahmad Tijani, the purest form of the saint is defined by the position of the *Khatm al-'Awliya* (Seal of the Saints), the *Qutb al-'Aqtab* (Pole of the Poles) or the *Qutb al-Maktum* (Hidden Pole); three titles referring simultaneously to the pinnacle of the hidden hierarchy of saints. The defining characteristic of this saint is his ascendant position of proximity to the Prophet, such that he becomes the intermediary between the spiritual flux from the presence of the *Haqiqa Muhammadiyya* to the rest of the saints, both past and future, without them having knowledge of his position.[414] Spiritual

411   Kitab al-Jami \ b. I, pp. 72-73.
412   Shaykh Hassan Cisse, interview, Medina Kaolack, Senegal, November, 2002.
413   Shaykh Hassan Cisse, interview, Rabat, Morocco, March, 2003.
414   Kitab al-Jami ', p. 18, Jawahir, p. 158.

emanation thus passes from the Divine presence through the *Haqiqa Muhammadiyya*, then to the rest of the Prophets, then to the Seal of the Saints before reaching the rest of the saints.[415]

It was on the basis of the reported words of the Prophet himself in a waking vision to Shaykh Ahmad Tijani that the latter claimed this most exalted position of the saintly hierarchy.[416] This position of mediation between the *Haqiqa Muhammadiyya* and the rest of the saints was not invented by the Shaykh, but was first elaborated in comprehensive fashion by Hakim al-Tirmidhi and later by Ibn 'Arabi. Al-Tirmidhi considered the Seal of the Saints to be the proof of sincerity, through his own humility, purity of heart and singularity of purpose being only to praise God, against the assembly of the saints for the proper usage of the Divine favor of which they were the recipient.

> *And he will be God's proof against all the other Friends (awliya', i.e., saints) on the Day of Judgment. By means of this seal will he possess the sincerity of Friendship with God the same way that Muhammad possesses the sincerity of Prophethood. The Enemy (Satan) will not speak to him and the carnal soul will not find the means to seize its share of the Friendship with God.*

> *Thus, when the Friends of God come forward on the Day of Judgement and they are asked for the sincerity of Friendship with God and the state of being God's bondsman ('ubada), the fulfillment (of this obligation) will be found with one who possesses completely, the seal of Friendship with God ... The Station of Intercession will be set up for him and he will praise his Lord with such praise and commend Him with such commendation that the Friends of God will recognize his superiority over them, with regard to knowledge of God.[417]*

---

415   Jawahir, p. 132.

416   Kitab al-Jami', p. 19.

417   Bemd Radtke and John O'Kane, The Concept of Sainthood in Early Islamic Mysticism: two works by al-Hakim al-Tirmidhi; an annotated trans-

Like the Seal of the Prophets (the Prophet Muhammad), the Seal of the Saints bears the stamp or seal God used to seal the treasures He distributes, meaning that anything arriving to any of the saints would bear the mark of this Seal (whether it was known to them or not), just as all the prophets before Muhammad bore the seal of the prophecy of the last messenger.[418]

Ibn 'Arabi conceived the Seal of the Saints in much the same manner as al-Tirmidhi, but distinguished between the Seal of general sainthood, who was Jesus, and the Seal of Muhammadan sainthood. This latter saint occupies a "tabernacle" through which the knowledge of God passes first, before reaching any of the other saints and is thus "one of the perfections of the Seal of the Messengers, Muhammad."[419] Ibn 'Arabi at one point claimed the position for himself after a vision seeing himself in the image of two bricks completing the structure of the Kaba, the sacred house in Mecca.[420] Tijanis claim that he in fact relinquished the claim after meeting Shaykh Ahmad Tijani on the "unseen," an encounter which Ibn 'Arabi detailed in his *Futuhat al-Makiyya,* saying that the Seal would live in Fes and that his claim would not be accepted by the majority of the people of his time.[421] Another prediction cited by Tijanis as evidence of their Shaykh's assumption of the title of the Seal is that of the Malian Qadiri scholar al-Mukhtar al-Kunti (d. 1811), who predicted that the Seal of the Saints would come in his own century, also that of Shaykh Ahmad Tijani.[422]

---

lation with introduction (Surrey: Curzon, 1996), p. 109.

418   Radtke and O'Kane, Concept of Sainthood, p. 102.

419   Fusus al-Hikam; quoted in Chodkiewicz, Seal of the Saints, pp. 123-124.

420   Chodkiewicz, Seal of the Saints, p. 128.

421   See Chodkiewicz, Seal o f the Saints, p. 118, and Abun-Nasr, The Tijaniyya, p. 30. According to Chodkiewicz, Ibn 'Arabi's description of this meeting is also described in his 'Anqa al-Maghrib as well as the Futuhat al-Makkiyya.

422   Abun-Nasr, The Tijaniyya, p. 30.

Shaykh Ahmad Tijani's own conception of the Seal of the Saints differed little from the idea's previous formulators, except that he laid an increased emphasis on this saint's subservient and essential connection to the Prophet as the defining characteristic of his position. The Seal of the Saints or the Pole of the Poles is simply he whose humility before God and knowledge of Him grant him the most complete inheritance from the Prophet Muhammad,[423] and he is thus his true *khalifa* (deputy)[424] and the "closest door to the Prophet."[425] Divine grace and knowledge passes "from the flood of the sea of the *Haqiqa Muhammadiyya*"[426] through him to the other saints, and even though "his position is hidden from the assembly of the saints;"[427] his "feet are upon the neck of every one of Almighty God's saints from the time of Adam until the horn is blown."[428]

---

423 Kitab al-Jami', b. I, pp. 18-20.

424 Jawahir, p. 158.

425 Cisse, Spirit of Good Morals, p. 29.

426 Kitab al-Jami", p. 18.

427 Kitab al-Jami', p. 20.

428 Shaykh Ahmad Tijani to his disciple, Muhammad al-Ghali, in Kitab al-Rimah; quoted in Abun-Nasr, The Tijaniyya, p. 39.

The Shaykh al-Tarbiyya or Spiritual Initiator

As for the role of the saint, his primary function among the people is to help them attain knowledge of God. The *Jawahir* relates of Shaykh Ahmad Tijani that he was "greatly concerned with pushing people towards God."[429] Unlike other *Tariqa Muhammadiyya* groupings such as the Sufis associated with Ahmad ibn Idris, the Tijaniyya affirms in this regard the classical notion of the *shaykh al-tarbiyya* or spiritual initiator. Tijani circles in Senegal quote the adage, "He who has no shaykh has Satan for a shaykh."[430] Shaykh Ahmad Tijani said that such a spiritual initiator was necessary to attain Divine favor, or the "overflowing support of God."[431]

The Shaykh's own career was marked by intense, if relatively brief, initiatory meetings with some of the most prominent shaykhs of the time. But in order to appreciate the Shaykh's own spiritual training, we must consider his own belief that

---

429   Jawahir, p. 47.
430   Interview with Shaykh Hassan Cisse, Kaolack, Senegal, February, 2003.
431   Jawahir, quoted in Triaud, "La Tijaniyya, voie infaillible," p. 186.

his true spiritual initiation was at the hands of the Prophet himself. Indeed, for Shaykh Ahmad Tijani, the Prophet, in both dream and waking visions, takes on all the characteristics of a living shaykh: taking him through various stages of enlightenment, granting him prayers and challenging him with any oversights. For his part, Shaykh Ahmad Tijani can be seen taking permission and advice from the Prophet for every sort of matter, from deciding where to live to the ascension of the highest spiritual ranks.

This sort of relationship between the guide and the aspirant was reflected in the Shaykh's own dealings with his disciples. He advised them to "run to him [your shaykh] in important affairs for indeed you shall be met with success at that immediate time."[432] He also advised them that, for the Sufi *murid* (disciple, aspirant), sitting with his shaykh was more benificial than making extra *dhikr* by himself.[433] Shaykh Ahmad Tijani did not go so far as to say it was obligatory for every Muslim to have a shaykh, but he nonetheless maintained the necessity of the shaykh if a person desired to attain real knowledge of God.[434] The point is taken up further by al-Hajj 'Umar in his *Rimah*, the heading of chapter thirteen reading,

> *Informing them that no ascetic aspirant attains to the presence of God and the planes of His Attributes and Names except through the agency of those specially authorized, no matter if he amass [all] the knowledge of the former [scholars] and associate with all kinds of people and perform worship, equivalent to that of the men and jinn combined.*[435]

---

432   Jawahir, cited in Shaykh Hassan Cisse, Spirit of Good Morals, p. 30.
433   Jawahir, p. 47.
434   Jawahir, p. 67.
435   Kitab al-Rimah, quoted in Hunwick, "An Introduction to the Tijani path," p. 22.

In the *Jawahir's* description of Shaykh Ahmad Tijani in his role as spiritual guide, we find the classic portrait of the Sufi shaykh. Nobody sees him except that they remember God.[436] He is endowed with a wondrous clairvoyance such that he is able to know the secrets of a person's heart; and "when any of us sit with him, we are afraid for our scandals and our states of ugliness."[437] Shaykh Ahmad Tijani explained this insight of the saint by saying,

> *Each knowledgeable person of God encapsulates in his intrinsic reality an integral knowledge of the assembly of creatures, angels and others, dispersed from the Divine Throne to the inferior spheres; he sees them in himself, in his own essence, of the sort that he perceives the integrated components in the Guarded Table. This supremacy pertains to the human being, and this is what justifies his being khalifa of Allah.*[438]

The true shaykh is also possessed of a forceful *himma* or spiritual energy, which inspires people towards God. Thus, Shaykh Ahmad Tijani was surrounded by an aura of majesty such that "no one comes upon him suddenly, except that he is in shock and awe of him and no one preoccupies himself with him except by his endowment and love."[439] As for "those who sit with him," they "forget of the material world, and achieve certainty of God and contentment with the blessings of God."[440]

The abode is sparked with light in the heart of him who sees him [Shaykh Ahmad Tijani], and he who is in his presence resolves on the love of God, and he who visits him is thrown into remembrance [of God], and who meets him is cast into

436   Jawahir, p. 46.
437   Jawahir, p. 31.
438   Jawahir, quoted in Benabdellah, La Tijania, p. 110.
439   Jawahir, p. 46.
440   Jawahir, pp. 46-47,

earnestness, and the vision of him is medicine for the hearts and his words healing from faults.[441]

Shaykh Ahmad Tijani was thus concerned to detail the qualities of a true *shaykh al-wasil* (an arrived shaykh), defining his miracle as the ability to open the door of illumination to his followers.[442] Elsewhere he spoke of the guide-aspirant relationship as one of love, which was capable of shaking the disciple to the core of his being.

> *The people are all animated by the love for the elect saint, but the content of spiritual knowledge is that you yourself are an object of love for this elect ... Your true shaykh is he to whom the attraction overwhelms your heart, masters your mind, and by his enveloping regard and his gripping spiritual energy (himma), penetrates to the depth of your being.*[443]

The necessity of having a shaykh in the Tijani order seems to be somewhat contested among some circles of Shaykh Ahmad Tijani's descendents in Fes, who insist upon the equality of all Tijanis and the founder's position of ascendancy over all other shaykhs, which obviates the need for any other shaykh after him.[444] This seems to be a minority position, however, not held by any Tijani scholar of renown. Doubtless the latter are aware of Shaykh Ahmad Tijani's own statement,

> *Whoever takes refuge with the living people of his time that are part of this special elite [the saints], accompanies them, making an example of them and searching for their approval, these succeed in obtaining the overflowing support of God. And he who turns from the*

---

441   Jawahir, p. 46.

442   Jawahir, pp. 48, 66. Kitab al-Jami', p. 55.

443   Jawahir, quoted in Benabdellah, La Tijania, p. 117.

444   Interview with some of the Shaykh's descendents, Fes, Morocco, October, 2002.

people of his time, declaring his satisfaction with the
words of deceased saints who have gone before, this one
is marked with the mark of exclusion.[445]

In any case the position of the Shaykh's descendants in this regard seems aimed not so much at denying the necessity of a shaykh, but more towards preserving the order from fracture due to the charisma of renowned Tijani *shaykhs,* for whom the enthusiasm on the part of their disiciples is thought to sometimes obscure the ascendency of the order's founder.[446] Those affiliated with prominent shaykhs of the order providing initiatory knowledge (*tarbiyya*), however, obviously consider their shaykhs as the medium by which they come to understand Shaykh Ahmad Tijani rathei than a lessening of this latters spiritual excellence.[447] In recent times, the Tijani notion of the *shaykh al-tarbiyya* seems most faithfully implemented by the followers of Shaykh Ibrahim Niasse. Shaykh Ibrahim stressed the notion of *tarbiyya* or spiritual education, and the consequent need to follow a shaykh, as essential to the Tijaniyya, citing the views of Shaykh Ahmad Tijani and al-'Arabi ibn Sa'ih as evidence.[448]

In regards to the *shaykh al-tarbiyya,* Shaykh Ahmad Tijani was a firm proponent of another of the *Tariqa Muhammadiyya* phenomenon's salient features, that of exclusive affiliation to one *tariqa* and even one shaykh. The Shaykh prohibited his followers from taking any other Sufi order or from going to any other shaykh for the sake of spiritual knowledge. In an untitled document concerning the subject,[449] Shaykh Ahmad

---

445   Jawahir, quoted in Triaud, "La Tijaniyya, voie infaillible," p. 186.

446   Observations from interviews with some of the Shaykh's descendents, Fes, Morocco, October, 2002.

447   Interviews with disciples of Shaykh Ibrahim Niasse and Mansur Sy (present khalifa of the Senegalese Sy family of the Tijaniyya), Senegal and Morocco, 2002- 2003.

448   Kashf al- 'Ilbas, pp. 26-28, 41-49, 113-114.

449   I obtained a copy and explanation of this document, in Shaykh Tija-

Tijani explained this requirement by elaborating on Ibn 'Arabi's famous idea of the saint's inheritance from a particular prophet. As such, according to the Shaykh, each saint has a special audience in the Divine presence. However, the saint (the *Khatm al-Awliya*) who has inherited directly from the Prophet Muhammad, and is sealed by the stamp of the *Haqiqa Muhammadiyya,* has inherited a comprehensive understanding superior to the other saints, and every spiritual benefit flowing from the prophets to the saints flows through this saint bearing the seal of the *Haqiqa Muhammadiyya.*

Even in the case of any of the saints, the aspirant's own spirit is mixed with his shaykh such that his own spiritual opening can only be found in the presence of his shaykh and the particular prophetic inheritance that is attached to him. Should he seek spiritual knowledge from another shaykh, the presence of his own shaykh will call to him that he has nothing to gain from such an endeavor. Should the aspirant change affiliation, he will be cut off from his previous shaykh and will still be unable to benefit from the new shaykh, his spiritual provision being effectively severed. The Shaykh quotes the Qur'an in this regard that Allah has not created for any person two hearts in one breast. The exception of course is for the aspirant who leaves a previous shaykh to follow one bearing the stamp of the *Haqiqa Muhammmdiyya.* Once he has found such a shaykh, it is especially important he give exclusive attention to his shaykh. Shaykh Hassan Cisse elaborates, "Why then will one go out to beg for what he has in excess in his house?"[450]

Many of the shaykhs have however, says Shaykh Ahmad Tijani, become careless of this reality to the detriment of their followers. Although a non-aspirant (non-*salik*) can visit any of the saints, a truthful seeker should only concern oneself with

---

ni's own handwriting, from Shaykh Hassan Cisse in Rabat, March, 2003.
450   Shaykh Hassan Cisse, Interview in Rabat (March, 2003) and Spirit of Good Morals, p. 18.

searching out his *shaykh al-tarbiyya*. His visitation to shaykhs other than his true shaykh only increases the exposition of his sins, because he is not free from base desires in the visitation of these other shaykhs. The shaykhs who have arrived and are thus free of the influence of their *nafs* are able to visit other saints, since they "are anhiliated in God and their existence is for God, from God, by God, and they are absent from everything except God."[451]

"If ye are grateful, I will add more (favors) unto you."

---

451   Citation from a document form Shaykh Ahmad Tijani, intreview with Shaykh Hassan Cisse, Rabat, March, 2003

The Principal of Shukr and God's grace in an age of corruption

Shaykh Ahmad Tijani was not the first saint to stress the principal of *shukr* (giving thanks or being grateful) and its relationship to Divine grace, but his placement of *shukr* as the only door remaining to arrive to God seems unprecedented. The Shaykh's ideas on this subject might be said to partly define the distinctiveness of the Tijaniyya order, and certainly, they are the essential ingredient in understanding how he was able to supply "a distinct vision of the destiny of his followers."[452] Indeed, it is through the concept of *shukr* that the Shaykh confronts the perceived corruption of the times and emphasizes the grace *(fadl)* or mercy of God and the course of its descent.

The *Qutb al-Maktum* or the *Khatm al-Awliya'*, being the closest saint to the Prophet and thus the most sincere in his praise *(hamd* or *shukr)* to God, becomes the receptacle and distributor of Divine favor or grace flowing through the Prophet. The appearance of such a position in a corrupt age, nearer to

---

452   Triaud, "La Tijaniyya, une confrerie musulmane pas comme les autres?" in Triaud and Robinson ed.s, La Tijaniyya, p. 14.

the End of Time, is no accident, but a favor from God, "which He bestows on whom He will, and God is the possessor of the highest bounty (*fadl*)."[453] Thus, for Shaykh Tijani, the *Tariqa Muhammadiyya* was a path of grace in a corrupt world whose core practice defined the essential behavior of the Prophet and the purpose of the Islamic message, that of giving thanks or praise to God.

Shaykh Ahmad Tijani places giving thanks on par with faith itself by citing the Qur'an, "What can Allah gain by your punishment, if ye are grateful (*shakartum*) and ye believe? Nay, it is Allah that recogniseth (all good) (*Shakir*), and knoweth all things."[454] For this, it is useful to recall the semantics behind the opposite of belief, the word *kufr*; usually translated as "disbelief," but also meaning "to cover up" or "to be ungrateful."[455] Thus the act of being grateful was the recognition and exposing or opening of oneself to Divine favor, which Shaykh Ahmad Tijani endowed with the greatest importance:

> *The closest of the doors to Allah is the door of Shukr, and who does not in this time enter through it, does not enter. [This because] the ego-selves (nafs) have become thick and they are not affected by spiritual exercises and devotions or obedience, nor are they restrained by accounting (hisab) or argumentation. So if one wants to become immersed in happiness and blessing, he should absent himself from all of that and end his distance [from God], and all goodness promised from God we find connected with having no other desire than to give thanks. For as the Most High has said: "If ye are grateful, I will add more (favors) unto you."*[456]

---

453 Qur'an, 62:4, quoted in the Jawahir, p. 28.

454 Qur'an, 4:147. The translation is that of Yusef 'Ali. See Jawahir, p. 48.

455 Toshihiko Izutsu, The Structure of the Ethical Terms in the Koran, A Study in Semantics (Japan, 1959), p. 38.

456 Jawahir, p. 48. The Shaykh quotes the Qur'an, 14:7. The translation is that of Yusef 'Ali. The verse continues, "But if ye show ingratitude (kafar-

Such a passage also helps to explain the Tijani deemphasis of excessive asceticism. For Shaykh Ahmad Tijani, the action of giving thanks, saying *alhamdulillah*, or praising God, was obviously intimately connected with the path of the Prophet and the ultimate expression of servitude before God. The emptying of the self of every desire except to praise or render thanks to God defines the closest station of proximity to God, where dwells the Prophet himself. Thus Shaykh Hassan Cisse comments, "Because of the humility displayed by the Prophet, the blessings and peace of Allah upon him, before his Creator, Allah granted him the highest position in the hereafter, known as 'the Praiseworthy Position.'"[457]

It is from this station of selfless proximity that flow God's favors to the rest of the saints and to creation. *Shukr* is the most important action for the servant to receive this grace: the servant must never believe that it is only through the merit of his good deeds that he may attain the good favor of God. Shaykh Ahmad Tijani, as was mentioned previously, cautioned the aspirant not to "err in pride in believing himself full of good qualities." The Shaykh himself used to entreat God, "I come, bringing no knowledge and no piety, rather all is defilement, my Lord, with me."[458] This idea was of course not new, and Hakim al-Tirmidhi once described the Prophet's own preeminence "because of what is contained in his heart, not because of his works."[459] The idea of grace *(fadl)* thus implies the complete submission of the servant to permit God's direct action, where, for Shaykh Ahmad Tijani, the saint becomes a letter *(harf)* among the letters *(huruf)* emanating from the Divine Essence, thereby "permitting him a direct action."[460]

---

tum), truly My punishment is terrible indeed."

457   Shaykh Hassan Cisse, Spirit o f Good Morals o f Shaykh Ibrahim Niasse, pp. 55-56.

458   Shaykh Ahmad Tijani, Ahzab wa Awrad, cited in Padwick, Muslim Devotions, p. 215.

459   Radtke and O'Kane, The Concept of Sainthood, p. 203.

460   Jawahir, quoted in Benabdellah, La Tijania, p. 110.

According to Shaykh Hassan Cisse, Shaykh Ahmad Tijani's emphasis on *shukr* and the grace *(fadl)* of Allah finds its parallel in the Hadith, for the Prophet once said nobody would enter Paradise except through the mercy of God. When asked if that included himself, he replied even himself.[461] Indeed Shaykh Ahmad Tijani himself declared, "We have nothing but the grace *(fadl)* of Allah and His mercy."[462] The Shaykh delimited within this grace from God the guidance and intercession of the Prophet and the presence of the saints, or the people of God *(ahl-Allah)*, "those who call on their Lord morning and evening, seeking His Face."[463] Such grace was necessary because the servant was painfully unable, especially in the present time, to fulfill God's commands by his own efforts. As the *Jawahir* poses the question, "Are you capable of fulfilling all the obligations of the Law, the explicit and the implicit? Are you able, without assistance, to triumph over your passions?"[464]

Clearly, what is meant by *shukr* is the recognition of God's grace and beauty, an essential action to avoid His punishment. In the words of the Shaykh,

---

461   Interview with Shaykh Hassan Cisse, Medina Kaolack, Senegal, February, 2003. There are plenty of examples from the Islamic tradition that speak of the idea of grace: "And ye have no good thing but it is from Allah" (16:53) or "And were it not for the grace and mercy (fadl) of Allah on you, not one of you would ever have been pure: but Allah doth purify whom He pleases" (24:20). Ibn al-'Arabi writes, "Mercy is acquired in two ways, by obligation, as in His saying, 'I will ordain it for those who are God-fearing and give alms (Qur'an 7:156),' together with the intellectual and practical qualities he attributes to them, or by Divine Grace, which is unlike any [human] action, as in His saying, 'My Mercy encompasses everything (Qur'an 7:156),' so that 'He might forgive you your earlier and later sins (Qur'an 48:2),' and 'Do what you will I have forgiven you (Hadith qudsi reported by Ibn Hanbal).'" See Ibn 'Arabi, Bezels o f Wisdom (translated by R.W.J. Austin, New York: Paulist Press, 1980), pp. 226-227.

462   Jawahir, p. 47.

463   Qur'an, 18:28, see Jawahir, p. 47.

464   Jawahir, quoted in Berque, L 'interieur du Maghreb, p. 249.

> *If Allah wishes the destruction of a servant, He empowers him to His [decreed] blessing, [but] without adding to it ... and if He wills mercy to a servant He makes known to him His blessing and makes him eager to show gratefulness and to avoid denial, and this [gratefulness] is the source of all good.*[465]

Elsewhere, the Shaykh likens gratefulness to love for God, for "the source of love is the witnessing of [God's] beauty and beneficence."[466] He was thus concerned to enumerate to his followers the grace or mercy of God. These passages of the *Jawahir* present a deeply compassionate idea of the Divine.

> *Indeed Allah has mercy on a servant for the sake of only one quality ... if He finds one trait of goodness in you, such as modesty, generosity or something of love, for example, or a peaceful heart or truthfulness of speaking, or something of this in your actions for His sake, He has sympathy for you and takes you by the hand.*[467]

However, even this is not enough to express God's mercy, and later the Shaykh simply declares, "Allah shows mercy without a reason."[468] Such an emphasis has subsequently provided the basis for a tradition of tolerance within the Tijaniyya, for God's mercy or *rahma* is present everywhere in the creation, even among wrongdoers or non-Muslims.[469] Shaykh Ahmad Tijani once said, "Wrongdoing is only an accident where the sick person remains enveloped by the Love of his Creator; his fate is between the Hands of his Lord. No other except God will know how to declare his fate."[470] Consequently, the Shaykh

---

465   Jawahir, p. 47.
466   Jawahir, p. 50.
467   Jawahir, p. 47.
468   Jawahir, p. 47.
469   For some reported favorable Tijani views on Christians, see Abun-Nasr, The Tijaniyya, pp. 58-59.
470   Jawahir, quoted in Benabdellah, La Tijania, p. 110.

often urged his followers to "ignore the evil of people."[471] Such a general emphasis on tolerance or not delving into another's shortcomings has been expanded by some Tijani scholars to include those who reject Sufism or the Tijaniyya, and thus has implications for modem divisions between Sufis and anti-Sufis. Shaykh Hassan Cisse advises Tijanis not to attack those hostile to them in the manner they themselves are attacked, since "it is just ignorance" that allows some other Muslims to label Sufis or Tijanis as unbelievers. Such behavior for any Muslim, concludes the Shaykh, "is dangerous, and very sad."[472]

Shaykh Ahmad Tijani's emphasis on the mercy or grace of God situated within the context of emptiness of the self presents the classic juxtaposition between hope and fear of God. On the one hand, we find the Shaykh assuring his followers of the unending mercy of the Creator, but in the majority of correspondences, we find him encouraging them nonetheless in the fear of God. Critics of the Tijaniyya are quick to isolate his assurances of mercy of God or His salvation from the totality of his teachings.[473] In the context of the *Jawahir*'s cautioning of the aspirant against God's anger or even misguidance *(makr Allah)*, it must be admitted that this seems to make about as much sense as taking in isolation the Prophet's assurances of salvation for anyone who once uttered the profession of faith, "There is nothing worthy of worship but God" *(la ilaha ill-Allah)*, without considering the hadith that not even the Prophet will enter Paradise without the mercy of God.

In any case, Shaykh Ahmad Tijani was enthusiastic to proclaim, based on what the Prophet reportedly told him, the wonder of God's mercy to his followers. Those who took his *wird* (the Tijani litany) and loved him are thereby a beloved of

---

471   Jawahir, p. 191.

472   Interview with Shaykh Hassan Cisse, Medina Kaolack, Senegal, August, 2001.

473   See Triaud, "La Tijaniyya, voie infailible."

the Prophet and would not die before becoming one of God's saints *(wali)*.[474] Those who gazed upon the Shaykh's face on Mondays or Fridays would die in faith and would enter Paradise, since the Prophet promised he would not separate himself from the Shaykh on these days.[475]

Obviously, this last guarantee is vehemently rejected by anti-Tijanis. Ibn Mayaba, the author of one of the most well known anti-Tijani polemics in West Africa, declared this to be impossible since the Prophet's own uncle, Abu Lahab, most certainly saw the Prophet on these days but was himself cursed by God in the Qur'an. A classic Tijani response is presented by Muhammad Niasse (1929) who wrote that Abu Lahab was seeing the Prophet in his corporal nature as the son of Abdullah rather than in his nature as the Messenger of God.[476] Remember that Shaykh Ahmad Tijani declared himself to be a normal man, except to those who had love for God and His Messenger. The implication is that the Shaykh's declaration concerned those who perceived his proximity to the Prophet.

In any case, such statements were not unique to the Tijaniyya. The Prophet appeared to such saints as Abu Madyan, Ibn 'Arabi, Muhammad Zawawi and al-Nabulsi, to shake their hands and inform them that others who shook their hand, sometimes up to the seventh person, would be saved from

---

474   Jawahir, p. 54.

475   Jawahir, p. 56. The passage goes on to say that such a person's name would be written in gold and presented by the angels to the Prophet, just as if he had sent blessings on the Prophet on those days. Thus seeing the Shaykh's face is linked to sending blessings on the Prophet, which is probably why Monday and Friday are singled out, these days being known as the best days to send blessings on the Prophet. According to the Jawahir, similar assurances were given to Abd al-Qadir Jilani, Abd al-Rahman al-Tha'alabi and Mawlay Tuhami.

476   Ousmane Kane, "Muhammad Niasse (1881-1956) et sa replique contre le pamphlet anti-tijan de Ibn Mayaba," in Triaud and Robinson ed.s, La Tijaniyya, pp. 229-230.

Hellfire.[477] The idea of the Prophet informing a saint that those who saw him would be saved was also present in Morocco prior to the Tijaniyya among the Jazuliyya, Nasiriyya and Wazzaniyya orders.[478] The Egyptian Tijani Shaykh Muhsin Shalaby contextualizes such an idea by citing the hadith where a wrongdoer is granted Paradise simply for giving a thirsty dog some water, and pointing out that the mercy of God is such that it sometimes appears as if "Allah is using any excuse to send people to Paradise."[479.] In any case, Shaykh Hassan Cisse explains the possibility of Shaykh Ahmad Tijani's pronouncements by saying they came not from him, but were statements made by the Prophet himself. Unless one is willing to accuse the Shaykh of lying on behalf of the Prophet, despite his having knowledge of the hadith where the Prophet says anyone lying concerning him should prepare his seat in Hellfire, there is no choice but to accept the Prophet's announcements as they were reported by the Shaykh.[480]

Whatever Shaykh Ahmad Tijani's emphasis of God's mercy, it apparently never eclipsed his stress on the necessity of having fear of God. The Tijani disciple should therefore not "take the promise of salvation as a trick to be safe from the punishment of God for his sins." In this case, God would veil him from the remembrance of God's grace and its means of distribution through the Prophet and the saints. "If so, God clothes his heart in ignoring us until he maligns us, and if he maligns us, God makes him die an unbeliever... [his] heart must be [ever]

477   Jonathan Katz, Dreams, Sufism and Sainthood, pp. 224-226.

478   See Katz, Dreams, Sufism and Sainthood, pp. 226-227 and fii. 56, p. 226 ; also Adnani, "Reflexions sur la naissance de la Tijaniyya," pp. 29-30. The Prophet was supposed to have said of Muhammad ibn Nasir that anyone who had seen him, and then anyone who had seen who had seen him, up the twentieth person, God would save his body from Hellfire. The statement was made during Abd Allah al-Atiqi's (alive 1788) visionary experience of the Prophet, recorded in his Kitab al-Durra, see Katz, Dreams, Sufism and Sainthood, pp. 226-227.

479   Muhsin Shalaby, interview, Fes, Morocco, December, 2002.

480   Shaykh Hassan Cisse, interview, Rabat, Morocco, March, 2003.

fearful of the punishment of God."[481] Even those most beloved of God, according to the Shaykh, never stop fearing Him, "Because the Prophets and the Saints themselves, despite their elevated ranks, did not believe themselves sheltered from Divine anger and always strove in the purification of their souls."[482]

* * *

The idea of accessing God's grace through contact with the Prophet was understood by Shaykh Ahmad Tijani to have a relationship to a new era of Islamic history. The Shaykh seemed concerned that the knowledge of God's favor or grace, itself perhaps the most important inheritance from the Prophet, was in danger of obscuration by the corruption of the times. He was specifically anxious about the prevalence of sin and the Muslim's increasing inability to live according to God's command. He warned his disciples, "Know that nobody in these times can keep away from sin since it falls on human beings like heavy rain, but do acts of penitence, the most assured of which is *Salat al-Fatih*."[483] Elsewhere he urged his disciples to have patience with the corruption of the times in the following terms:

> *This time is one in which the bases of divine ordinance have been destroyed and it is beyond the capacity of any person to carry out God's command in every respect in this time, except those attired in knowledge of Him or who approach it. However, things being what [as] they have been described, and as the servant has no escape from that in which God has placed him, the gray is better than the black. Abstain from acting contrary to God's command as much as it is within your powers, and carry out His ordinance as much as possible; but do for yourself numerous acts of penitence day and night.*[484]

---

481   Jawahir, p. 56.
482   Ifadat al-Ahmadiyya, quoted in Samb, Tariqah Tidjaniyyah, p. 202.
483   Jawahir, quoted in Abun-Nasr, The Tijaniyya, p. 42.
484   Jawahir, p. 190. The translation is Abun-Nasr, The Tijaniyya, p. 42.

In such a time the saint, or "those attired in knowledge of Him," had a particularly important role to play. The saint, as was explained previously, was for Shaykh Ahmad Tijani the true inheritor of the Prophet, so his presence among the people, especially in difficult times, served as an opening to God's favor or grace that would not otherwise be available given the near impossibility of fulfilling Divine ordinance in such a time. The legal scholars were thus unable by themselves to pass on the Islamic message to the people, and the *Jawahir* asks the negatively rhetorical question, "The *'ulama* of today, are they capable of transmitting guidance to the people?"[485] The saints alone, due to their access to God's grace through their spiritual relationship with the Prophet, were capable of serving the people in this regard. The Shaykh was of course not implying the saints had the power to change the law to fit the new age, but only that his position as *ibn waqtihi*, the son of his time, required him to act within Divine ordinance "according to what his time requires"[486] in order to maintain access to God's grace.

It is tempting to conclude that what the Shaykh meant by the corruption of the times was the onset of modernity and the beginnings of non-Muslim colonial control of Muslim societies. However, even if Napoleon's conquest of Egypt in 1798 can be seen in hindsight as ushering in a new era for the Muslim world, it is doubtful Shaykh Ahmad Tijani was speaking of the encroaching age of European modernity when he spoke of the corruption of his age. There is no reference to the Europeans in the *Jawahir*, nor to any of the elements of European style modernity, such as increasing technological progress, secularization, urbanization, etc. More likely the Shaykh, as with many an Islamic reformer before him, saw his own time as the most recent, lowest state of deterioration from the time of the Prophet; a time whose corruption was itself a testament to the approaching End of Time. For Shaykh Ahmad Tijani, the most

485   Jawahir, quoted in Berque, L 'interieur du Maghreb, p. 250.
486   Jawahir, p. 161.

serious result of this decline was the disappearance of the people of knowledge who were capable of providing guidance to the Muslims.[487]

Such a notion of guidance or grace in a corrupt age defines the historical purpose the Shaykh saw his own *Tariqa Muhammadiyya* as playing from his own time until the Last Day. The fact that he believed that the *Mahdi* (a deliverer whose coming will precede the return of Jesus) would himself come from the ranks of the Tijaniyya[488] is evidence enough of his conception of the order's distinct historical role.

It is with such a notion of Divine mercy, grace or preference *(fadl)*, that is found the most valuable definition of the *Tariqa Muhammadiyya* as both an abstraction and an historical phenomenon. Thus, for Shaykh Ahmad Tijani, the *Tariqa Muhammadiyya* was a path of grace through contact with the enduring guiding spirit of the Prophet, seeing its culmination in the formation of the Tijaniyya order as a favor from God to face the difficulties of a world full of sin and increasingly bereft of knowledge.

---

487   Jawahir, p. 214.
488   Abun-Nasr, The Tijaniyya, p. 33.

Conclusion

This study has attempted to produce a closer, though not exhaustive, reading of primary texts to help clarify the understanding of the mysterious figure of Shaykh Ahmad Tijani and the nature of the *Tariqa Muhammadiyya* he left behind. Such an understanding is an important part of comprehending the character of Islam and Sufism on the eve of European conquest and the advent of the modem era in Muslim societies. The story of scholars such as Shaykh Ahmad Tijani helps to question the prevailing notions of Islam's eighteenth-century intellectual decline and the mistaken assumption of the invariable irreconcilibility between Sufism and Islamic "orthodoxy." Study of the founder of the Tijaniyya is also important given his order's central role in spreading Islam in nineteenth and twentieth-century Africa and on account of its continued pervasiveness in many areas of the world today. We have been concerned with understanding what the Shaykh actually said or did in isolation from the polemics that have often sprung up around his person and teachings, polemics that often serve more to obscure than to elucidate any genuine understanding of the Tijaniyya, and most certainly any understanding of how Tijanis themselves have perceived their Shaykh and their own identity as Muslims and Sufis.

Study of the most important primary text of the order, the *Jawahir al-Ma'ani,* has revealed a picture of a highly intelligent, benevolent and charismatic spiritual leader, well acquainted with the important personalities and events of his day. The primary subject of this work has been Shaykh Ahmad Tijani's contact with and ideological relationship to the tradition of scholarly Sufism that had culminated by the end of the eighteenth century through the development of the loosely defined phenomenon of the *Tariqa Muhammadiyya.* Reconstruction of the Shaykh's biography reveals his exchange with some of the more prominent movements of reform in both the Middle East proper and his native land of the Maghreb. He not only had contact with some of the important branches of the Shadhili tradition, such as the Jazuliyya, the Nasiriyya and the Wazzaniyya, orders representing a socially conscious, reform heritage of scholarly Sufism, but with the Egyptian Khalwatiyya of Mustafa al-Bakri. This later relationship linked Shaykh Ahmad Tijani to one of the central movements of renovation and scholarly renaissance in the eighteenth-century Muslim world. The Shaykh's teachers in this Khalwati tradition, Mahmud al-Kurdi and Muhammad al-Samman, were themselves foremost in the formulation and practice of the *Tariqa Muhammadiyya* phenomenon, and also had direct links to al-Bakri, who in turn inherited from Abd al-Ghani al-Nabulsi, the first to write a book situating the nomenclature of the *Tariqa Muhammadiyya* firmly within scholarly Sufism.

The biography of Shaykh Ahmad Tijani also reveals his close relationship to the Moroccan Sultan of the time, Mawlay Sulayman, who was himself, engaged in an important campaign of reform. The Sultan objected to certain practices of popular Sufism, emphasizing instead, on a traditional, scholarly form of Islam as it had come to be defined in the Maghrebi context. Thus, while the Sultan's movement was decidedly reform-minded, it ended in accentuating traditional scholarship both in the field of the Shariʻa, which meant for Morocco the affirmation of the Maliki school of jurisprudence, and in Sufism. It seems likely that the Sultan found in Shaykh Ahmad Tijani the epitome of the ideal Islamic scholar, balanced between knowledge of the Law and of Sufism, and himself became a member of Tijaniʼs *Tariqa Muhammadiyya*.

The Shaykhʼs own ideology closely mirrors the phenomenon of the *Tariqa Muhammadiyya* as it has been characterized by recent academic research, with a few important exceptions. This movement, it is recalled, has been characterized as having a number of elements: 1) an emphasis on the Sunna of the Prophet, leading to an objection to certain popular manifestations of Sufism and a de-emphasis of the *madhahib* (schools of jurisprudence), 2) prominence of the idea of the *Haqiqa Muhammadiyya* (Muhammadan Reality) in esoteric conceptualizations, leading to a from of spiritual concentration on the spirit of the Prophet and a deemphasis of the role of the shaykh in spiritual instruction, 3) stress on the dream and waking vision of the Prophet for transmission of knowledge and 4) a tendency to restrict the discipleʼs adherence to one preeminent *tariqa*.

We have seen that Shaykh Ahmad Tijani did indeed stress the external elements of the Prophetʼs Sunna, the *Haqiqa Muhammadiyya*, the waking vision of the Prophet and the need for exclusive affiliation to one *tariqa*. However, his emphasis on the Sunna cannot be said to have lead to a rejection of the Islamic legal tradition, or the *madhahib*, or the permissibility for free *ijtihad*, even if the Shaykh did articulate the ascendency of the Sunna and its best interpreters, the true scholars possessing both external and esoteric knowledge. His opinion on *ijtihad* restricted its performance to the absence of a clear text and warned against the exclusion of divergent interpretations, provided such interpretations were made by qualified scholars. Shaykh Ahmad Tijani also differed from the above characterization in the terms of the *Haqiqa Muhammadiyya*, since he did not see its existence as grounds to reject the importance of the shaykh-disciple relationship and the necessity of spiritual education *(tarbiyya)* at the hands of a living shaykh.

In general, Shaykh Ahmad Tijani's interpretation of the *Tariqa Muhammadiyya* seems more an accentuation (if of a slightly renovated version) of the tradition of Islamic scholarship in both the external field of the *Shari'a* and the esoteric field of *tassawuf* or Sufism. He urged his disciples to both respect the *fuqaha,* the "bearers of the Law," and the past saints of God. In both cases, he simply emphasized their connection to the essential source of all knowledge of God and His laws, the Prophet Muhammad himself. Of course, this was a double-edged sword, for those scholars who divorced themselves from following the Prophet, both internally and externally, were not to be considered capable of transmitting guidance to the Muslim community. However, Shaykh Ahmad Tijani's own conception of the forebearance, mercy or "grace" implicit in the Prophetic Sunna limited his denunciation or excommunication of diverging opinions or Muslims who were not following the Sunna in the ideal fashion.

The idea of Divine grace might be said to contain the Shaykh's essential contribution to the *Tariqa Muhammadiyya* phenomenon. Since the aspirant was incapable of satisfying God's commands (which did not mean he should not still try), he was only granted God's satisfaction through His grace. The *Tariqa Muhammadiyya* for Shaykh Ahmad Tijani thus was essentially a path of *Shukr,* or giving thanks to God for His favor or grace, the bestowal of which had nothing to do with the merits of the benificiary. The Shaykh bound the path of *Shukr* with the *Tariqa Muhammadiyya* by his detailing of how God's grace reached the creation through the state of pure worship God had bestowed on His most beloved Prophet Muhammad. Those who were best able to receive God's grace after the Prophet were the saints who were closest to the Prophet's spirit, an existent force even after the Prophet's death. The Seal, or most perfect, of the Saints was thus he who was the most beloved of the Prophet and whom God had marked with the stamp of the *Haqiqa Muhammadiyya*. The dispensation of God's grace in this way was not arbitrary, but came at a time when God's servants were increasingly incapable of fulfilling Divine ordinance due to the corruption of an age more and more bereft of true knowledge.

Shaykh Ahmad Tijani's own conception of the *Tariqa Muhammadiyya*, then, can best be summarized from the perspective of academic scholarship as having four elements:

1) Emphasis of the Prophetic Sunna and the grounding of Sufism within the Shari'a, where the Law obviously can come to affect the expression of Sufi practice, but where the Sufi scholar also can be provided direct access to the Law and become its most qualified interpretor.

2) The notion of the *Haqiqa Muhammadiyya* and the Prophet's integral role in the distribution of Divine knowledge, both in abstraction as the locus of Divine manifestation and tangibly through visionary contact with the Prophet's essential being *(dhat)*.

3) the ascendency of the *Tariqa Muhammadiyya* and the saint (Seal of the Saints) who comes to epitomize it, who bears the seal of the *Haqiqa Muhammadiyya*, thereby requiring exclusive affiliation over other Sufi orders and shaykhs.

4) the accentuation of God's preference or grace *(fadl)* on His Prophet, which provides access to Divine favor despite the corruption of the age and inability of the aspirant to fulfill Divine commands. This last element might be said to provide the Tijaniyya with its own notion of historical distinction.

Such a characterization of Shaykh Ahmad Tijani's thought in relationship to the *Tariqa Muhammadiyya* is not meant to

describe the whole of his doctrine as the founder of the Tijaniyya order, but it is hoped it will help to contextualize his life,
ideolgy and the emergence of his *tariqa*. It is not to be claimed
that such Sufis in the late eighteenth century as Shaykh Ahmad
Tijani always interpreted, or had contact with, the Islamic tradition in ways of which modem Salafist or other types of Muslim reformers would approve. However, it cannot be denied
that the *Tariqa Muhammadiyya,* as conceived by Shaykh Ahmad Tijani, affirms the essential relationship between Sufism
and the Islamic tradition. This link is given cogent expression
by Ahmad Sukayrij's characterization of Shaykh Ahmad Tijani
as the *muqaddam* (teacher or propagator) of the *Tariqa Muhammadiyya* while the Prophet is its real Shaykh.[489]

---

489   Adnani, "Les origines de la Tijaniyya," p. 47.

Epilogue: Reflections on the later spread of the Tijaniyya

The later spread of the Tijaniyya in the nineteenth century, as was the case with some of the other groups associated with the *Tariqa Muhammadiyya* phenomenon, has often found itself victimized by one of two polemics. Either the order is described, by those of the "Neo-Sufi" consensus, as one of reactionary, messianic Jihad against the European colonial mission or it becomes admidst the Arab nationalist or Salafist constructions, the collaborator with the infidel who betrayed the Arab nation to the European occupiers. That the Tijaniyya could be simultaneously appropriated by two opposite polemics, itself demonstrates the range of roles the order has played in the diverse societies in which it spread. However, the characterizations of the Tijaniyya within the context of Colonialism and Arab nationalism dertainly disguises a more complex picture of the order's societal integration.

The obvious protagonist of the Tijaniyya for followers of the "Neo-Sufi" consensus is the West African al-Hajj 'Umar al-Futi (or Tal). Al-Hajj 'Umar (1794-1864) of the Futa Toro region in modem Senegambia/Mali was a Tijani scholar of great renown who, on the way back from his Pilgrimage to Mecca (where he studied under the Tijani *khalifa* in the Hijaz and companion of Shaykh Ahmad Tijani, Muhammad Ghali), spread the Tijani order in some important regions of West Africa, such as Sokoto, where it is probable he initiated the kingdom's Emir, Muhammad Bello (d. 1837).[490] In 1852, his community of followers was attacked by a neighboring rival, helping to provoke him to lead a Jihad that was to temporarily establish an Islamic state in the Senegambia and Western Mali region. Towards the end of his campaign, he had begun to fight the French armies attempting to penetrate deeper into West Africa. Caught between the hostility of local rulers to the East and the French to the West, al-Hajj 'Umar died in battle in 1864 and his newly created state only lasted some twenty years before being dismantled by the French.[491]

Obviously the thought of armed and unified Muslim resistance to French colonial interests was a frightening prospect for the French, and the Jihad of al-Hajj 'Umar led to a certain hysteria among the colonial adminstrators against any kind of Muslim, especially Tijani, organization in West Africa well into the twentieth century. Despite the short-lived successes of Tijani jihadists such as Ma Ba Diakhou (d. circa 1870) and Lat Dior Diop (d. 1886) in Senegal after the demise of al-Hajj 'Umar,[4923] the tradition of West African Tijani Jihad quickly evolved into a withdrawal of the Tijani shaykhs from all but essential contact with the French. It was this later influence of a peaceful and scholarly Tijani elite, focused inwardly on the societies in which they lived, that was responsible for the large scale spread of Islam and the Tijaniyya that is today witnessed in West Africa. As one writer put it, "A small army of humble and unarmed marabouts won the final victory that had eluded Ma Ba's proud warriors."[493] The activity of Tijani scholars in

---

490   Hunwick, "Introduction to the Tijani path," p. 18.
491   David Robinson, The Holy War of Umar Tal, the Western Sudan in the midnineteenth century (Oxford: Clarendon Press, 1985), p. 316.
492   Leonardo Villalon, Islamic Society and State Power in Senegal (London: Cambridge University Press, 1995), pp. 62, 67.
493   Martin Klein, Islam and Imperialism in Senegal, Sine-Saloum 1847-

West Africa, as mentioned in the Introduction, has led some to remark that, "It is this Tijani push that Islamicized Africa. And if there had not been this [European colonial] occupant, all of Africa would have been Islamicized."[494]

But such a narrative of the ultimately peaceful spread of Islam in West Africa through the hands of the Tijaniyya makes little sense unless the nature of al-Hajj 'Umar's legacy as understood by the colonial or "Neo-Sufi" misconception is itself reinterrogated. That the famous jihadist was first and foremost a scholar of great intelligence and spiritual charisma is evident from any study of his seminal work, the *Kitab al-Rimah*. Indeed, most of the literature concerning the Tijaniyya in West Africa has neglected the scholarly aspect of the famous Tijani leaders, "ignoring their intellectual underpinnings as well as their links with wider and deeper streams of Islamic thought."[495] The result is that the nineteenth-century West African Tijani leaders are too easily glossed over as reactionary and even cultic local organizers marginalized from the larger context of the Islamic and Sufi traditions.

The role of the Tijaniyya in nineteenth-century Algeria provides the primary fodder for the narrative of the Tijaniyya's betrayal of the Arab nation, so important within the Salafist and Arab nationalist discourse. But deeper study of this story also complicates the polemic, this time of the order's supposed isolated elitism and subservience to French authorities being the "most salient aspects of the history of the Tijaniyya order in the Maghrib."[496] The Tijaniyya in Algeria, mostly under the leadership of Shaykh Ahmad Tijani's son,

---

1914 (Stanford: Stanford University Press, 1968), p. 206.

494   Abdelaziz Benabdellah citing Chakib Arsalane, The Presence of the Islamic Civilization, and Maury Bonnet, L'Islam et la Chretiente. See Benabdellah's interview with the Senegalese daily, Le Soleil (www.abdelaziz-benabdellah.org, date not included in reprinting).

495   Hunwick, "An Introduction to the Tijani path," p. 17.

496   Abun-Nasr, The Tijaniyya, p. 98.

Muhammad al-Saghir (d. 1853), is blamed for manipulating the turmoil of the French occupation to attempt to build an independent Tijani state, and also for supporting the French against the native Algerian jihad of Emir Abd al-Qadir.[497] A recent letter discovered in the Tijani zawiya at Tammasin, Algeria, provides the basis for a reexamination of this narrative. The letter dates from 1839 and follows the Emir's seige of Ain Madi in order to secure the loyalty and tribute of this Tijani stronghold. In it, the Emir writes to Muhammad al-Saghir, "I have just discovered the truth and know that our differences simply and surely are only [the result of] a dissension provoked by people."[498] Filali asserts that the "people" mentioned here were meant to refer to French spies working within the Emir's forces to prevent cooperation between the Sufi orders. This viewpoint is to some extent supported by the recorded statements of the French commanding general in Algeria, General Amaud, who wrote that if the Emir had succeeded in "making enter into his party the Tijaniyya, who were disposed of a large moral force, they would have without doubt created for us a very serious obstacle."[499] As for Muhammad al-Saghir, his true intentions seem to have been simply to stay out of any conflict, and he once wrote the Emir, "I am neither an enemy nor a rebel, but a simple brother who is only occupying himself with spiritual things; I want to avoid all opposition with the princes to the extent possible. I confirm again my peaceful intentions."[500]

Although the polemics surrounding al-Hajj 'Umar and Muhammad al-Saghir come to nearly opposite conclusions, they serve to conceal a similar narrative. In both West and North Africa, the spread of the Tijaniyya was the work of large-

---

497   Abun-Nasr, The Tijaniyya, p. 68.
498   Kamel Filali, "Le Differend Qadiriyya-Tijaniyya," in Revue d'Histoire Maghrebine (24/87-88, 1997), p. 313.
499   Filali, "Le Differend Qadiriyya-Tijaniyya," pp. 311-312.
500   Filali, "Le Differend Qadiriyya-Tijaniyya," p. 309.

ly peaceful, charismatic and independently minded scholars whose professed motivation was the establishment and renewal of the "path of the Prophet," the *Tariqa Muhammadiyya*.

Any discussion of the later spread of the Tijaniyya cannot escape the mention of of the Senegalese Shaykh Ibrahim Niasse (1900- 1975). Shaykh Ibrahim was appointed *khalifa* of the Tijaniyya by Ahmad Sukayrij during his 1936 visit to Morocco.[501] It might be estimated that over half of all the Tijanis in the world today trace their lineage through him,[502] and there is little doubt that his loosely organized *Jama'at al-Fayda* (community of the flood, also known as the *Jama'at Nasr al-Din)* became "the largest single Muslim organization in West Africa."[503] Shaykh Ibrahim epitomized the peaceful, independent Tijani scholar committed to renewing the path of the Prophet in both its external and esoteric applications. As was mentioned in the Introduction, he was named *Shaykh al-Islam* by the Azhar mosque in Cairo (where in 1961 he became the first black African to lead the Friday prayer).[504]

---

501   John Paden, Religion and Political Culture in Kano (Berkely and Los Angeles: UC Press, 1973), p. 97-98. Shaykh Ibrahim also had his status as khalifa of Shaykh Ahmad Tijani confirmed by the muqaddam of the Tijani zawiya in Fes, Abd al- Salam al-Sa'id. After his meeting with Sukayrij, his most important silsilah to the founder became: Shaykh Ahmad Tijani - Ali al-Tamasani - Ahmad al-Abdalawi - Ahmad Sukayrij - Shaykh Ibrahim Niasse.

502   A newspaper article estimates the number of Shaykh Ibrahim's followers at sixty million (see "Senegalese Imam in Hyde Park," West Africa (London), 16 November 1987, p. 2281). Some estimates of the number of Tijanis in the world put it at 120 million (Ashaki Taha-Cisse, "The Tariqa Tijaniyya," p. 1). It is impossible to verify either number. Shaykh Hassan Cisse believes Shaykh Ibrahim's followers to comprise eighty percent of all Tijanis, since those who follow him comprise nearly all the Tijani populations of Nigeria, Niger, Ghana, Mali, Mauritania and nearly every other West African country.

503   Mervyn Hiskett, The Development of Islam in West Africa (London and New York: Longman, 1984), p. 287.

504   Ousmane Kane, "Shaikh al-Islam al-Hajj Ibrahim Niasse," in Robinson and Triaud ed.s, Le Temps des Marabouts (Paris: Karthala, 1997), p. 309.

He was also appointed a member of the academy of research at the Azhar University, named secretary general of the World Islamic League based in Mecca and vice-president of the World Muslim Congress founded in Karachi, Pakistan.[505] He had personal relations with some of the prominent Muslim and African nationalist leaders of the day, such as Jamal Abd al-Nasser (Egypt), Kwame Nkumah (Ghana), Sekou Toure (Guniea) and Leopold Senghor (Senegal).[506]

As an Imam and propagator of Islam in many non-Muslim areas in West Africa, Shaykh Ibrahim evidenced the clear accentuation of the external Sunna of the Prophet, sometimes in transcendance of the Islamic legal tradition, permitting him the use of scholarly *ijtihad* that is characteristic of the *Tariqa Muhammadiyya* phenomenon. He once wrote, "If I am asked what is your *madhhab*, and who is your beloved, I will definitely answer that they are the Prophet."[50718] He is also widely quoted as having said, "If the best of mankind, the Prophet is moving, even I shall follow him step by step; and the day he stops, from there I shall never move."[508]

Nevertheless, like Shaykh Ahmad Tijani, Shaykh Ibrahim was trained and situated his perspective of Islamic law largely within the tradition of the *madhhab*, which in his case also was the Maliki School. However, Shaykh Ibrahim made *ijtihad* on a few key issues that demonstrated his independence from *taqlid* of the legal tradition. He stressed, contrary to the Maliki practice in North and West Africa, that the Sunna of the Prophet was to pray with the hands folded on the chest (*qabd*), to raise the hands before and after bowing (*raf-al-ya-*

505   John Paden, Religion and Political Culture in Kano, pp. 144-145; Shaykh Hassan Cisse, Shaykh Ibrahim Niasse, Revivalist of the Sunnah (New York, 1984), p. 19.

506   Kane, "Shaikh al-Islam," p. 309; interview with Shaykh Hassan Cisse, Medina Kaolack, August, 1997.

507   Cisse, Spirit of Good Morals, p. i.

508   Cisse, Revivalist of the Sunnah, p. 14.

dayn) and to say the *basmallah* (in the name of Allah the Most Compassionate the Most Merciful) out loud before beginning recitation when the prayer is to be said out loud.[509]

Shaykh Ibrahim also continued Shaykh Ahmad Tijani's stress on the esoteric elements of the *Tariqa Muhammadiyya*, all the while situated within the tradition of earlier Sufism. As previously mentioned, he was particularly famous for emphasizing the importance of the *shaykh al-tarbiyya* in undergoing spiritual training to attain knowledge of God (*ma'arifa*). He also elaborated on principals such as the *Haqiqa Muhammadiyya*, the vision of the Prophet and sainthood.[510]

He especially emphasized the idea of God's grace in a difficult time through the idea of *fayda*, meaning flood or overabundance. Shaykh Ibrahim quoted Shaykh Ahmad Tijani's own prediction of the coming of the *fayda* in his community to support the idea: "A *fayda* will overwhelm my companions to the point that people with enter our path in multitudes. This *fayda* will come at a time when mankind will be in a state of utmost difficulties."[511]

In 1930, at the time of the worldwide Great Depression, Shaykh Ibrahim publicized his claim to possess the *faydat al-Tijaniyya*. Essentially the idea seems to closely mirror Shaykh Ahmad Tijani's own ideas about the flux of Divine grace, mercy and love passing through the Prophet to God's creation. Of course, the highest expression of this love was God's permitting His creation to know Him. Shaykh Ibrahim presented a parable to conceptualize the flow of Divine gnosis to the creation through the intermediary of the Prophet and the saints;

509   Cisse, Revivalist of the Sunnah, p. 15.
510   Shaykh Ibrahim Niasse, Dawawin al-sit (Dakar: Muhammad Ma'mun Niasse, unknown date); Shaykh Ibrahim Niasse, Najum al-Huda (Rabat, 1381 A.H.); also interviews with Shaykh Hassan Cisse.
511   Abu Bakr 'Aniq Khadir al-Tijani, Ifadat al-Murid, chapter 4; quoted in Shaykh Hassan Cisse, Revivalist of the Sunnah, p. 11.

God is said to be a well, "whose Being is continuous and without end;" knowledge of God is the water, "so precious it cannot be thrown away and yet cannot be put back into a well already overflowing;" the Prophet is a bucket "that never wants repair" drawing the water from the well; Shaykh Ahmad Tijani is the "tireless worker who continually draws water from the well;" and Shaykh Ibrahim himself is a basin next to the well, "an extraordinary spiritual adept who has received so much in the way of Divine Gnosis that he must communicate this Gnosis to others or it will overflow."[512]

The emergence of Shaykh Ibrahim also helped to develop Shaykh Ahmad Tijani's own vision of his order's role of historical distinction in a corrupt age. Shaykh Ibrahim has thus been described as manifesting "the possibility of attaining spiritual perfection in the modem age."[513]

---

512   Parable related by Shaykh Ibrahim Niasse to Ibrahim Mahmud Diop and quoted in Shaykh Hassan Cisse, Revivalist of the Sunnah, pp. 11-12.
513   Shaykh Hassan Cisse, Revivalist of the Sunnah, p. 15.

Appendix:

Some Prayers of Shaykh Ahmad Tijani

The following are prayers that are all found in Shaykh Tija-ni's *Ahzab wa Awrad,* a book of common litanies the Shaykh encouraged his followers to do. The exception is the second prayer in the series, which I have translated directly from the *Jawahir al-Ma 'ani.* All the others from the *Ahzab wa Awrad* are translated in Constance Padwick's *Muslim Devotions,* except for the first prayer which is translated in George Appleton's *The Oxford Book of Prayer.* I have reserved the right to make minor alterations in the translations based on my copy of the *Ahzab wa Awrad.*

Prayer from "Forgiveness for all Sins."

O my God, my unworthiness is clear enough to You. The state I am in is not concealed from You. My request is that I might draw near to You, that I might have Your directive. Guide me then to Yourself by Your own light. Make me to stand in the truth of servanthood between Your hands.

My prayer to You is through the hiddeness of Your gentleness, the gentleness of Your way of dealing, through the very beauty of Your elusiveness, through the greatness of Your might and the utter secret of Your power, by all that is untold in Your transcendence.

I have taken Your Name for my citadel and pleaded the intercession of Your messenger Muhammad – the blessing and peace of God be upon him.

O my God, draw me to Yourself, You my Lord, my Master. Nurture me, that I may pass away from myself into You. Let me not be ambushed in myself, hindered and held in the world of sense. Make me pure in word and deed.

O God, You clothe the hearts of those who understand in the light that is divine where angels cannot lift their heads, so overwhelming is the omnipotent glory, You have said in the decree of Your mighty Book and in Your words from eternity: *"Call upon Me and I will hear you and answer."* O God, answer us, for what we have remembered and what we have forgotten. Hear our cry of Your grace. Amen, Amen, Amen, You who say to anything: "Be" and it is.

"Ya Man Azhahara al-Jameel"

O One who has made manifest what is beautiful, and concealed what is ugly,

Who has not taken us for our crimes, nor snatched away the veil (covering our faults),

O One who is prodigious in pardon,

Splendid in transcendence,

Expansive in forgiveness, hands outstretched in mercy

O One who hears every intimate discourse, who ends every complaint

O Bountiful in remission, Great in bestowal O Refuge for stumblers

O source of unearned blessing;

O my Lord, 0 my Master, O my Protector,

O Purpose for my longing:

I ask that You not disfigure my character by the affliction of the world

Or by the punishment of the Fire.

Other prayers expressing humility and asking for forgiveness.

O Lord, endow me with a lowly, humble, prostrate heart, and a weeping eye ... and sincere acceptable repentance.

My God, You are the Forgiver and I the wicked one. Does any one, save the Most Forgiving, show mercy to the wicked?

O God, You have commanded us to call on You and have promised that You will answer. And now we have called on You according to Your command, answer us then, according to Your promise.

You are worthy of my thanks for answering my call when I lift up my voice calling, and when I whisper to You in longing, and when I call to You in humiliation and sincere supplication, and when I look to You for hope. Indeed, I find You sufficient.

Our God, it was You who moved and again stilled every good and every evil that came into existence. In Your power is the loosing and binding of all things. In Your hand and through Your will are the disposal of fate and the predetermination of decree. And You have caused us to stand at Your door and we seek the protection of Your Majesty. We stand at Your threshold asking for help through You.

Prayers expressing love for the Prophet Muhammad

Make him to us a spirit and the very secret of our worship. And make his love to us a food aiding us to magnify him. And make our magnifying him, life in our hearts by which I may arise and with its aid make mention of him and make mention of his Lord.

At the door of the best of creation my purpose has stationed me, from my knowledge that the chosen one is generous in succor. I come, bringing no knowledge and no piety, rather all is defilement, my Lord, with me.

Invoking the Glory of God

Glory to Him who girds Himself with might.

Glory to Him who wraps Himself in greatness.

Glory to Him who is unique in His soleness.

Glory to Him who is veiled in light.

Glory to Him who quells His servants with death.

O Light of Light who illumines the obscurity of non-being with the effulgence of Your Light, make Your Light the lamp of my subconscious being and of my mind and my soul and spirit and heart and body and all of me and each part of me, until I shall be only light and flooded with the Light of Your Unity.

Bibliography

Primary Sources

Abayawo, Abubakar Sadiq Yusef, *Toriqat Tijaniyat, the Way of. Allah and His Messenger from the Holy Quran and Traditions of the Prophet (S.A.W.).* Ilorin, Nigeria: Medinat Faedat Tijaniyyah, unknown date.

Barada, Ali Harazem al-, *Jawahir al-Ma'ani wa bulugh al-amani.* Cairo: Dar al-Fikr, 2001.

Bey, Ali, *The Travels of Ali Bey, Volume I.* London: Longman, 1816.

Cisse, Shaykh Hassan 'Ali, *Sincere Advice.* New York, M.I.l Publishing, 2000.

---- *Translation and Commentary of the Spirit of Good Morals by Shaykh of Islam Shaykh Ibrahim Niasse.* Michigan: The African American Islamic Institute, 1998.

Cornell, Vincent, *The Way of Abu Madyan: the Works of Abu Madyan Shu'ayb.* Cambridge: Islamic Texts Society, 1996.

Futi, al-Hajj Umar al-, *Kitab al-Rimah.* Cairo: Dar al-Fikr, 2001.

Ghazali, Abu Hamid al-, *Jawahir al-Qur'an.* Translated Muhammad Abdul Quasem, *The Jewels of the Qur'an.* Bangi, Malaysia: Quasem, 1977.

---- *Remembrance of Death and the Afterlife.* Translated TJ. Winter, Cambridge: Islamic Texts Society, 1989.

Houdas, Octave V., *Le Maroc de 1631 a 1812, extrait de l'ouvrage de Abd al-Qasim ibn Ahmad al-Zayyani (d. 1833).* Amsterdam: Philo Press, 1969.

Ibn al-' Arabi, *The Bezels of Wisdom.* Translated R. W. J. Austin. New York: Paulist Press, 1980.

---- *Les Illuminations de la Mecque, textes choisis.* Trans. Michel Chodkiewicz. Paris: Sinbad, 1988.

Ibn al-Farid, 'Umar, *Diwan Ibn al-Farid.* Fes: al-Bilabil al-Batha', unknown date.

Ibn al-Sabbagh, *Durrat al-Asrar wa Tuhfat al-Abrar.* Translated Elmer Douglas, *The Mystical Teachings of al-Shadhili, including his life, prayers, letters and followers.* Albany: SUNY Press, 1993.

Ibn Sa'ih, Muhammad Al-Arabi, *Bughyat al-Mustafid.* Cairo: Sharakat Maktab Mustafa al-Babi, 1959.

Jabarti, Abd al-Rahman al-, *History of Egypt.* Trans, and ed. by Thomas Philipp and Moshe Perlmann. Stuttgart: Franz Steiner ' Verlag, 1994.

Jilani, Abd al-Qadir, *Futuh al-Ghaib: Revelations of the Unseen.* Trans. M. Aftab-ud-Din Ahmad. New Delhi: Kitab Bhavan, 1998.

---- *The Secret of Secrets.* Translated Tosun al-Helveti. Cambridge: Islamic Text Society, 1992.

Keller, Nuh Ha Mim, *Reliance of the Traveller of Ahmad ibn Naqib al-Misri.* Maryland: Amana, 1991.

Kinberg, Leah, *Ibn Abi al-Dunya: Morality in the Guise of Dreams, a Critical Edition of Kitab al-Manam.* Leiden: Brill, 1994.

McCarthy, Richard, *The Theology of al- 'Ash 'ari: The Arabic texts of al-Ash 'ari's Kitab al-Luma ' and Risalat Istihsan al-Khawdfi 'Ilm al- Kalam, with briefly annotated translations, and Appendices containing material pertinent to the study of al-Ash'ari,* Beirut: Imprimerie Catholique, 1953.

Nabulsi, Abd al-Ghani al-, *Ta'teer al-anam ta'bccr al-Manan.* Beirut, Dar al-Kutub, 1997.

Nawawi, Imam, *Riyad al-Salihin.* Translated Muhammad Zafrulla Khan, *Gardens of the Righteous.* New York: Olive Branch Press, 1975.

Neveu, Francois Edouard de, *Ordres Religieux chez les Musulmans de l'Algerie.* Paris: A. Guyot, 1846.

Niasse, Ibrahim, *Jawahir al-Risala.* Senegal, 1390 A.H. (1970).

---- *Kashf al- 'Ilbas 'an al-Khatm Abi al- 'Abbas.* Cairo, 2001.

---- "Lumieres sur la Tijaniyya et les Tijan." Trans. Gane Samb Lo, Dakar: GARSIS, unknown date.

Radtke, Bemd, and John 0'Kane, *The Concept of Sainthood in Early Islamic Mysticism:two works by al-Hakim al-Tirmidhi; an annotated translation with introduction.* Surrey (England): Curzon, 1996.

---- and O'Kane, Vikor and O'Fahey, *The Exoteric Ahmad Ibn Idris : A Sufi's Critique of the Madhahib and the Wahhabis: four Arabic texts with translation and commentary.* Lieden: Brill, 2000.

Razi, Najm al-din, *The Path of God's Bondsmen from Origin to Return.* Trans. Hamid Algar. New York: Caravan Books, 1982.

Sail, Ibrahim, *Le Guide du parfait Tijani aspirant a la perfection.* Beirut: al-Bouraq, 1999.

---- *La Prophetie, la Saintete et leur fruits.* Dakar: Multi-Services-

Excellence G.I.E., 1997.

Samb, Amadou Makhtar, *Introduction a la Tariqah Tidjaniyya ou Voie Spirituelle deCheikh Ahmad Tidjani.* Dakar: Imprimerie Saint- Paul, 1994.

Shinqiti, Ahmad al-Amin, *Al-Futuhat al-Rabbaniyya fi al-Tariqa al- Ahmadiyya al-Tijaniyya,* in Muhammad al-Tasafawi al-Tijani, *Al- Fath al-Rabbani fima mahtaj ilayhi al-murid al-Tijani.* Casablanca: Dar al-Kitab, unknown date.

Sijilmasi, Ahmad ibn al-Mubarak Lamati al-, *Kitab al-Ibriz fi kalam sayyidi 'Abdal-'Aziz.* Beirut: Dar al-Kutub, 1998.

Sufyani, al-Tayyib al-, *Ifadat al-Ahmadiyya li murid al-sa'ada wal- abdiyya.* Edited and commentary by Muhammad al-Hafiz. Cairo: Khairiya, unknown date.

Sukayrij, Ahmad, *Kashf al-Hijab.* Casablanca: Dar al-Kitab, unknown date.

Taha-Cisse, Ashaki H., "The Tariqa Tijaniyya: a means of approach to Allah." New York: African American Islamic Institute, 1992.

Tijani, Shaykh Ahmad al-, *Ahzab wa Awrad al-Qutb al-Rabbani wal-'arif al-Samadani.* Casablanca: Dar al-Rashad al-Haditha, 2001.

---- Document of unknown title concerning the *shaykh-mu-rid* relationship. Copy from the private collection of Shaykh Hassan Cisse.

Tijani, Salah al-din al-, *Kashf al-Ghuyum 'an ba'd israr al-Qutb al- Muktum.* Cairo: Dar al-Taysir, 1999.

Tijani Zawiya of Heliopolis, "Ithbat jawaz ru'ya sayyidina rasulullah salla Allahu aleihi wa salam fi al-yaqzha ba'da intiqalihi ila al-rafiq al-'ala" ("The proof of the permissibility of seeing our master the Messenger of God, the blessings and peace of God upon him, in a waking state after his passage to the Most High Companion."). Cairo, Ramadan, 1422 (2002).

Tishiti, 'Ubayda ibn Muhammad al-Saghir al-Shinqiti al-, *Mizab al- Rahmat al-Rabbaniyya.* Beirut: Dar al-'Ilm, 1973

Secondary Sources

Abdellah, A. Dedoud Ould, "Le passage au sud: Muhammad al- Hafiz et son heritage," in Triaud and Robinson ed.s, *La Tijaniyya, Une Confrerie musulmane a la conquete de l'Afrique.* Paris: Karthala, 2000.

Abu Habib, Sa'di, *Hayat Jalal al-Din al-Suyuti.* Damascus: Dar al- Manahil, 1993.

Abun-Nasr, Jamil M., *A History of the Maghreb.* Cambridge: Cambridge University Press, 1975.

---- *The Tijaniyya, A Sufi Order in the Modern World.* London: Oxford University Press, 1965.

Adams, Charles, *Islam and Modernism in Egypt, a Study of the Modem Reform Movement Inaugurated by Muhammad 'Abduh.* London: Oxford University Press, 1933.

Adnani, Jillali El, "Les origines de la Tijaniyya: quand les premiers disciples se mettent a parler," in Triaud and Robinson ed.s, *La Tijaniyya, Une Confrerie musulmane a la conquete de VAfrique.* Paris: Karthala, 2000.

---- "Reflexions sur la naissance de la Tijaniyya. Emprunts et surencheres," in Triaud and Robinson ed.s, *La Tijaniyya, Une*

Confrerie musulmane a la conquete de l'Afrique. Paris: Karthala, 2000.

Andre, Capitaine P.J., *L'is lam noir.* Paris: Geuthner, 1924.

Azmy, Ahmad al-, *Al-Tariqa al-Tijaniyya fi al-Maghrib w'al-Sudan al-Gharbi khilal al-qarn al-tisi '- 'ashr al-mayladi.* Muhammadiyya, Morocco: Matbi'a Fadala, 2000.

Baldick, Julian, *Imaginary Muslims: the Uwaysi Sufis of Central Asia.* London: I.B. Tauris, 1993.

Behrman, Lucy, *Muslim Brotherhoods and Politics in Senegal,* Cambridge: Harvard University Press, 1970.

Benabdallah, Abdelaziz, *La Tijania: une Voie Spirituelle et Sociale.* Marakech: Al Quobba Zarqua, 1998.

---- *Le Soufisme Afro-Maghrebin aux XIXe et XXe siecles.* Rabat:

Media Strategie, 1995.

Berque, Jacques, *L'Interieur du Maghreb XV-XIX siecle.* Paris: Editions Gallimard, 1978.

---- *Al-Yousi, Problemes de la Culture Marocaine au XVII siecle.* Paris: Mouton, 1958.

Bousbina, Said, "Les merites de la Tijaniyya d'apres Rimah d'al- Hajj 'Umar," *in Islam et Societes au Suddu Sahara.,* no. 3, 1989.

Brenner, Louis, "Sufism in Africa in the Seventeenth and Eighteenth Centuries, " *Islam et Societes au Sud du Sahara,* no. 2, May 1988.

---- *West African Sufi, The Religious Heritage and Spiritual Search of Cemo Bokar SaalifTaal.* London: C. Hurst & Co. Ltd., 1984.

Brown, Kenneth, "Profile of a Nineteenth-Century Moroccan Scholar," in Keddie ed., *Scholars, Saints and Sufis: Muslim Religious Institutions in the Middle East since 1500.* Berkely: University of California Press, 1972.

Buehler, Arthur F., *Sufi Heirs of the Prophet, the Indian Naqshbandiyya and the Rise of the Mediating Sufi Shaykh.* Columbia, South Carolina: University of South Carolina Press, 1998.

Burke, Edmund III, "The Moroccan 'Ulama, 1869-1912," in Keddie ed., *Scholars, Saints and Sufis: Muslim Religious Institutions in the Middle East since 1500.* Berkely: University of California Press, 1972.

Callaway, Barbara and Creevey, Lucy, *The Heritage of Islam: Women, Religion and Politics in West Africa.* Boulder: Lynne Rienner, 1994.

Chatalier, A. Le-, *Les Confreries Religieux Musulmans.* Paris: E. Leroux, 1887.

Chih, Rachida, "Les debuts d'une tariqa, la Halwatiyya," in Chich and Gril ed.s, *Le Saint and Son Milieu, ou Comment lire les sources hagiographiques.* Cairo: IF AO, 2000.

Chittick, William, *Faith and Practice of Islam.* Albany: SUNY Press, 1992.

---- "Ibn 'Arabi and His School," in Seyyed Hossein Nasr ed., *Islamic Spirituality, Manifestations*. New York: Crossroads, 1991.

---- *Imaginal Worlds: Ibn al-'Arabi and the problem of religious diversity.* Albany: SUNY Press, 1994.

---- *The Sufi Path of Knowledge, Ibn al- 'Arabi's Metaphysics of Imagination.* Albany: SUNY Press, 1989.

Chodkiewicz, Michel, *Emir Abd el-Kader, Ecrits spirituels.* Paris: Editions du Seuil, 1992.

---- *An Ocean Without Shore, Ibn 'Arabi, The Book, and the Law.* Albany: SUNY Press, 1993.

---- *Seal of the Saints, Prophethood and Sainthood in the Doctrine of Ibn al-'Arabi.* Cambridge: Islamic Texts Society, 1993.

Cisse, Shaykh Hassan 'Ali, *Shaykh Ibrahim Niasse, Revivalist of the Sunnah.* New York: Tariqa Tijaniyya of New York, 1984.

Clancy-Smith, Julia, *Rebel and Saint, Muslim Notables, Populist Protest, Colonial Encounters: Algeria and Tunisia, 1800-1904.* Berkeley: University of California Press, 1997.

Clarke, Peter, *West Africa and Islam.* London : Edward Arnold, 1982.

Corbin, Henry, *Imagination Creatrice dans le Soufisme d'Ibn Arabi.* Paris: Flammarion, 1958.

Cornell, Vincent, *Realm of the Saint: Power and Authority in Moroccan Sufism.* Austin: University of Texas Press, 1998.

Danner, Victor, "The Shadhiliyyah and North African Sufism," in Seyyed Hossein Nasr ed., *Islamic Spirituality, Manifestations.* New York: Crossroads, 1991.

De Jong, Frederick, "Mustafa Kamal al-Din al-Bakri (1688-1749): Revival and Reform of the Khalwatiyya Tradition?" in Levtzion and Voll ed.s, *Eighteenth-Century Renewal and Reform in Islam.* Syracuse, New York: Syracuse University Press, 1987.

DeLong-Bas, Natana, *Wahhabi Islam: from Rrevival and Reform to Globlal Jihad.* New Yourk: Oxford UP, 2004.

Depont, Octave, and Coppolani, X., *Les Conferies Religieuses Musulmanes.* Algiers, 1897.

Dirks, Nicholas, "History as a Sign of the Modem," in, *Public Culture.* Vol. 2, No. 2, Spring 1990.

Doi, Abdur-Rahman Ibrahim, "Sufism in Africa," in Seyyed Hossein Nasr ed., *Islamic Spirituality, Manifestations.* New York: Crossroads, 1991.

Eikelman, David, *Moroccan Islam: traditions and society in a pilgrimage center.* Austin: University of Texas Press, 1976.

Fahd, Toufic, *La Divination Arabe.* Leiden: Brill, 1966.

---- "The Dream in Medieval Islamic Society," in Grunebaum and Caillois eds., *The Dream and Human Societies. Berkeley and Los Angeles'.* UC Press, 1966.

Filali, Kamel, "Le Differend Qadiriyya-Tijaniyya en Algerie," in *Revue d'Histoire Maghrebine.* 24/87-88, 1997, pages 301-313.

Friedlander, Shams, "A Note on the Khalwatiyya-Jarrahiyyah Order," in Seyyed Hossein Nasr ed., *Islamic Spirituality, Manifestations.* New York: Crossroads, 1991.

Gellner, Ernest, *Muslim Society.* Cambridge: Cambridge University Press, 1981.

Geoffroy, E., "Le traite de soufisme d'un disciple d'Ibn Tay-miyya : Ahmad 'Imad al-din al-Wasiti (m. 1311)." *Studia Islamica* 82 (1995).

Gibb, H.A.R., *Mohammadanism: an historical survey.* London and New York: Oxford University Press, 1949.

Goldziher, Ignaz, "The Appearance of the Prophet in Dreams," in *Journal of the Royal Asiatic Society.* London, 1912, pages 503-509.

Gouda, Yehia, *Dreams and their meanings in the Old Arab Tradition.* New York: Vantage Press, 1991.

Gran, Peter, *Islamic Roots of Capitalism: Egypt, 1760-1840.* Cairo: American University in Cairo Press, 1999.

Gray, Christopher, "The Rise of the Niassene Tijaniyya, 1875 to the Present," *Islam et Societes au sud du Sahara.* Volume 2, May, 1988, pages 34-60.

Green, A.H., "A Tunisian Reply to a Wahhabi Proclamation: Texts and Contexts," in Green ed., *In Quest of an Islamic Humanism.* Cairo: AUC Press, 1984.

Grunebaum, G.E. Von, "Introduction, The Cultural Function of the Dream as Illustrated by Classical Islam," in Grunebaum and Caillois ed., *The Dream and Human Societies.* Berkely and Los Angeles: UC Press, 1966.

Hamet, Ismael, *Histoire du Maghreb.* Paris: Editions Leroux, 1923.

Hiskett, Mervyn, "The Community of Grace and its opponents, the rejectors," in *African Language Studies,* no. 17, 1980, pages 99-140.

---- *The Development of Islam in West Africa.* London and New York: Longman, 1984.

Hoffman, Valerie, "Annihilation in the Messenger of God: The Development of a Sufi Practice," *International Journal of Middle East Studies,* v.31, 1999.

Hunwick, John, "An Introduction to the Tijani Path: Being an Annoted Translation of the Chapter Headings of the *Kitab al-Rimah* of Al-Hajj 'Umar," in *Islam et Societes au Sud du Sahara.* No. 6, 1992.

Hutson, Alaine S., "The Development of Women's Authority in the Kano Tijaniyya, 1894-1963," in *Africa Today.*

Izutsu, Toshihiko, *The Structure of the Ethical Terms in the Koran, A Study in Semantics.* Japan, 1959.

Jabre, Farad, *La notion de la Marifa chez Ghazali.* Beirut: Editions les lettres orientales, 1958.

Joffe, George, "Maghribi Islam and Islam in the Maghrib, the Eternal Dichotomy," in Westerlund and Rosander eds., *African Islam and Islam in Africa, Encounters between Sufis and Islamists.* Athens: Ohio University Press, 1997.

Kane, Ousmane, "La Confrerie 'Tijaniyya Ibrahimiyya' de Kano et ses liens avec la zawiya mere de Kaolack," in *Islam et Societes au Suddu Sahara,* no. 3, May 1989.

---- "Muhammad Niasse (1881-1956) et sa replique contre le pamphlet anti-tijani de Ibn Mayaba," in Triaud and Robinson ed.s, *La Tijaniyya, Une Confrerie musulmane a la conquete de VAfrique.* Paris: Karthala, 2000.

---- "Shaikh al-Islam Al-Hajj Ibrahim Niasse," in Robinson and Triaud ed.s, *Le Temps des Marabouts, Itineraires et stratifies islamiques en Afrique occidentale francaise v. 1880-1960.* Paris: Karthala, 1997.

Karrar, Ali Salih, *The Sufi Brotherhoods in the Sudan.* London: C. Hurst, 1992.

Katz, Jonathan G., *Dreams, Sufism and Sainthood, The Visionary Career of Muhammad al-Zawawi.* Leiden: Brill, 1996.

---- "Visionary experience, Autobiography and Sainthood in North African Islam," in *Princeton Papers in Near Eastern Studies,* v.l, 1992.

Kinberg, Leah, "Literal Dreams and Prophetic Hadits in classical Islam – a comparison of two ways of legitimation, in *Der Islam,* 70 2, 1993.

Klein, Martin A., *Islam and Imperialism in Senegal: Sine-Saloum 1847-1914.* Stanford, California: Stanford University Press, 1968.

Lapidus, Ira Marvin, *A History of Islamic Societies.* Cambridge: Cambridge University Press, 1988.

Lecerf, Jean, "The Dream in popular culture: Arabic and Islamic," in Grunebaum and Caillois ed.s, *The Dream and Human Societies.* Berkeley: University of California Press, 1966.

Lings, Martin, *A Sufi Saint of the Twentieth Century, Shaikh Ahmad al- 'Alawi, his spiritual heritage and legacy.* Britain: Unwin Brothers, 1973.

Manas, Francisco Rodriguez, "Supplanting the Ruler: the Levying of Taxes by Sufi Zawiya-s in the Maghrib," in *Islamic Quarterly,* v. 40, no. 2, 1996.

Mansour, Mohamed El, *Morocco in the reign of Mawlay Sulayman.* Wisbech, England: Middle East and North African Studies Press, 1990.

Marsot, Afaf Lutfi al-Sayyid, "The Wealth of the Ulama in late Eighteenth Century Cairo," in Naff and Owen ed.s, *Studies in Eighteenth Century Islamic History.* Carbondale, Illinois: Southern Illinois University Press, 1977.

Martin, B.G., *Muslim Brotherhoods in Nineteenth Century Africa*. Cambridge: Cambridge University Press, 1976.

Melliti, Imed, "La ruse maraboutique: le statut du *Hayal* et du *Itlaq* dans Phagiographie des Tijaniyya," in *Annuaire d VAfrique du Nord*, volume 33, 1994.

Miner, Horace and Vos, George, *Oasis and Casbah: Algerian Culture and Personality in Change*. Ann Arbor: University of Michigan, 1960.

Monteil, Vincent, *L 'islam noir*. Paris: Editions du Seuil, 1971.

Naff, Thomas, "Introduction" to Naff and Owen ed.s, *Studies in Eighteenth Century Islamic History*. Carbondale, Illinois: Southern Illinois University Press, 1977.

Nasr, Seyyed Hossein, "Oral Transmission and the Book in Islamic Education," in George Atiyeh ed., *The Book in the Islamic World, The Written Word and Communication in the Middle East*. Albany: SUNY Press, 1995.

Nicholson, Reynold A., *Studies in Islamic Mysticism*. England : Curzon, 1994.

Nizami, Khaliq Ahmad, "The Qadiriyyah Order," in Seyyed Hossein Nasr ed., *Islamic Spirituality, Manifestations*. New York: Crossroads, 1991.

O'Fahey, R.S., *Enigmatic Saint, Ahmad Ibn Idris and the Idrisi Tradition*. London: C. Hurst, 1990.

---- and Bemd Radtke, "Neo-Sufism Reconsidered," in *Der Islam*, v.70, 1993.

Paden, John N., *Religion and Popular Culture in Kano*. Berkeley: University of California Press, 1973.

Padwick, Constance, *Muslim Devotions: a study of prayer manuals in common use.* London: SPCK, 1961.

Pierce, Leslie, *The Imperial Harem.* Leiden: Brill, 1993.

Radtke, Bemd, "Ibriziana: Themes and Sources of a Seminal Sufi Work," in *Sudanic Africa.* No. 7, 1997.

---- "Ijtihad and Neo-Sufism," in *Asiatische Studien.* V. 19, issue iii, 1994.

---- "Sufism in the 18th Century: an attempt at a provisional appraisal," *Die Welt des Islams,* 36, 3, 1996.

Rahman, Fazlur, "Dream, Imagination and 'Alam al-mithal," in Grunebaum and Caillois ed.s, *The Dream and Human Societies.* Berkeley: University of California Press, 1966.

---- *Islam.* London: Weidenfeld &Nicolson, 1966.

Reichmuth, Stefan, "Islamic Scholarship between Imperial Center and Provinces in the 18th Century: the Case of Murtada al-Zabidi (d. 1205/1791) and His Ottoman Contacts," in *The Great Ottoman- Turkish Civilization, Volume III.* Ankara: Yeni Turkiye, 2000.

Robinson, David, *The Holy War of Umar Tal, the Western Sudan in the mid-nineteenth century.* Oxford: Clarendon Press, 1985.

Rosander, Eva Evers, "The Islamization of 'Tradition' and 'Modernity,'" in Westerlund and Rosander ed.s, *African Islam and Islam in Africa, Encounters between Sufis and Islamists.* Athens: Ohio University Press, 1997.

Schimmel, Annemarie, *And Muhammad is His Messenger: the Veneration of the Prophet in Islamic Piety.* Chapel Hill: UNC Press 1985.

---- *Mystical Dimensions of Islam.* Chapel Hill: UNC Press, 1975.

Sedgwick, Mark, *The Heirs of Ahmad Ibn Idris, The Spread and Normalization of a Sufi Order, 1799-1996.* Doctoral thesis at University of Bergen (Norway), 1998.

Sells, Michael A., *Early Islamic Mysticism: Sufi, Qur'an, Mi'raj, Poetic and TheologicalWritings.* New Jersey: Paulist Press, 1996.

Schleifer, Abdullah, "Sufism in Egypt and the Arab East," in Nasr ed., *Islamic Spirituality, Manifestations.* New York: Crossroad, 1991

Shahin, Emad, *Political Ascent: Contemporary Islamic Movements in North Africa.* Boulder: Westview Press, 1997.

Shoshan, Boaz, "High Culture and Popular Culture in Medieval Islam," in *Studia Islamica,* v. 83, 1991.

Shuval, Tal, *La ville d'Alger vers la fin du XVIIle siecle: population et cadre urbain.* Paris: CNRS Editions, 1998.

Sirriyeh, Elizabeth, *Sufis and Anti-Sufis: The Defence, Rethinking and Rejection of Sufism in the Modern World.* Surrey, England: Curzon, 1999.

Triaud, Jean-Louis, "La Tijaniyya, une confrerie musulmane pas comme les autres?" in Triaud and Robinson ed.s, *La Tijaniyya, Une Confrerie musulmane a la conquete de l'Afrique.* Paris: Karthala, 2000.

---- "La Tijaniyya, voie infallible ou voie soufie inventee: autour du pamphlet anti-tijani d'Ibrahim al-Qattan," in Triaud and Robinson ed.s, *La Tijaniyya, Une Confrerie musulmane a la conquete de l'Afrique.* Paris : Karthala, 2000.

Trimingham, J. Spencer, *A History of Islam in West Africa.* London: Oxford University Press, 1962.

--- *The Sufi Orders in Islam*. London: Oxford University Press, 1971

Umar, Muhammad S., "Sufism and its Opponents in Nigeria: the Doctrinal and Intellectual Aspects," in de Jong and Radtke ed.s, *Islamic Mysticism Contested: Thirteen Centuries of Controversies and Polemics*. Leiden: Brill, 1999.

Van Bruinessen, Martin, "Controversies and Polemics involving the Sufi orders in Twentieth Century Indonesia," in de Long and Radtke ed.s, *Islamic Mysticism Contested*. Leiden: Brill, 1999.

Vikor, Knut S., *Sufi and Scholar on the Desert Edge, Muhammad b. 'Ali al-Sanusi and his Brotherhood*. London: C. Hurst, 1995.

Villalon, Leonardo, *Islamic Society and State Power in Senegal: Disciples and Citizens in Fatick*. London: Cambridge University Press, 1995.

Voll, John O., *Islam, Continuity and Change in the Modem World*. Boulder: Westview, 1982.

Watt, Montgomery, *Faith and Practice of al-Ghazali*. London: Unwin Brothers, 1953.

Willis, John Ralph, "The Writings of al-Hajj 'Umar al-Futi and Shaykh Mukhtar b. Wadi at Allah: Literary Themes, Sources and Influences," in John Ralph Willis ed., *Studies in West African Islamic History*, v. *1, The Cultivators of Islam*. London: Frank Cass, 1979.

---- *In the Path of Allah, the Passion of al-Hajj Umar: An Essay into the Nature of Charisma in Islam*. London: Frank Cass, 1989.

Yapp, Malcolm, *The making of the modern Near East, 1792-1923*. London: Longman, 1987.

Index

A

Abdalawi, Ahmad al- 217

Abd al-Hamid, Sultan, 94

Abd al-Nasser, Jamal, 218

Abd al-Qadir, Emir, 216

Abd al-Salam, Mawlay 101

Ablution (wudhu') 87

Abu Bakr al-Saddiq 80, 118

Abu Madyan 77, 98, 148, 201

Abun-Nasr, Jamil 37, 38, 114

Ahl al-Bayt 118

Akhdari, al 53

Alawi dynasty (Morocco) 93

Ali ibn Abi Talib 65, 118, 158

Amaud, General 216

Andalib, Muhammad Nasir 69

Andalusi, Andalusi, Ahmad ibn Abdullah Ma'n al- 41

Angels 76, 79, 126, 167, 189, 225

Aql 173

Ash'ari, Abu Hassan Ali al 80, 239

'Attar, Farid al-Din 82

Azhari, Abd al-Rahman al- 60, 79

Azhar University 218

B

Bakri, Muhammad al 141, 153

Bakri, Mustafa al 16, 60

Barada, Ali Harazem al 39, 40, 70, 71, 106, 116, 125, 159

Baraka 98, 107

Basri, Hassan al 65

Bello, Muhammad 214

Benabdellah, Abdelaziz 9, 37, 38, 44, 46, 54, 57, 92

Berque, Jacques 37, 242

Birgawi, Muhammad ibn 'Ali 66, 67, 68, 70

Bistami, Abu Yazid al 148

Bughyat al-Mustafid 43, 44, 57, 58, 98, 100, 149, 182

Burdah 183

Busiri, al- 183

C

Charity (*zakat, sadaqa*) 99, 124, 140

Christian(s) 16, 80, 94, 199

Cisse, Ali 42

Cisse, Hassan ibn Ali 41, 46, 117, 120, 130, 135, 142, 183, 192, 198, 200, 202

Corruption 95, 100, 113, 125, 195, 203, 204, 211

Crise Maraboutique 102

D

Dabbagh, Abd al-Aziz al 68, 134, 150, 171, 173

Dahsa 52

Dala'il Khairat 142, 152

Damrawi, Ibn 'Arabi al-Tazzi 70, 71

Dandarawiyya 29

Darqawiyya 92, 103, 124

Detractors (of the Tijaniyya) 143

Dhat-Allah 173

Dhat al-Rasul 67, 68, 82, 166, 174, 182, 211

Dhikr 103, 119, 120, 123, 140, 141, 153, 188

Diakhou, Ma Ba 214

Diop, Lat Dior 214

Disbelief (*kufr*) 104, 196

E

Excommunication (*takfir*) 68, 104, 132, 210

F

Fadl (grace, bounty, preference) 35, 124, 137, 141, 156, 161, 179, 195, 197, 205, 211

Fana '(annihilation) 68, 159, 174, 182, 247

Fath al-Rabbani 43, 87

Fayda 217, 219

Fear of God (*taqwa*) 128, 200, 202

Fiqh 52, 86, 102, 105, 114, 115, 123, 127, 128, 130, 133

France 46

French, the 214, 216

Fuqaha 123, 127, 130, 132, 133, 134, 137, 138, 210

Futi, al-Hajj Umar al 43, 129, 130, 213

G

Ghali, Muhammad 106, 214

Ghazali, Muhammad Abu-Hamid al 19, 76, 80, 81, 166

Ghazwani, Abdullah al 68

H

Hadith 140

Hafiz, Muhammad al 106, 115, 116

Hallaj 19, 112, 172

Haqiqa Muhammadiyya 171, 172, 175

Hassan ibn 'Ali 85

Hassan II, Sultan 101

Hell 77

Hell-fire 140, 164, 165, 202

Hifhi (Hifnawi), Muhammad al 16, 61, 64, 65, 134, 151

Himma 189, 190

Hindi, Ahmad ibn Abdullah al 63

House of Mirrors 99, 106

Human Purpose 156, 163

I

Ibn Abi al-Dunya 75, 239

Ibn al-Farid 182

Ibn al-Subqy 80

Ibn al-Subqy, Abu Nasr 'Abd al- Wahhab 78

Ibn Arabi al-Hatimi 148

Ibn 'Ata Allah 60

Ibn Azzuz 71

Ibn Ibrahim 152

ibn Idris 16, 22, 29, 31, 34, 62, 70, 128, 150, 168

Ibn Idris 30

Ibn Idris, Ahmad 16, 22, 29, 31, 34, 62, 70, 128, 150, 168

Ibn Mashish 148, 172

Ibn Mu'an 152

Ibn Nasir 85, 151, 202

Ibn Rushd 52

ibn Sa'ih Muhammad al-' Arabi 43, 191

Ibn Taymiyya 67, 168

ibn waqtihi 204

Ibn Zayd, Tariq 80

Ibrahim ibn Abdullah Niasse 42

idrak 165

Idris II, Mawlay 98, 106

Ijtihad 48, 81, 114, 123, 127, 128, 129, 130, 135, 138, 155, 209, 218

Ikanasus 101

Innovation (*bida* ') 22, 23, 36, 103, 111

Intercession (*shaf'a*) 85, 103, 104, 198, 225

J

Jabarti, Abd al-Rahman al 61

Jami', Abd al-Rahman al 79

Jawahir al 35, 39

Jazuliyya 66, 83, 85, 151, 152, 153, 202, 208

Jihad 104, 157, 213, 214, 216

Jihad al-Akbar 157

Jilani, Abd al-Qadir 114, 238

Jili, Abd al-Karim al 64, 66

K

Kadizadelites, Kadizadeli 68

Kashf al-Hijab 41, 44, 71, 88, 94, 98, 99, 100, 106, 107, 124

Kashf al-'Ilbas 44, 143, 150, 169, 191

Khalil, Sidi (author of al-*Mukhtasar*) 52

Khalwa 51, 74, 106

Khalwatiyya 16, 26, 34, 60, 62, 64, 65, 69, 70, 134, 208, 245

Khatm al-Awliya 148, 192

Khatmiyya (see also Mirghaniyya) 29

Khidr 61, 153

Kiran, al-Tayyib ibn 98, 106

Kitab al-Jami 40, 43, 84

Kitab al-Maqsid 41

Kitab al-Rimah 44, 149, 215

Kitab Ifadat al-Ahmadiyya 43

Kunti, Mukhtar al 185

Kurdi, Mahmud al 60, 61, 65, 69, 151, 208

L

Lewis, Bernard 20

M

Ma'arifa (knowledge of God) 117, 150, 166, 167, 168, 169, 175, 219

Madhhab 33, 68, 104, 127, 128, 130, 131, 134, 135, 138, 218

Mahdi 205

Makr Allah 200

Maliki *madhhab* 104

Manners (*adab*) 99, 126

Material world (*dunya*) 87, 117, 125, 173, 189

Mawlid 51, 103, 119

Mercy (*rahma*) 126, 153, 159, 160, 195, 198, 199, 200, 202, 205, 210, 219

Mir Dard 69

Mirghani, Muhammad Uthman al 29

Mirghaniyya 29

Mishry 70, 71, 116, 165

Mizab al-Rahma Rabbaniyya 43

Modernity 15, 17, 204

Mu'awiya ibn Abi Suffyan 80

Mukhtar, Muhammad ibn al 94

Mursi, Abu Abbas al 82

Mu'tazilite 80

N

Nabulsi, Abd al-Ghani al 16, 68, 208

Nafs (Ego, Self, Soul) 76, 113, 133, 151, 156, 157, 163, 164, 173, 192, 196

Napoleon 204

Naqshbandiyya 69

Nasiriyya 55, 83, 85, 101, 151, 202, 208

Nasr, Seyyed Hosseifa 37, 38

Nawawi, Abu Zakariyya Yahya al 19

Neo-Sufism 22, 112, 129, 130, 133, 135, 168

Niasse, Ibrahim ibn Abdullah 30, 42, 44, 46, 115, 116, 118, 120, 132, 133, 142, 143, 168, 169, 191, 217, 237, 239, 244

Nkrumah, Kwame 218

O

Orthodoxy 11, 19, 20, 48, 66, 114, 118, 207

Ottoman Caliphate (Turks) 92, 93, 94, 95

P

Paradise 57, 62, 132, 164, 165, 198, 200, 201

Popular Sufism 19, 67, 68, 101, 103, 113, 119, 137, 151

Q

Qabd 218

Qadiri, Muhammad Abd al-Salam al 41

Qadiriyya 21, 148, 245

Qarawin University 9, 97

Qur'an

    Surat al-Duha 86
    Surat al-Fatiha 140, 142
    Surat al-Ikhlas 140
    Surat al-Qadr 140

Qushayri 61, 148, 160

Qutb 40, 43, 58, 63, 70, 106, 137, 148, 181, 183, 195

Qutb al-Aqtab 106

Qutb al-Maktum 183, 195

Qutbaniyya 58, 63, 77, 86, 158

R

Rahmaniyya 60, 71, 92

Raks (Sufi dance) 120

Rashid, Ibrahim 29

Rashidiyya 29, 67

Razi, Najm al-Din al 136

Rifa'i, Ahmad 81

Riyahi, Ibrahim 61, 94, 115, 143

Ruhanis 167

Ruh (Soul, Spirit) 67, 76, 82, 163, 164, 165, 172, 173, 174

258

S

Sahaba 118, 174

Salafis 16, 40, 103, 111, 212, 213, 215

Salafiyya 40

Salat al-Fatih 43, 114, 139, 141, 142, 153, 203

Salihiyya 16, 22, 29

Sama' 120

Sammaniyya 16, 64

Samman, Muhammad al 60, 63, 152, 153, 158, 174, 208

Sanusi, Muhammad al 16, 29, 52, 115

Sanusiyya 16, 22, 29, 52

Satan 77, 184, 187

Sa'ud 104

Sects (Islamic) 21, 169

Senghor, Leopold 218

Shadhili, Abu-Hassan al 21, 58, 148

Shadhiliyya 21, 30, 149, 152

Shafi'i, Imam al 81

Shafi'i madhhab 130

Sha'rani 132

Sharawi 84

Sharia (Islamic Sacred Law) 101, 102

Sharqawi, Abdullah 62

Shaykh al-tarbiyya 57, 115, 156, 179, 187, 191, 192, 219

Shaykh al-Wasil 190

Shinqiti, Ahmad al-Amin al 43

Sijilmasi 84, 150

Sirhindi, Ahmad 69, 83

Sufyani, Muhammad al-Tayyib al 43

Suhrawardi 19

Sukayrij, Ahmad 41, 44, 46, 70, 94, 100, 119, 212, 217

Sulayman 97, 99, 101, 102, 103, 104, 105, 113, 119, 138, 208

Sunna 33, 48, 56, 64, 66, 68, 85, 112, 114, 118, 119, 120, 121, 127, 128, 129, 131, 138, 172, 209, 210, 211, 218

Suyuti 79, 82

T

Tamanarti 83

Tamasani, Ali al- 217

taqlid 127, 130, 218

Tarbiyya 43, 57, 115, 156, 179, 187, 191, 210, 219

Tayyib, Ahmad al- 64

Tobacco 102

Toure, Sekou 218

U

Ubayda ibn Muhammad al-Saghir 43

Ulama 16, 25, 26, 65, 106, 117, 129, 138, 204

Umar ibn Abd al-Aziz 80

Umar ibn al-Khattab 80

Uthman ibn 'Af fan 80

Uways 81, 82

Uwaysi transmission 81

Uzgen 79

W

Wahdat al-Wujudl 168

Wahhabism, Wahhabiyya 103, 104, 105

Waliullah 83

Wasiti 66, 67, 70

Wazzaniyya 41, 55, 151, 202, 208

Wealth 17, 26, 107, 123, 124

Wird 73, 75, 99, 152, 200

World Islamic League 218

World Muslim Congress 218

Z

Zarruq, Ahmad 152

Zarruqiyya 151

Zawawi 83, 201

Zawiya 9, 78

Zawiya Tijaniyya (Fes) 37, 127, 128

Zaytuna University 60, 62, 94

Zhahir 21

Ziyara 64, 104, 119, 138

CPSIA information can be obtained
at www.ICGtesting.com
Printed in the USA
BVHW041339010519
547057BV00029B/1841/P